T0289647

THE WEALTH OF A NATION

THE PRINCETON ECONOMIC HISTORY
OF THE WESTERN WORLD

Joel Mokyr, Series Editor

A list of titles in this Series appears at the back of the book.

The Wealth of a Nation

INSTITUTIONAL FOUNDATIONS OF ENGLISH CAPITALISM

GEOFFREY M. HODGSON

PRINCETON UNIVERSITY PRESS

PRINCETON & OXFORD

Published by Princeton University Press
41 William Street, Princeton, New Jersey 08540
99 Banbury Road, Oxford OX2 6JX

press.princeton.edu

All Rights Reserved
ISBN 978-0-691-24701-4
ISBN (e-book) 978-0-691-24751-9

British Library Cataloging-in-Publication Data is available

Editorial: Joe Jackson and Emma Wagh
Production Editorial: Jenny Wolkowicki
Jacket design: Karl Spurzem
Production: Danielle Amatucci
Publicity: William Pagdatoon and Charlotte Coyne
Copyeditor: Anita O'Brien

Jacket credit: *Coalbrookdale by Night*, 1801 (oil on canvas) by Philip James de Loutherbourg. © Science and Society Picture Library / Bridgeman Images

This book has been composed in Arno Pro

Printed on acid-free paper. ∞

Printed in the United States of America

10 9 8 7 6 5 4 3 2 1

To Deirdre McCloskey, Joel Mokyr and the memory of
Douglass North, who have done a great deal to
enhance my interest in economic history.

CONTENTS

THE HISTORY of capitalism is one of violence, inequality, exploitation, colonialism and slavery. But eventually capitalism led globally to huge increases in economic output per capita and major worldwide extensions in average human longevity. In recent decades, extreme poverty in developing countries has been greatly reduced. But economic inequality has persisted. Billions are still deprived of adequate nutrition, housing, healthcare and education. The expansion of capitalism has also threatened the natural environment and may bring catastrophic global warming. Military conflict continues. Appreciating both its achievements and its limitations, we need to understand how capitalism evolved and how it radically transformed human existence.[1]

Capitalism is more than a market economy with private enterprise. Trade and private business have existed for thousands of years. Capitalism is also based on finance capital. With important precursors in medieval Italy and the Netherlands, such a system emerged in England in the eighteenth century and led to the Industrial Revolution. It developed new institutional arrangements, including those that facilitated the mortgaging of collateralizable property, a central bank, a national debt, markets for private and public debt, and a substantial private banking sector. Although banks and credit were found in ancient China, Greece, Rome and Sumer, modern finance developed in England in the seventeenth and eighteenth centuries. Also relevant was the development of a modern state that could project its trading arrangements using military force.

This book follows many others, including the Nobel Laureate Douglass C. North, in underlining the importance of institutions in economic development. It places particular emphasis on legal institutions. This conceptual approach, described as *legal institutionalism*, builds on the work of precursors including the nineteenth-century British economist Henry Dunning MacLeod

1. See also Hodgson (2019c, 2021c), Koyama and Rubin (2022, 1–8).

(1821–1902), who was one of the first to bring law and economics together, and some American institutional economists, including John R. Commons (1862–1945) and Warren J. Samuels (1933–2011). Legal institutionalism here dovetails with ideas from pragmatist psychology and pragmatist philosophy, including those developed by another American institutional economist, Thorstein Veblen (1857–1929). Veblen's insights on the differential impacts of external disturbances on human adaptation and economic change are particularly important in this context. On the role of finance in modern economies, another key influence is the work of Joseph A. Schumpeter (1883–1950).

Understanding the drivers of English economic development in earlier centuries can help us appreciate problems of underdevelopment around the world today. Of course, we have to be cautious about generalizations. Every country is unique. History, culture, population, area and institutions all differ. The problems of catching up with powerful rival economies are different from those of forging ahead as a pioneer. But still, important lessons can be learned from the English example. Recent research by several scholars has underlined the wider importance of financial institutions in economic development. To be fully effective, these financial institutions require a workable legal system and an effective national government. These lessons are stressed by the English case.

I have been writing on issues in social science for over fifty years. My research has covered a wide and varied list of topics. This book links many of these topics together. It touches on institutional economics, legal institutionalism, economic history, the evolution of institutions and culture, the roles of habit and instinct, the importance of adequate definitions, the strengths and limits of Marxism, and much else. My excursions into economic history stem from my longstanding interest in history in general. Economic history is a major laboratory for economics. Here empirical research can actually make a difference. And it can sometimes challenge core assumptions.

I thank Benito Arruñada, Michael Bordo, Stephen Broadberry, Goncalo Fonseca, Oscar Gelderblom, Peter Grajzl, Michelle Liu, Deirdre McCloskey, Joel Mokyr, Nicos Moushouttas, Anne Murphy, Peter Murrell, Sheilagh Ogilvie, Dmitri Safronov, Gerhard Schnyder, Alex Trew, Mehrdad Vahabi, Jan Luiten van Zanden, Makio Yamada, anonymous referees and many others for help, advice and discussions. I am also grateful to Millennium Economics Ltd for permission to use here some material from three essays published in the *Journal of Institutional Economics* (Hodgson 2017b, 2021b, 2022a). Peter Grajzl and Peter Murrell kindly gave permission, along with Millennium Economics, to reproduce their images in figure 4.4 (Grajzl and Murrell, 2021b, 209).

INTRODUCTION

Economic development . . . is essentially a knowledge process . . . but we are still too much obsessed by mechanical models, capital-income ratios, and even input-output tables, to the neglect of the study of the learning process which is the real key to development.

— KENNETH E. BOULDING, 'THE ECONOMICS OF KNOWLEDGE
AND THE KNOWLEDGE OF ECONOMICS' (1966)

The development of more efficient economic organization is surely as important a part of the growth of the Western World as is the development of technology, and it is time it received equal attention.

— DOUGLASS C. NORTH, 'INSTITUTIONAL CHANGE
AND ECONOMIC GROWTH' (1971)

A MAJOR TASK for economic historians is to explain the innovation and growth that started largely in England in the seventeenth and eighteenth centuries and spread to other countries around the world. After 1700, gross domestic product (GDP) per capita increased in Europe and accelerated further upwards. Western European GDP per capita was about twenty times larger in 2003 than it was in 1700. World GDP per capita in 2003 was about eleven times larger than it was in 1700.[1]

The global outcomes in terms of human longevity were spectacular. As a result of technological developments in medicine and the improved average standard of living, between 1800 and 2000 life expectancy at birth rose from a

---

1. Maddison (2007).

global average of about thirty years to sixty-seven years, and to more than seventy-five years in some developed countries.[2]

The Focus of This Book

With these huge global changes in mind, this book concentrates on the English economy from 1300 to about 1820. England was one of the major pioneers of economic development. Figure 0.1 uses data processed by Stephen Broadberry and his colleagues, showing GDP per capita for England from 1300 to 1700, and for Britain from 1700 to 1870. The figure dramatizes the huge expansion in GDP per capita from the seventeenth century. Previously there were over two hundred years of stagnation or decline in GDP per capita and in all three of its sectoral components. A sustained upward trend in GDP per capita is evident from about 1651, after the disruption of the Civil War. Much of this expansion in GDP per capita is explained by increases in industrial output. GDP per capita more than doubled from 1650 to 1820. Industrial output per whole population tripled in the same period. Agricultural output per whole population reached a peak in 1781. Its decline after 1781 was due largely to a marked contraction of agricultural employment, partly alleviated by increases in productivity. Industry had become the leading sector of the British economy.

This book considers the institutional and other changes that spurred the dramatic rise in economic activity. The impressive expansion from about 1651 to 1820 was followed by an acceleration in the growth of industrial output and GDP per capita. But the post-1820 acceleration is a topic for another study. We focus here on the foundational conditions that enabled a dramatic transition from stagnation to growth. The key changes occurred in the seventeenth and eighteen centuries.[3]

From 1300 to 1600 agricultural output took up an average of about 43 per cent of GDP. After 1600 agricultural output as share of GDP trended downwards, reaching 27 per cent in 1700, 22 per cent in 1800 and 8 per cent in 1870. Rising industry took up most of the remaining share, with the service sector

2. Riley (2001), Fogel (2004), Deaton (2013).

3. Broadberry et al. (2015, 194, 227–44). Figure 0.1 shows average GDP and sectoral shares per person, i.e., GDP and sectoral outputs divided by the size of the total population. Broadberry et al. (2015, 365) also provided estimates of labour productivity. Agricultural output per agricultural worker more than doubled from 1522 to 1801 and continued increasing (albeit more slowly) into the nineteenth century.

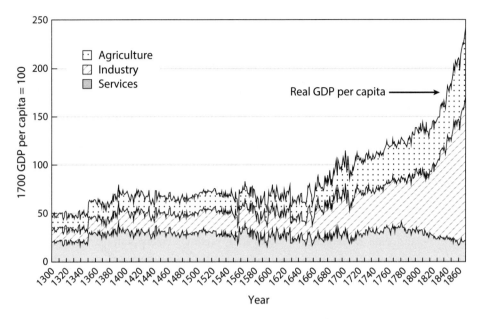

FIGURE 0.1. Sectoral shares of English/British real GDP per capita, 1300–1870
This is a stacked graph. GDP per capita is the top line, where 1700 GDP per
capita is 100. Before 1700 the data are for England. From 1700 the data are for
Great Britain. Data from Broadberry et al. (2015, 194, 227–44).

growing less dramatically. From 1600 to 1870 industrial output as a share of
GDP trended upwards, from 37 per cent in 1600 reaching 41 per cent in 1700,
47 per cent in 1800 and 62 per cent in 1870. In the early nineteenth century,
Britain became an industrial economy.

Why is England in the subtitle of this book? Some people wrongly describe
the whole of the UK as England. The United Kingdom consists of Great Britain and Northern Ireland. Great Britain is made up of three nations—England,
Scotland and Wales. Wales was colonized in 1536 by Henry VIII, and since
then it has had the same legal system as England. The Crowns of Scotland,
England and Wales became one when James VI of Scotland came to the
throne in London in 1603, becoming James I of Great Britain. The Act of
Union of 1707 disbanded the Scottish Parliament and brought England, Scotland and Wales under a single government from Westminster. This created a
united trading area free of internal tariffs. But Scotland retained separate legal
and financial institutions. From 1801 to 1922 the whole of Ireland was part of the

United Kingdom. Most of Ireland became independent in 1922, leaving Northern Ireland as part of the UK.

The census of 1851 found that England made up 81 per cent of the population of Britain.[4] Estimates for earlier dates confirm similar degrees of population dominance by England. The principal focus in this book on England is partly justified by the physical, economic and demographic weight of that nation within Britain, and by avoiding the complication of giving separate accounts for Wales and Scotland. This does not diminish the distinctiveness and importance of these smaller nations.

Another problem is that the available datasets are sometimes for England alone and sometimes for England and Wales. For data after 1707 there is a tendency to look at the whole of Britain. So while there is a primary focus on England, data for Scotland or Wales are sometimes incorporated in the narrative. But legal changes applying to Scotland alone are generally overlooked here: they would be better addressed in a separate study.

The choices of start and end points for any historical narrative are typically arbitrary. The fourteenth century brought the Black Death, then followed a decline in classical feudalism and the growth of a market economy using wage labour. Wage labour is arguably a key feature of capitalism, so this is our starting point. A fuller account of England's modern economic development would extend to the twentieth century. But the focus of the present study is on key changes in financial and other institutions that enabled the economic take-off in the seventeenth, eighteenth and early nineteenth centuries. The Industrial Revolution is often dated from 1760 to 1820 or thereabouts. Thomas S. Ashton put it at 1760–1830, and Eric Hobsbawm pushed it up to 1780–1840.[5] Major technological developments and important changes in financial and corporate institutions occurred after 1820, but the narrative would have to be greatly extended to incorporate them. Circa 1820 is also a useful ending point because it was just after the beginning of the century of Pax Britannica, which led to expanded trade and further British imperial expansion.

The 1820–1914 period, which saw accelerated growth and a massive further expansion of trade, warrants treatment in a separate work. It would cover an era when industrialization was consolidated, extended and promoted by new and reformed institutions. Instead, this volume focuses on the creation of the

4. Cheshire (1854).
5. Ashton (1968), Hobsbawm (1969). See also Berg and Hudson (1992)

institutional conditions that enabled the industrial take-off, and on the constraints on growth that persisted into the early nineteenth century.

Confusion over the Meaning of Capital

Financial institutions are central to the argument. Unfortunately, economic historians, with some notable exceptions, have given insufficient attention to the evolution and influence of finance. An ongoing confusion between *finance capital* and *capital goods* has diverted attention and clouded understanding. At the root of this is the peculiar usage by economists of the word *capital,* which dates from Adam Smith in his *Wealth of Nations* of 1776.

In the real world, the word has a different meaning. Even today, in everyday business and accounting usage, *capital* means a sum of money to be invested, or already invested, in material or immaterial assets. Inspired by the triumph of Newtonian science and the growing use of machines, Smith changed the meaning of *capital.* As Edwin Cannan put it, instead of the money value of property, 'Smith makes it the things themselves'. This decisive shift in the meaning of *capital,* from a monetary evaluation to a physical asset, has muddled social scientists ever since. It is found in the confusion of *capital goods* with *finance capital* and in the mistaken treatment of finance as a 'factor of production'. These confusions are sadly still commonplace in economics, sociology and elsewhere. Yet in the real world of business and accounting, *capital* still means money or the money value of alienable assets.[6]

Capital goods are useful in production, but finance produces nothing. Money is not a tool for making physical things. Money may be used to purchase factors of production, but this does not mean that finance itself does any producing. For millions of years, humans have produced things without money or finance. Finance capital—or *capital* as businesspeople call it—is historically specific. Capital goods are not.

Smith's change of the meaning of *capital* has received minority criticism from within economics. In a work published in 1888, the Austrian economist Carl Menger made clear that economists did not have the right to 'arbitrarily redefine popular terms' like capital: 'only sums of money are denoted by the above word.' As Eduard Braun put it, Menger was of the opinion that capital must be interpreted in terms of common parlance, 'as a homogeneous concept depicting sums of money on ordinary business accounts. In fact, he vigorously

---

6. Smith (1976, 282), Cannan (1921, 480).

opposed all theories that dissented from this ordinary business view on capital, including the one that is commonly imputed to him.'[7]

On this point, Menger was not alone among German-speaking social scientists. Werner Sombart returned to the pre-Smithian meaning of *capital* by defining it as 'the sum of exchange value which serves as the working basis of a capitalist enterprise.' Similarly, Max Weber wrote that '"capital" is the money value of the means of profit-making available to the enterprise at the balancing of the books.'[8]

Likewise, the British diplomat and economist Alfred Mitchell Innes wrote in 1914: 'Every banker and every commercial man knows that there is only one kind of capital, and that is money. . . . And yet every economist bases his teaching on the hypothesis that capital is not money.'[9] The American economist Frank Fetter—who was influenced by both Austrian economics and the original institutionalism—was one of the few to attempt to restore the pre-Smithian meaning. Fetter wrote: 'Capital is essentially an individual acquisitive, financial, investment ownership concept. It is not coextensive with wealth as physical objects, but rather with legal rights as claims to uses and incomes. It is or should be a concept relating unequivocally to private property and to the existing price system.'[10] Fetter insisted that capital is both a monetary and a historically specific phenomenon: 'Capital is defined as a conception of individual riches having real meaning only within the price system and the market where it originated, and developing with the spread of the financial calculus in business practice.'[11]

Joseph A. Schumpeter also argued that the term *capital* should be applied to money or money values alone:

> The word Capital had been part of legal and business terminology long before economists found employment for it. . . . [It] came to denote the sums of money or their equivalents brought by partners into a partnership or company, the sum total of a firm's assets, and the like. Thus the concept was essentially monetary, meaning either actual money, or claims to money, or some goods evaluated in money. . . . What a mass of confused, futile, and downright silly controversies it would have saved us, if economists had had

7. Menger (1888, 6, 37), Braun (2015, 78; 2020).
8. Sombart (1919, 324), Weber (1968, 1:91).
9. Mitchell Innes (1914, 152).
10. Fetter (1927, 156).
11. Fetter (1930, 190).

the sense to stick to those monetary and accounting meanings of the term instead of trying to 'deepen' them![12]

This advice was largely ignored. Even the Cambridge capital controversy of the 1960s and 1970s neglected the issues raised by Schumpeter and others. In their models, both sides of the debate treated capital as physical rather than financial, with Cambridge UK insisting on the heterogeneity of physical capital goods and on the problems of their aggregated measurement. Money and finance were largely left out of the picture.[13]

If Menger, Sombart, Weber, Mitchell Innes, Fetter, Schumpeter and others are broadly right on this question, then economists have subverted a central concept. They have been aided and abetted by sociologists such as Pierre Bourdieu and James Coleman. These two widened the concept of capital to include *social capital*, which, unlike *capital* in its everyday business meaning, and unlike *capital goods*, cannot be owned or sold, and it has no evident and meaningful price. Bourdieu and others expanded the meaning of *capital* further, to cover anything of social use, including social networks and interpersonal trust. These expansions fail to treat capital as historically specific, as if economics and other social sciences must be based solely on the study of universal and ahistorical laws. I try to avoid terms like *human capital* and *social capital* because they add little to the understanding of the phenomena involved, and they muddle the essentially monetary and financial meaning of *capital* proper.[14]

Smith's physicalist view of the economy, and his accordant redefinition of the word *capital*, led him into trouble when dealing with money and credit. Smith did not think it possible to detach money from the metals that it was seen to represent: 'The whole paper money of every kind which can easily circulate in any country, never can exceed the value of the gold and silver, of

---

12. Schumpeter (1954, 322–23). Schumpeter (1956, 174) wrote in 1917: 'The capital market is the same as the phenomenon that practice describes as the money market. There is no other capital market.' Schäffle (1870, 101 ff.) and Hobson (1926, 26) also argued that capital was monetary. For other dissenters, see Hodgson (2014; 2015a). To his credit, Piketty (2014) reverted to a pre-Smithian definition of capital.

13. Sraffa (1960), Harcourt (1972), Robinson (1979a), Cohen and Harcourt (2003).

14. Bourdieu (1986), Coleman (1988). As Piketty (2014) pointed out, waged workers are not capital because they cannot be used as collateral, and they do not appear as assets on the firm's balance sheet. By contrast, slaves can be mortgaged: they are literally human capital, and the term was first used in that context (Hodgson, 2014).

which it supplies the place.' Henry Thornton criticised Smith's views on money and credit in 1802, arguing that the Scottish economist had failed to consider possible variations in the velocity of circulation of money and the wide range of paper assets in circulation. Thornton also pointed out that banks are important not only because they mobilize finance capital, but also because, by supplying paper money or bills, they can create credit. This additional credit adds to the amount of finance available. Thornton thus hinted, like Schumpeter much later, that credit can defy the then-assumed physical laws concerning the conservation of matter and energy and create more value, as if 'out of nothing'. A physicalist ontology is inapplicable to finance.[15]

Capital, Capitalism and the Neglect of Finance

Up to about 1990, the conventional wisdom, including from orthodox economists at the World Bank to heterodox economists at Cambridge UK, was that investment in capital goods was a leading factor in economic development. Finance was simply a means to that end. Addressing the causal relation between the two, the heterodox Cambridge economist Joan Robinson proposed that 'where enterprise leads finance follows'. H. John Habakkuk argued similarly that financial institutions grow up to satisfy any large need for finance. The accumulation of capital goods was primary. Finance would take care of itself.[16]

This widespread view was undermined by arguments and empirical work by a number of authors. For example, William Easterly attacked the 'capital fundamentalism' of approaches to economic development that put priority on investment in capital goods. Using the standard production function $Q = f(K, L)$, 'capital fundamentalism' upholds the supreme importance of K, which refers to capital goods, not to finance. Easterly showed that, within a production function approach, the impact of K is limited. He argued that 'increasing buildings and machinery' is not the prime cause of growth. He collaborated with Ross Levine in publishing a survey of the evidence that

15. Smith (1976, 300). There are conflicting interpretations of Smith's views on money (Curott, 2017), which cannot be resolved here. See Thornton (1802, 44–46, 53–58, 176–77), Schumpeter (1934, 73). On how bank credit creates money, see Robertson (1928), Moore (1988), Minsky (1991), McLeay et al. (2014), Werner (2014), Jakab and Kumhof (2015), Keen (2022).

16. Robinson (1952, 86; 1979b, 20), Habakkuk (1962, 175), Pollard (1964).

similarly undermined the role of *K* (capital goods) in development. They made it clear that they were rebutting the claim that 'physical capital accumulation' was paramount. Their argument about finance is different. One of their conclusions is that 'a higher level of financial development boosts economic growth', particularly by aiding innovation. Other studies have also underlined that finance capital remains important for economic development. The effects of finance capital and capital goods on economic development are very different.[17]

Deirdre McCloskey supported Easterly's attack on 'capital fundamentalism'. But while Easterly criticized explanations centred on capital goods (factors of production), he did not attack those focusing on finance capital. McCloskey ignored this difference and misleadingly cited Easterly and others in her attempt to rebut Schumpeter's claim that finance capital is vital. Easterly, and especially his collaborator Levine, supported the Schumpeterian idea that finance is important for development. McCloskey's argument exhibits a confusion between two very different meanings of *capital*.[18]

McCloskey saw *capitalism* as referring to the accumulation of capital goods, or 'piling brick on brick' as she put it. On this basis she rejected the word *capitalism*. Of course she is right that economic growth is much more than the piling up of bricks or machines. But she did not consider that the word *capitalism* might better refer to *capital* in the sense of finance, and not primarily to the accumulation of physical objects.[19]

The confusion has led to different outcomes. Using historical case studies, Bas van Bavel developed an ambitious thesis about economic development. He argued that economic systems involving 'factor markets' in 'land, labour, and capital' experience cycles of expansion and decay. Van Bavel insisted: 'Everything that is necessary for human life is made by combining the three factors of production: land, labour, and capital.' *Capital* (presumably capital goods) is thus omnipresent in human history. But van Bavel shifted meanings in a footnote: 'When factor markets are discussed . . . this concerns the land market . . . the labour market . . . and the credit market (the borrowing of capital for a specific period).' Throughout the book, *capital* generally refers to

17. Blomstrom et al. (1996), Easterly (2001, 47–50), Easterly and Levine (2001, esp. 177–78, 211), Levine (2005), Beck et al. (2003), Rousseau (2003), Carlin and Mayer (2003), Sarma and Pais (2011), Kendal (2012), Heblich and Trew (2019), Raghutla and Chittedi (2021).

18. McCloskey (2010, 132–39), King and Levine (1993).

19. McCloskey (2016b, 93).

money and finance, and less to capital goods. Van Bavel first treated capital as a 'factor of production' and then, for most of the book, as finance. Financial markets are mistakenly described as factor markets. But money and finance are not productive instruments. They grow no crops. The relevant productive resources are capital *goods*, alongside land and labour. Capital goods have existed since our prehuman ancestors picked up sticks or stones and used them as tools. But finance capital is only a few thousand years old, and it is of supreme importance in the modern era only.[20]

For these mistaken reasons, van Bavel shared McCloskey's distaste for *capitalism* as a description of a historically specific era. While the arguments of McCloskey and van Bavel are different, these two authors reveal the problems caused by the persistent ambiguity and Smithian distortion of the term *capital*. They also show how confusion on this key concept leads to challengeable rejections of the term *capitalism*. Such conceptual errors are widespread in economic history. Several other instances are revealed later.

Consider another example of the neglect of finance. In a stimulating book addressing the institutional and other long-term preconditions of the Industrial Revolution, Jan Luiten van Zanden drew inspiration from the stress on knowledge and the cumulative development of skilled labour in endogenous growth theory. Accordingly, endogenous growth theory has helped to shift the emphasis from K to L. Inspired by these models, van Zanden concentrated on the growth of knowledge production in pre-industrial and industrial Europe. He provided impressive evidence on the expanding production of manuscripts, the spread of printed books, the growth of literacy, increasing female participation in the labour market, the development of skills and the expansion of the knowledge economy.[21]

But although there is an emphasis on the role of institutions throughout van Zanden's book, institutional changes are often treated as parametric rather than structural. Omitted are factors that do not appear as key variables in standard versions of endogenous growth theory. This puts the modelling cart before the horse of historical investigation. But it is mostly up to historians to tell modellers what is important, not the other way round. Seemingly because much of endogenous growth theory says little about financial institutions, these features are neglected. Accordingly, neither banking, credit nor finance

20. Van Bavel (2016, 1–2), Hodgson (2021a).
21. Romer (1994), Aghion and Howitt (1998), van Zanden (2009).

appears in the index of his volume. There is no consideration of major institutional developments that led to the growth of finance during the Industrial Revolution. They are simply ignored.[22]

The term *capital market* appears a few times in his book. These and other markets are treated as eternal verities, with the focus on improving their efficiency, not on the processes of their institutional creation, nor on the creation of property rights that are alienable and thus tradeable on markets. Misled by prestigious mathematical growth models that overlook finance, van Zanden neglected these crucial institutional developments.[23]

On the contrary, finance is vital. If we regard capital as money or finance, and neither a factor or production nor a capital good, then the historical specificity of capitalism is sustained by the unique features of modern financial institutions. Developed financial institutions make capitalism historically specific. Hence the use of the word *capitalism* in this book and its subtitle signals the importance of those modern financial arrangements.

An opposite error exists. While some economic historians reject the *capitalism* label for unsound reasons, others apply it too broadly, thus diluting its meaning. Both Marxist and non-Marxist economic historians have associated capitalism and capitalists principally with commercial trade and profit-seeking, sometimes with the additional criterion of wage labour. (Some examples are given in the following chapter.) But trade and profit-seeking have both existed for thousands of years. This might suggest that capitalism too has existed for millennia. Even if we add wage labour as a criterion, waged employment was widespread in England from the early fifteenth century. These criteria make capitalism at least six centuries old, and they are insufficient to demarcate capitalism as a finance-driven system that was actually consolidated in England in the eighteenth century. Finance was not the only institutional development that then mattered. But the role of finance has been silenced in part by an enduring confusion over whether the word *capital* refers to financial capacity, or to non-monetary assets, including physical stuff.

---

22. Finance is mentioned only briefly in the mammoth Aghion and Howitt (1998, 71) textbook on endogenous growth theory. Van der Ploeg and Alogoskoufis (1994) developed an endogenous growth model where increases in the money supply can stimulate growth. Laeven et al. (2015) introduced a more substantial financial sector in their endogenous growth model, where financial innovation is as vital as technological advance.

23. Van Zanden (2009, 24, 100, 104, 131, 140, 222–23, 295), Hoffman et al. (2019).

Defining Capitalism

Once we understand *capital* primarily as finance and not goods, then it is reasonable to describe what was developed in Britain in the eighteenth century as *capitalism*. Finance is definitionally central to this system. As Schumpeter pointed out, 'Capitalism is that form of private property economy in which innovations are carried out by means of borrowed money, which in general . . . implies credit creation.' Money is often borrowed on the basis of collateral. Schumpeter also emphasized 'the importance of the financial complement of capitalist production and trade'. Hence 'the development of the law and the practice of negotiable paper and of "created" deposits afford perhaps the best indication we have for dating the rise of capitalism.' As Geoffrey Ingham summarized: 'Capitalism is distinctive in that it contains a social mechanism by which privately contracted debtor-creditor relations . . . are routinely monetized.'[24]

The role of taxonomic definitions is not to describe or analyse, but to list the minimum number of essential features that can successfully demarcate one kind of entity from another. Capitalism can be defined as a social formation with the following five features:[25]

1. A legal system supporting widespread individual rights and liberties to own, buy, and sell private property
2. Widespread commodity exchange and markets, involving money
3. Widespread private ownership of the means of production, by firms producing goods or services for sale in the pursuit of profit
4. Widespread wage labour and employment contracts
5. A developed financial system with banking institutions, the widespread use of credit with property as collateral, and the selling of debt

24. Schumpeter (1939, 223). Schumpeter (1954, 78 n.) dated the rise of capitalism to the sixteenth century. But modern mortgaging rules were not established in England before the 1670s, and secure markets for debt were consolidated only after 1750 (see Hodgson 2021b and this text below). The final quotation is from Ingham (2008, p. 73).

25. See Hodgson (2019a) on taxonomic definitions. Previously I suggested a definition of capitalism with six features, including 'much of production organized separately and apart from the home and family' (Hodgson, 2015a, 20, 259, 385). This criterion was inspired by Weber. But Chinese family firms and the COVID-19 pandemic show that businesspeople are capable of efficient work and rational pecuniary calculation even when they are in their home and family environments. Weber's point was important, but it is not vital for an effective taxonomic definition of capitalism. I now think that, in the interests of parsimony, the 'apart from the home and family' feature can be removed, while doing little harm to the remaining integrity or value of the definition.

To emphasize, the task of a taxonomic definition is demarcation, rather than to provide an adequate or complete description or analysis. Important aspects of capitalism in history are omitted from the definition, including the role of violence, slavery and imperial conquest. Such features were also present in pre-capitalist societies, albeit often on a smaller scale. Despite their historical importance, they do not demarcate capitalism from non-capitalism. Capitalism can exist without imperial conquest or slavery, and arguably with much diminished violence. We understand their importance via historical analysis, not by their placement in the taxonomic definition itself.

There are important features of English and other capitalisms that are not included in the five-point definition. All capitalisms rely a great deal on the intervention of the state. But the point about taxonomic definitions is not to include everything necessary for a type of phenomenon to exist. The point is to provide parsimonious but adequate criteria of demarcation. English capitalism was built on empire and slavery. But several other capitalisms were different in these respects. State intervention and slavery are examples of *impurities* within capitalism. Impurities can be necessary or contingent for the system. Some state intervention was arguably necessary, but slavery was not. Accounts of real existing capitalisms should refer to their major impurities. But they do not have to be part of the taxonomic definition. Analysis, description and definition are not the same.

Returning to the five-point definition of capitalism, the first three criteria are necessary but insufficient. Private ownership, money and markets have existed for thousands of years. We need more than these three criteria to pin capitalism down. But they are necessary, because any society lacking one or more of them would not be capitalist.

Marx emphasized widespread wage labour and employment contracts as an additional definitional feature of the capitalist mode of production. But because extensive wage labour stretches back to the early fifteenth century, it is less useful for marking the beginning of capitalism. Nevertheless, widespread employment contracts are still an important feature of all modern economies, and their widespread replacement by (say) worker cooperatives or self-employed entrepreneurs would mark a radical system change. Hence, by this logic, the end of wage labour could mark the end of capitalism.

As noted earlier, Schumpeter emphasized the fifth and final criterion, involving developed financial institutions including credit and the sale of debt. It provides a much better means of identifying the emergence of capitalism. As elaborated in later chapters of the present book, such financial institutions became prominent in England in the eighteenth century. We can date the birth of capitalism in England from sometime in the seventeenth or eighteenth centuries, coinciding with upward trends in industrial output and GDP per capita, as noted in figure 0.1.

Financial institutions enable the raising of money for innovation and investment. But economists have paid insufficient attention to the institutional conditions required to mortgage assets or otherwise use them as security for loans. For example, in 'the economics of property rights'—as developed by Armen Alchian, Yoram Barzel and others—property is regarded as mere possession or control. Legal title is seen as significant only if it aids control of an asset. Otherwise, 'property' is simply what you control, and you can have a 'property right' even if you have stolen it. Critics point out that de facto possession does not necessarily constitute a *right*. This dismembered view of property ignores its multifaceted legal nature. Possession (*usus*) is only part of the real story. Ownership is not simply a matter between buyer and seller, but it requires some legal authority. As John R. Commons put it: 'In the end, the actual title to property rests on the sovereign power of the state to enforce its decrees.' Neglecting this question of legal title, the 'economics of property rights' places no emphasis on the possible use of property as collateral. But such legal issues are vitally important for economic development.[26]

It is shown in this book that the mortgaging of English land was inhibited by legal constraints and was rare before the seventeenth century. More widespread mortgaging began around 1670, growing thereafter and making more finance available. This again gives us a historical marker of the beginnings of capitalism in England. Institutionally grounded and historically specific concepts of *property* and *capital* are essential to understand modern economic development.

Reconceptualizing the Economics of Production and Innovation

We think with the aid of metaphors. The metaphors of much of economics—classical, Marxist, Sraffian and neoclassical—have been generally physical in nature. This applies to the $Q = f(K, L)$ production function and its more

---

26. On the 'economics of property rights', see Alchian (1965), Furubotn and Pejovich (1972), Barzel (1989). The concepts of collateral and mortgage are absent from these works. For contrasts and criticisms, see Honoré (1961), de Soto (2000), Cole and Grossman (2002), Steiger (2006, 2008), Heinsohn and Steiger (2013), Hodgson (2015a, 2015b, 2015c), Arruñada (2016). The quote is from Commons (1893, 110).

sophisticated descendants, including endogenous growth theory. It also applies to the representation of the economy as an input-output matrix, including the Sraffian (Cambridge) formulation, where capital goods are heterogenous and labour can be too. These all invoke metaphors of physical stuff, with labour as a vital force to move and transform it.[27]

The problem of the heterogeneity of capital goods never goes away. In any modern economy there are millions of commodities. Even with production functions or matrices with heterogenous capital goods, the theory has to be simplified to deal with this. It is necessary to combine groups of things, to avoid the problem of addressing equations with millions of variables. Different things must be aggregated via some vector of their values. There is always the temptation to use prices. To make it measurable, physical stuff becomes monetized. Finance enters the production process by the back door. The lure is then to conflate finance with capital goods, or to treat them as moving in parallel with one another. But when relative prices change, aggregation by price becomes doubly problematic.

There is also the problem of dealing with technological innovation, which concerns unknown future technologies. It is widely accepted that innovation is central to economic growth, but the physical metaphor of the production function, assuming known inputs of capital goods and labour, within a fixed structural form, has difficulty dealing with future technology in an adequate manner. Innovation is often treated as manna from heaven, leading to unexplained shifts in the function itself.[28]

Some economists assume that innovation is a process where agents estimate their expected returns from different types of investment; they make choices between them and adjust their expectations as further information is revealed. This depiction assumes away uncertainty (where, by definition, probabilities are incalculable) and replaces it by risk (which means that probabilities are calculable). Long ago, Frank Knight and John Maynard Keynes distinguished risk from uncertainty. When uncertainty is present, we cannot depict learning or discovery as probabilistic, and subject to a standard rational calculus. Frank Hahn pointed out that the concept of 'rational learning' is problematic. As North wrote: 'It is necessary to dismantle the rationality assumption underlying economic theory in order to approach constructively

27. Robinson (1953), Solow (1956, 1957), Sraffa (1960), Leontief (1966), Harcourt (1972), Romer (1994), Aghion and Howitt (1998).
28. Dosi et al. (1988).

the nature of human learning.' Learning and innovation are not processes whereby agents can maximize calculable expected returns.[29]

Future knowledge is uncertain and unknowable. Too often the uncertainties surrounding innovation and events in the future are forced into a probabilistic framework. Economists give priority to mathematical models, which require probabilistic estimates. Learning is not simply an individual acquiring new information. It is about individuals and communities discovering or creating new knowledge in highly complex circumstances with radical uncertainty. Invention and innovation are leaps into the unknown.

The physical metaphor of the production function diverts our attention from the actual processes involved. As Axel Leijonhufvud wrote, the production function approach is 'more like a recipe . . . where ingredients are dumped in a pot. . . . This abstraction from the sequencing of tasks . . . is largely responsible for the well-known fact that neoclassical production theory gives us no clue to how production is actually organized.' We must understand production and innovation as relational, transformative processes, not as inputs into a static function.[30]

To make progress we need to consider the knowledge held by the producers, based on their experience of what works and of the difficulties or constraints. Much of this knowledge is in the form of rules. For example, 'every Monday morning this machine should be oiled and tested'. This is a working technological rule, relating to the design of the machine and to the pattern and circumstances of its use, and depending in part on the laws of physics and chemistry. Much of technological knowledge consists of rules.

Another example of a rule would be that 'if you are late by more than ten minutes in the morning, then £10 will be deducted from your pay'. This is an institutional rule, intended to motivate workers to turn up promptly. It may result from some (true or false) notion of how people are motivated. It may or may not serve its purpose, but a key feature is the extent of its arbitrariness. Unlike the rules emanating from the laws of physics and the design of a machine, the penalties could be smaller or bigger, or non-existent, or non-pecuniary, or whatever.

Hence there are technological rules and institutional rules. The former are heavily constrained by physical laws; the latter are often more malleable (although constrained by culture, nature and social practicalities). Some

29. Knight (1921), Keynes (1921, 1936, 1937), Hahn (1991, 49), North (1994, 362).
30. Leijonhufvud (1982, 203).

institutional rules depend on legislated laws (the other meaning of *law*). Legislation can be changed, although it is often costly to do so. Many other institutional rules are not necessarily juridical laws, including rules of communication (language), rules governing behaviour in organizations, cultural rules, and so on. Again, there are different degrees of difficulty in establishing or changing them.[31]

Accordingly, we should understand economic innovation and development as centred on the changing and creation of rules—both technological and institutional—and the spreading and assimilation of knowledge of these rules among those engaged with the processes involved. This entails an alternative ontology of rules and rule-systems, serving as a rival to the physicalist view of the economy as evidenced in production functions. The emerging ontological fundamentals involve technologies, institutional structures and algorithmic learning processes, made up of programs or systems of rules. As Kurt Dopfer, John Foster and Jason Potts put it: 'An economic system is a population of rules, a structure of rules, and a process of rules.' Rules are the basic operational units in evolving social systems. For an individual or group, a prominent rule provides a normative guide for thought or action. Knowledge of a prevalent rule provides an imperfect but often necessary means of predicting the behaviour of others.[32]

Knowledge is an adaptation to circumstances. It is often acquired through social interaction. It becomes ingrained in habits. It involves a tacit or codified rule structure, subject to triggers and stimuli, often in organizational or other social contexts. Organizational knowledge is an emergent property of

---

31. There is a near-consensus that institutions are defined as systems of rules (Rowe, 1989; North, 1981, 201–2, 1990a; Ostrom, 1990; Knight, 1992; Crawford and Ostrom, 1995; Mantzavinos, 2001). This suggests that organizations are a kind of institution (Kornai, 1971; Parsons, 1983; Giddens, 1984; Scott, 1995; Miller, 2010; Guala, 2016). Despite a widespread belief, there is no clear evidence that North took a different view (Hodgson 2006, 2019a). When North (1990, 4) made a 'crucial distinction . . . between institutions and organizations', he may have implied, but did not clearly state, that they were mutually exclusive. Institutions and organizations are definitely different concepts, just like mammals and humans. North (1981, 18–19) more than once implied that organizations were institutions. Barzel (2002, 14n.), Dam (2006b, 22–23) and Faundez (2016) have criticized the stance that organizations are not institutions.

32. Dopfer et al. (2004, 263). See also Arthur (2006), Crawford and Ostrom (1995), Dopfer (2004), Dopfer and Potts (2008), Hodgson (1997, 2004, 2007, 2019b), Hodgson and Knudsen (2004), Holland et al. (1986), Ostrom (2005), Parra (2005), Potts (2000) and Vanberg (2002, 2004).

structured and shared individual knowledge. It depends on the existence of routines that can trigger behaviours as a result of interactions within the group. Just as individuals develop knowledge to deal with adaptive problems, organizations too are problem-solving entities. They are 'epistemic communities' and 'machineries of knowing'.[33]

Production is a goal-oriented process involving purposeful individuals. Both manual and mental labour involve the development of habits. Production is purposeful, problem solving and informational, played out on the register of material things. Production is organized in terms of structures and networks that process, filter and screen large amounts of information, which can be used to help generate useful knowledge. Production is informational as well as physical.

We may define *information* very broadly, in the famous sense of Claude Shannon and Warren Weaver, where a message has 'information content' when its receipt can cause some action. The information consists of signals with the potential to be retained, used by the receiver or communicated to others. This definition does not mention meanings and interpretations. This does not mean that they are unimportant. It is a mistake to think that taxonomic definitions must include every vital feature. The advantage of the Shannon-Weaver definition is that it highlights the rule-like structure (if in receipt of signal X, then carry out action Y) of a piece of information. This applies to genetic information and computer algorithms as well. When we discuss human social evolution, then, it is essential to bring meanings and interpretations into the picture, and to establish a richer concept of human knowledge that fully involves them.[34]

The informational mechanisms involved in socio-economic evolution are conditional, rule-like structures that are made up of habits of behaviour and thought that are ingrained in individuals and harboured in groups and organizations. They may be communicated using ideas, body language and other stimuli. We are not fully aware of some of the rules that we habitually follow. Much knowledge is unavoidably tacit and unavailable. The transmission of

---

33. For a selection of the large relevant literature, see Reber (1993), Plotkin (1994), Nonaka and Takeuchi (1995), Hendriks-Jansen (1996), Clark (1997), Wenger (1998), Keijzer (2001), Beinhocker (2006), Nonaka et al. (2006), Collins (2010), Knudsen et al. (2012), Luo et al. (2012), Gascoigne and Thornton (2013).

34. Shannon and Weaver (1949), Hodgson and Knudsen (2010, 123–27), Hodgson (2019a).

tacit knowledge is difficult. It often requires close study, social interaction and repeated practice.[35]

In modern economies, production is a materially grounded information system that is tied up with key institutions such as property and contract. They function as information registries of what is produced and owned, and of rules governing their use and allocation. In earlier societies, custom and tradition would play these informational roles. Any complex economy is a structure of organisations and sub-organisations, each subsystem playing its role in storing and processing information in habits, customs and routines.

This is a paradigm shift away from the physical metaphors that still infuse mainstream economics, as represented by production functions, maximising behaviour and other key concepts. Instead we need to develop another metaphor, where the processing, retention and replication of information, in complex and uncertain contexts, is central. This information-based metaphor admits an evolutionary perspective, using principles of variation, selection and inheritance, synthesized with notions of entropy and negentropy taken from thermodynamics, and with insights from the study of complexity. The kind of evolutionary thinking signalled here is arguably better placed to deal with issues such as adversity, conflict, cooperation, innovation, variety, complexity and uncertainty, which are all central to historical processes.[36]

Paradigm shifts are notoriously difficult to accomplish. As Thomas Kuhn, Michael Polanyi and Donald T. Campbell all pointed out, they meet the ingrained resistance of any organized academic discipline, with many good scientists habituated in old ways of thinking and with vested interest in the status quo. As Max Planck observed, sciences often progress not by persuasion, but by a new generation taking over as their elders die. Science advances, funeral by funeral.[37]

35. Polanyi (1966), Lave and Wenger (1991), Reber (1993), Cohen and Bacdayan (1994), Hutchins (1995), Nonaka and Takeuchi (1995), Lane et al. (1996), Clark (1997), Collins (2010).

36. On the roots of neoclassical economics in physics, see Mirowski (1989). For relevant modern evolutionary approaches, see Georgescu-Roegen (1971), Holland et al. (1986), Wicken (1987), Plotkin (1994), Depew and Weber (1995), Corning (2003, 2005), Beinhocker (2006), Mayfield (2013) and Wallast (2013).

37. Kuhn (1962), Polanyi (1962), Campbell (1969), Hodgson (2019d, chaps. 6–7). Planck (1949, 33–34) wrote that 'a new scientific truth does not triumph by convincing its opponents and making them see the light, but rather because its opponents eventually die, and a new generation grows up that is familiar with it'. This was quoted by Kuhn (1962, 150) and reportedly

Some seeds of this paradigm shift in economics were sown long ago. Alfred Marshall emphasized that knowledge 'is our most powerful engine of production' and that organization is an 'agent of production' that 'aids knowledge'. Thorstein Veblen noted the abuse of physical metaphors in economics and stressed the importance of habitual knowledge and evolution. Friedrich Hayek and Kenneth Boulding attempted to put knowledge—including its discovery and distribution—at the centre of economics.[38]

But grand sentiments about the informational paradigm and evolutionary analysis are not enough. The advantages of a shift in the required direction have to be demonstrated by detailed studies of concrete phenomena. In economic history and economic development, empirical evidence and its application have played a major role. A hope of this work is to show that changing some underlying principles may be of some significant help in improving both analysis and policy in these areas.

Scope and Content of This Book

My book on *Conceptualizing Capitalism* attempted to establish clear meanings of *capital* and *capitalism*, and to stress the nature and importance of such features as money and property rights. The present book is more about the detailed causes behind the rise of capitalism and of the Great Enrichment—to use McCloskey's term. *Conceptualizing Capitalism* is more about the 'what?'; this book is more about the 'why?' and the 'how?'

Marx was one of the first authors to write on the structures and dynamics of capitalism. We can still learn a great deal from him, even if several of his arguments are flawed. Chapter 1 is an appraisal of the Marxist theory of history. There are severe difficulties in the Marxist class analysis of historical change. It is argued here that institutions rather than classes are fundamental. The legal system is one of these institutions, which Marx erroneously regarded as part of the 'superstructure', somehow reflecting the (vaguely defined)

---

summarised with the distinctive 'funeral by funeral' wording in a 1975 *Newsweek* article by the economist Paul Samuelson.

38. Marshall (1920, 138–39), Veblen (1898a, 1898b, 1898c, 1906a, 1908a, 1908b, 1908c), Hayek (1948), Boulding (1966). On Veblen and Marshall on knowledge and evolution, see, respectively, Hodgson (2004, chaps. 7–8; 2013b). Endogenous growth theory (Romer, 1994; Aghion and Howitt, 1998) has put much more stress on the growth of knowledge and skill-creation, but it has placed this in the production function framework.

'economic' foundations beneath. But the 'economic' sphere itself relies on law to constitute some of its basic social relations and structures.

Chapter 2 reviews a selection of other explanatory approaches. Several authors have seen technology as the driver of change, with institutions following and adjusting in its wake. Some statements by Marx suggest this. Similar views are found in the writings of William Ogburn, Clarence Ayres, Erik Reinert and Justin Yifu Lin. Of course, without technological innovations there would have been no Industrial Revolution and no Great Enrichment. But the development of technology and its application require institutions. Most basically, the institution of language is required for communication. More particularly, there must be sufficient political freedom of enquiry. Science must be organized to consolidate, test and adapt ideas. In modern economies, financial institutions and business companies must be there to raise money for investment and to empower productive activity.

Also discussed in chapter 2 is Weber's claim that the Protestant ethic stimulated the capitalist spirit. Recent empirical research suggests that the likely chain of causality is that Protestantism gave greater encouragement to literacy, which then in turn aided innovation and economic growth. McCloskey likewise emphasized ideas but highlighted liberalism rather than Protestantism. She suggested that institutions did not change very much from the seventeenth to the nineteenth century. But liberalism grew in influence. Her claim of institutional stasis is countered at length below, by pointing to several major institutional changes in the seventeenth and eighteenth centuries, particularly in the financial sector. Joel Mokyr also emphasized ideas, but he focused on those that gave rise to modern experimental, practically oriented science and technology. He spotlighted 'intellectual entrepreneurs' such as Francis Bacon and Isaac Newton. But in contrast to McCloskey, he accepted a role for institutions in his explanation. He also placed the cultural advance of ideas in a Darwinian evolutionary framework.

Mokyr briefly considered the role of exogenous pressures and disruptions, alongside endogenous processes of institutional and technological development. Exogenous shocks (coming from outside a politico-economic system) are emphasized in the present work. Many of these shocks involved war. By contrast, writers including Marx and Schumpeter emphasized development 'from within' and paid less explanatory attention to external shocks. By contrast, external disruptions and conflicts, and their role in the development of European states, are a major theme of the work of Charles Tilly, and some of his insights are used in this book. But Tilly treated capital as *capital goods* and thus gave an inadequate account of the role of financial institutions in economic development. Nevertheless, exogenous shocks have to be considered alongside the complex dynamics of national systems.[39]

Chapter 2 is not intended to be exhaustive. Other important contributions, including by Douglass North, Daron Acemoglu, Francis Fukuyama and others, are considered later in the volume, in the context of explaining particular historical developments.[40]

Part 2 looks at historical developments in detail. Chapter 3 begins with the exogenous shock of the Black Death, which killed about half the English population and undermined key feudal institutions. After the end of serfdom, there were changes in landowning rights, including the introduction of copyhold tenure. The need to mobilise the rural population in the case of war was a major reason why the Tudor monarchs curbed enclosures and gave yeoman farmers some legal protection. Consequentially, the logic of economic growth was not entirely commercial. Exogenous and military matters greatly affected development.

The Reformation and the Dissolution of the Monasteries were highly disruptive, in religious, political and economic terms. The Dissolution created new landowners. Henry VIII revived some of their feudal obligations, to raise further revenues for war. The early Stuart monarchs had similar problems raising money for military purposes. Conflicts with Parliament over this led to the Civil War of 1642–51. The Protectorate under Oliver Cromwell abolished the feudal provisions reintroduced by Henry VIII. At the behest of the large landowners, the Restoration government quickly reaffirmed their abolition in 1660. The Stuart governments of Charles II and James II also furthered the interests of the big landowners, including by a crucial reform of mortgage law in the 1670s.

Chapter 4 looks at the impact of the Glorious Revolution of 1688 on British economic development. Contrary to some authors, the constitutional settlement of 1689 did not lead to significant changes in the nature and security of

39. Hodgson (1989, 1996, 2015a) stressed the importance of both exogenous and endogenous disruptions in economic development.

40. North had an extraordinary, virtuous capacity to admit sometimes that his critics were right, and to modify creatively his arguments in response. This led to a corpus of work that adapted and evolved; hence it is difficult to summarize briefly. Perhaps partly because of his shifting arguments, his work has more than a fair share of imprecision of meanings of key terms (Hodgson, 2006, 2017a, 2019a).

property rights. But the de facto balance of power between Crown and Parliament shifted in the direction of the latter. The effects of 1688 were international as well as domestic. The Glorious Revolution overturned Britain's alliances with France and Spain. After wars with the Dutch in 1652–54, 1665–57 and 1672–74, the Dutch United Provinces became Britain's foremost ally. This led to over a century of global war, interrupted by short periods of peace. The needs of war, combined with the new working accord between Crown and Parliament, led to major revolutions in British financial institutions and state administration. A new financial system developed with the Bank of England at its core, alongside a growing number of private banks. Extensive state borrowing was partly financed by loans from private banks and the sale of state bonds and annuities. Further measures had to be introduced to extend markets for debt and to increase borrowing. To finance the sinews of war, the national debt soared skywards. Waves of parliamentary enclosures after 1750 led to the consolidation of large estates. Inequalities of wealth and income increased. These changes were more important for the Industrial Revolution than the constitutional settlement of 1689. Financial innovations, developed in the crucible of war, were paramount.[41]

Having established the importance of financial institutions for economic development, and charted their evolution into the eighteenth century, the book considers in chapter 5 the possibility that the limited availability of finance remained a constraint on growth during the Industrial Revolution. It questions the prominent argument that there was 'no shortage of capital' for entrepreneurs at that time, and that they could rely on family and friends if any finance were needed. Against this, there is evidence to suggest that finance was inadequate, and the relatively underdeveloped state of the banking and financial system restricted economic growth. Specific cases, such as the famous partnership of Matthew Boulton and James Watt, show that their enterprise was held back for lack of finance, especially in its early years. Entrepreneurs often relied on the country banks, which were legally limited in size to six partners and highly vulnerable to financial shocks. Mortgaging was inhibited by a lack of a national land registry and by other factors. Nevertheless, there

41. Although this explanation of the British economic take-off has clear precedents in the work of Commons, Schumpeter and others, it is still neglected. For example, in their excellent text on the role of institutions in economic development, Koyama and Rubin (2022) list several explanations of the British Industrial Revolution. Novel financial institutions are not mentioned.

was sufficient finance to enable a major industrial transformation. The importance of financial institutions is thus underlined by both this positive achievement and by the financial constraints under which it operated. The chapter calls for more empirical research to get a more accurate picture.

Part 3 underlines some lessons from the analysis and makes some further points. Chapter 6 draws from psychology, philosophy and elsewhere to consider the conditions under which agents are impelled to try to solve pressing problems, during their struggles for power, wealth or recognition. Agents make decisions and act in ways that may promote or constrain socio-economic change. The basic argument is that disruptions of various kinds can bring emotional, cognitive and deliberative challenges, plus opportunities for individuals, families and organizations. These interruptions to habituated behaviour and daily routine pose problems that require some kind of resolution. Attempted problem solving takes place in a context of uncertainty and complexity. Posited solutions may draw on religious, scientific or other ideas to frame or justify an action. A variety of solutions may be tried. Conscious or unintended processes of selection may determine which of these solutions persist through time. By undertaking and responding to new actions, people establish new habits and routines, and socio-economic change is accomplished.

Ideas are still important in this account because they are used to rationalize and communicate current and changing activities. People are motivated by ideas, but their adoption must also be explained. Ideas and beliefs are founded on habits that are formed in particular social contexts. As the philosopher Charles Sanders Peirce put it, the 'essence of belief is the establishment of habit'. By contrast, 'ideas first' or 'mind first' explanations ignore the need to address and explain the processes through which ideas are selected and adopted. These accounts are often based on a mistaken 'folk psychology', where ideas and beliefs are seen as the primary sources of intentions, preferences, choices and actions.[42]

Ideas-first explanations have problems explaining the origins of ideas. Fortuitous mutations of ideas are not enough. But some accounts, particularly that of Mokyr, point also to impulses to solve pressing practical problems. If this perspective is broadened to include disruptions to ongoing behaviour, adaptive responses and changes to underlying habits, then our explanations

42. Peirce (1878, 294), Dewey (1922), Bunge (1980), Stich (1983, 1996), P. M. Churchland (1984, 1989), P. S. Churchland (1986), Damasio (1994), Rosenberg (1995, 1998), Rudolph et al. (2009).

no longer rely on ideas alone. Instead of an atomistic perspective that concentrates on individuals and their ideas, we need also to consider social relations, and the interactions of individuals with others in changing environments.[43]

We pay particular attention to legal institutions. Legal institutionalism involves four basic ontological claims. First, rules (including legal rules) infuse human society. Systems of rules support structures of power and perception, providing some social coherence and cognitive guidance. Second, law (in its most developed sense) necessarily involves both the state (broadly the realm of public ordering) and supportive private or customary arrangements. Reduction of law to either private (customary) or public (state) aspects alone is mistaken. This applies to systems of common law, as well as to civil or statute law. Law involves an institutionalized judiciary and a legislative apparatus. Third, law accounts for many of the powerful rules and structures of modern capitalist society. Consequently, law is not simply an expression of authority but is also a constitutive part of the institutionalized power structure, and a major means through which control is exercised. Fourth, law is a great motivational force. It works not simply through threat of punishment but also because of commitments to what is perceived as legitimately sovereign. Law builds on cultural (and possibly genetic) dispositions to honour legitimate authority. Many other rules do not have this motivational advantage, and obedience to them depends more on the expected benefits and costs of compliance versus non-compliance. Law, like religion, has enhanced moral power.[44]

Accordingly, law helps to constitute key economic institutions, including money and property. As Georg Knapp put it: 'Money is a creature of law. A theory of money must therefore deal with legal history.' As the legal theorist James Penner wrote, property is 'a creature of . . . the legal system'. These claims apply especially to modern developed economies, where property and its monetary valuations are crucial for economic decision-making. In underdeveloped societies, the rule of law may be compromised by greater arbitrary or unconstitutional power. But even in these cases, law often plays an important role. An understanding of history is impossible without reference to law.

43. Mokyr (2016).

44. Features of legal institutionalism are found in Commons (1924), Samuels (1971, 1989), Field (1991), Fukuyama (2011), Hodgson (2015a), Deakin et al. (2017) and Pistor (2019). On the nature and functions of law, see Hart (1961) and Ehrenberg (2016). On obedience to authority and law, see Milgram (1974), Tyler (1990), Haidt (2012). On legitimation, see Weber (1968, 1: 212 ff.).

And economic historians are not exempt. Law is far from the only thing that matters. But it does matter.[45]

Chapter 6 concludes with a discussion of whether the kind of institutional changes discussed in the preceding chapters can be understood in terms of the variation-selection-replication framework of generalized Darwinism, and if so, what peculiarities need to be added to that scaffolding. This poses an agenda for future theoretical and empirical research.

Chapter 7 considers the possibility that some English institutional innovations may have relevance for other countries today. Japan, South Korea and Taiwan are among the few economies that moved from underdevelopment in 1950 to a high level of development by the end of the twentieth century. Despite major differences with England, in their histories, cultures and institutions, these three countries fostered land collateralization, the extensive use of credit and related financial institutions, which are argued here to be generally crucial for modern economic development. Hence, despite the enormous differences between England and Japan, they both depended on modern financial institutions for economic progress. A final section draws the threads together and concludes the volume.

The evolution of the institutions of science is crucial for modern economic development, and this is briefly discussed in chapter 6. Science is an institutionalized process. Mokyr pointed to the 'Republic of Letters' that developed in Europe in the seventeenth and eighteenth centuries and enabled scientists from different countries to share and develop ideas. But while it was crucial, it was a limited institutional mechanism. More extensive organizations of science emerged in the nineteenth century. They were boosted in Prussia after 1809, with the university reforms of Karl Wilhelm von Humboldt. Later in the nineteenth century, universities in the United Kingdom, France, the United States, and elsewhere began to organize their scientific endeavours on a more systematic and professionalized basis. The role of science in technological and economic development became more important in a later period, after the years covered in this book.[46]

This volume stresses the importance of legal property relations and financial institutions in the development of capitalism. But while these are common features of developed capitalism throughout the world, there is enormous

45. Knapp (1924, 1), Penner (1997, 3).

46. Polanyi (1962), Campbell (1969), Kitcher (1993), Hodgson (2019d), Mokyr (2016) Koyama and Rubin (2022, 171–74).

variation in the institutional structures of different capitalisms. While global-ization has led to some convergence, pressures have been insufficient to force all the different capitalisms to meet on one developmental path. England is spe-cial because it was the first fully developed capitalist economy. It is also special because it is different, and it will remain so.

Some see countries as going through preordained developmental stages. Marxists, the German historical school, and numerous other scholars extensively developed such a view of history. But stages theories typically overgeneralize. At many historical junctures, diverse options are possible. Development is often path dependent, with branching possibilities at key points of bifurcation. Co-existing systems often exhibit varied tracks of development.[47]

Some systems adorn and encapsulate institutions from their past. Britain today is an example. It hybridizes aristocratic elements with business and fi-nance. Britain is a form of aristocratic capitalism. The survival of its ancient nobility is imprinted on its institutions and in the backgrounds of many of its powerful individuals. As a system it harks back to its past, to draw selective comfort from its past international hegemony and its historic achievements. England's past is played out in Britain's politics and economics today. But that is another story.

47. Stages theories of historical development are countered by the literature on path depen-dence (North, 1990a; Arthur, 1994; David, 1994) and on institutional complementarities (Aoki, 2001; Hall and Soskice, 2001). Some critics describe the stages view of development as 'evolu-tionary' and reject all 'evolutionary' approaches because of that association. (e.g., Giddens, 1979, 233; Graeber and Wengrow, 2021, 319, 442, 446–49, 454, 474). But it is a big mistake to reject all 'evolutionary' theories on such grounds. Graeber and Wengrow (2021, 446) explicitly dismissed Darwinism, with the profoundly mistaken claim that it too entails a stages theory. In fact, Dar-winism rejects the notion of preordained development and all other teleological explanations of change (Veblen, 1906b; Mayr, 1988). Ironically, Graeber and Wengrow's account of a rich diversity in scale and organization among early cultures is redolent of a Darwinian view.

Scotland

1. Huntingdonshire
2. Bedfordshire
3. Buckinghamshire
4. Hertfordshire
5. Middlesex
6. Isle of Wight
7. Lancashire
8. Shropshire

Yorkshire – North Riding

Yorkshire – West Riding

York

Yorkshire – East Riding

⑦ Bury
Manchester
Liverpool
Styal
Sheffield

Chester

Nottingham

Norfolk

Wales

⑧
Coalbrookdale

Birmingham
Coventry
Naseby
1645

Fenland

① Ely
Cambridge

Suffolk

South Wales

Oxford
③
② St Albans
④

⑤
London
Putney
Uxbridge

Bristol

Langport
1645

Salisbury

Devon
Exeter

River Tamar

Cornwall
Plymouth
Brixham

Weymouth

⑥

0   50   100   150
Miles
0   50   100   150   200
Kilometres

France

MAP 1. Places mentioned in the text, with English county boundaries circa 1844

PART I

Some Prominent Explanatory Frameworks

1

Karl Marx's Theory of History

What Marx accomplished was to produce such a comprehensive, dramatic, and fascinating vision that it could withstand innumerable empirical contradictions, logical refutations, and moral revulsions at its effects. The Marxian vision took the overwhelming complexity of the real world and made the parts fall into place, in a way that was intellectually exhilarating and conferred such a sense of moral superiority that opponents could be simply labelled and dismissed as moral lepers or blind reactionaries.

—THOMAS SOWELL, *MARXISM, PHILOSOPHY AND ECONOMICS* (1985)

I enrage my friends on the right by stating the obvious, that Marx was the greatest social scientist of the nineteenth century, without compare. But then I enrage my friends on the left by adding . . . that he was nevertheless mistaken on almost every point of economics and of history. Which is why I haven't got any friends.

—DEIRDRE MCCLOSKEY, *WHY LIBERALISM WORKS* (2019)

NOTWITHSTANDING THE FLAWS in his analysis, Karl Marx is one of the greatest social scientists of all time. His thinking still frames debate. His portrayal of history going through stages, from antiquity and feudalism to capitalism, is still prominent among his supporters and critics. His emphasis on the technological 'forces of production' as drivers of change still inspires many different writers. We need to address his intellectual legacy.

This book considers how England developed from a backward feudal state to become a rich capitalist country. Marx's influence is present in how the problem is presented and what concepts are used. Marx's thought is often valuable when it was wrong, as well as when it is right. The gaps and mistakes require us to develop different ideas. Marx posed important questions, even when he gave flawed answers.

Marxism is used here as a foil to introduce some contrasting ideas. For example, I side with Schumpeter against Marx as seeing modern finance as definitionally central to capitalism. Also against Marx, I argue that social class is not a foundational category—it rests upon more fundamental phenomena. Major socio-economic changes are better described as institutional transformations than in terms of the rise and fall of social classes. Marxism is a prominent example of endogenous 'unfolding' or 'stages' views of historical development. This emphasis on endogenous change downplays the importance of exogenous shocks in politico-economic transformations. Also against Marx, I propose that the state cannot be reduced to class interests. Finally, I stress the additional importance of legal powers and relations, which are not 'superstructural' as Marx suggested. Despite all my criticisms, the fact that Marx's work can be used in this way is a tribute to its importance and influence.

Marx's Historical Materialism

Marx insisted that capitalism was a historically specific social formation. He shared this view with members of the German historical school. Together they differentiated between concepts that related to a particular mode of production and concepts that applied to all human existence.[1]

Marx distinguished the 'natural' or 'material' content of economic activity, on the one hand, from its (historically specific) social and relational forms, on the other. For example, he differentiated labour in general from the historically specific form of wage labour. The former is present in all human societies throughout history. Marx's distinction is redolent of John Stuart Mill's claim in 1848 that material production is essentially a matter of the laws of nature, whereas distribution is a contingent matter of specific social organization.

---

1. On Marx and the German historical school on historical specificity, see Hodgson (2001). Marx mostly used the term *capitalist mode of production* rather than *capitalism*. The word *Kapitalismus* does not appear in the original German edition of the first volume of *Das Kapital*. In the German edition of the second volume, which was edited by Engels, *Kapitalismus* appears just once. It does not appear at all in the German edition of the third volume. I thank Dmitri Safronov for these observations.

Both Mill and Marx created a dichotomy between material production and social relations.[2]

Accordingly, Marx considered the interplay between the material 'productive forces' of technology and the social 'relations of production' or 'property relations' between social classes. As he wrote in his famous *Preface to the Critique of Political Economy* in 1859:

> The mode of production of material life conditions the general process of social, political and intellectual life. . . . At a certain stage of development, the material productive forces of society come into conflict with the existing relations of production . . . with the property relations within the framework of which they have operated hitherto. From forms of development of the productive forces these relations turn into their fetters. Then begins an era of social revolution.[3]

These words have proved controversial. Gerald Cohen's defence of Marx's stance is one of the most rigorous, but other Marxists contest it. A controversial part of Cohen's argument is his 'Primacy Thesis', which he summarized as follows: 'The nature of the production relations of society is explained by the level of development of its productive forces'.[4]

Addressing Marx's distinction between 'material' forces and 'social' relations of production, where do work relations—concerning the organization of work—fit in? Are work relations part of the 'material productive forces' or part of the 'relations of production'? One option is to put work organization among the productive forces. We may accept that industrial output depends on and is affected by the organization of the production process. Production is necessarily tied up with organization, and it cannot be grounded solely on physical conditions, without the inclusion of organizational and motivational matters as well. The constitution and use of much tacit and explicit knowledge in production depend on organized social relations.[5]

2. Mill (1909, 199) wrote: 'The laws and conditions of the Production of wealth partake of the character of physical truths.' Cohen (1978, 108–11) showed that Marx's attempt to criticize Mill on this point is a failure.

3. Marx (1971, 20–21).

4. Cohen (1978, 134). Other Marxist accounts include Elster (1983), Callinicos (2009), Blackledge (2019) and Laibman (2019).

5. For example, Suchman (1987, 2007), Button (1993), Star (1995), Collins and Kusch (1998), Latour (2005), Orlikowski (2010).

But work organization is not independent of wider social relations. To a degree, the organization of work reflects the power relations in society as a whole. The boundaries between the 'material productive forces' and the (historically specific) social relations of productive organization become so fuzzy that the distinction (attempted by both Mill and Marx) begins to break down.

Cohen tried to rescue Marx from this difficulty by regarding work relations as neither 'social relations' nor 'material productive forces'. Cohen upheld three mutually exclusive categories: (a) work relations, (b) productive forces and (c) social relations. He excluded work relations from the productive forces with this argument: 'We agree that *something* in this conceptual area is a productive force, but not the work relations themselves. On our account, knowledge of ways of organizing labour is a productive force, part of managerial labour power, but the relations established when that knowledge is implemented are not productive forces.'[6] Here Cohen adopted a questionable view of the nature of productive knowledge. He assumed a separation of conception and implementation, redolent of Taylorist management theory, where all relevant knowledge can in principle be held by management and communicated to others. It sees knowledge as an individual matter, to the neglect of the social relations and structures that are necessary for its retrieval, deployment and operation. In reality, the constitution and deployment of knowledge are inseparable from social relations.[7] This mounts a challenge to Cohen's solution. The boundaries between (a), (b) and (c) all become blurred.

Another major problem is that some explanation of the autonomous development of the productive forces is required to sustain the view that they eventually 'come into conflict with the existing relations of production'. If there were no autonomous pressure from the productive forces, with their growth solely determined by the relations of production, then this conflict would not happen. Such autonomous tendencies must also be presumed to make sense of the notion that the relations of production sometimes 'fetter' or constrain the productive forces.

Marx saw the need for such an explanation. He wrote in an 1846 letter: 'The productive forces are the result of man's practical energy.' And 'developing his productive forces' results from him 'living' in a given material environment.

6. Cohen (1978, 112–13), Marx and Engels (1976a, 47), Hodgson (1999, 184–86, 267–68).
7. Taylor (1911), Polanyi (1966), Lave and Wenger (1991), Reber (1993), Cohen and Bacdayan (1994), Hutchins (1995), Nonaka and Takeuchi (1995), Lane et al. (1996), Clark (1997), Goldman (1999, 2009), Collins (2010).

This attempted a general explanation of why productive forces tend to grow independently of the relations of production, creating the possibility that the latter can 'fetter' the former.[8]

Cohen tried to improve on Marx's account. Unconfined to capitalism or to any other particular mode of production, Cohen suggested 'a perennial tendency to productive progress, arising out of rationality and intelligence in the context of the inclemency of nature'. His argument for both the primacy and the autonomous development of the productive forces throughout history is 'based . . . on such generalities as human rationality and intelligence, and the fact of scarcity'.[9]

But Cohen's explanation of the autonomous growth of the productive forces also falls short. Human 'rationality and intelligence', ingenuity and 'practical energy' while 'living' in the context of 'scarcity' can account at best for only minimal incremental changes in the productive forces and technology. Cohen ignored the historically specific social relations that empower the deployment of 'rationality and intelligence' when dealing with scarcity and the challenges of nature. Rational analysis, ingenuity and practical energy all depend on social relations and interactions. Remarkably, when he wrote of 'man's practical energy', Marx added these words: 'The social history of man is never anything else than the history of his individual development.' It seems that he saw productive forces as the aggregate of individual efforts. Marxism exhibits here a remarkably individualistic view of the nature and retention of knowledge.[10]

Changes in technology and productivity that involve new forms or work organization cannot be explained by 'rationality and intelligence' or ingenuity of a single worker facing 'the inclemency of nature'. Workers must coordinate their activities. Through their interaction they trigger procedural knowledge

8. Marx (1971, 21), Marx and Engels (1982, 96, 100).

9. Cohen (1978, 155, 159). By 'rationality' Cohen seemed to mean 'subject to reason'. There is no evidence here that he was adopting the model of rational choice in mainstream economics. Cohen did not define 'scarcity' carefully. We should distinguish between global and local scarcity. Some resources—like oil—are globally limited, but others—like love and trust—are not. Local scarcity is a universal feature of the human condition. Love and trust are not globally limited, but they are locally scarce. Even if some resources are globally abundant, it always takes time and energy to focus on them and to bring them into practical use. For Cohen, local scarcity is the relevant concept.

10. Marx and Engels (1982, 96–100), Cohen (1978, 154–60).

and utilize complementary tacit skills. Without these interactions, these forms of interpersonal knowledge cannot be adequately deployed.

Capitalism is by far the most innovative and productive system in human history, multiplying wealth and productive capacity many times over. It exploits large-scale organization and economies of scale. In 1848 Karl Marx and Frederick Engels acknowledged this achievement: 'The bourgeoisie, during its rule of scarce one hundred years, has created more massive and more colossal productive forces than have all preceding generations together.'[11]

Marx and Engels attributed this creation of 'more massive and more colossal productive forces' to 'the bourgeoisie', who 'cannot exist without constantly revolutionising the instruments of production, and thereby the relations of production, and with them the whole relations of society'. Capitalists need to make profits to survive. They innovate, invest and accumulate. The economic success of the bourgeoisie is largely attributable to the way capitalist social relations accelerate the growth of the productive forces. By acknowledging the power of these social structures, Marx and Engels admitted that relations of production can greatly stimulate the forces of production. Any general, ahistorical impulses for the development of the productive forces solely through intelligence and ingenuity are miniscule by comparison to the additional forces provided by capitalism. The productive forces alone are not the major drivers of change in modern societies. Relations of production matter much more.[12]

We may agree with Marx that capitalism and markets can fetter the productive forces. Problems with markets are well known. Mainstream economics abounds with discussions of business cycles, recessions, market failures, transaction costs, problems with externalities, and difficulties with the provision of public goods. Such problems within capitalism are not confined to markets. Alfred Marshall understood that the ability of the worker to exit from an employment relationship could deter employers from investing sufficiently in worker training. Marshall's observation is among the most pertinent, but it is rarely discussed. It identifies an irremovable structural limitation within capitalism. Marxism is not alone in identifying such problems.[13]

11. Marx (1973a, 70).
12. Marx (1973a, 70, 72; 1976).
13. See Marshall (1920, 565) and Hodgson (2015, chap. 9) for a discussion. Worker cooperatives may be a possible solution, as they provide enhanced incentives for workers to remain with the organisation.

Historical materialism has very limited explanatory power. For example, it does not identify the most important causal factors in the decline of serfdom in England in the fourteenth century—it had relatively little to do with technology or the productive forces. Historical materialism is of meagre help in explaining the key institutional and other conditions that enabled the rise of English capitalism in the seventeenth and eighteenth centuries, and which underpinned the industrial take-off after 1760. Historical materialism serves more as a historical schema to foretell the end of capitalism, on dubious and unelaborated grounds, and with an unjustified presumption that socialism is its only possible progressive replacement. The Marxist assumption that the replacement of private by common ownership would unfetter the productive forces is unproven in theory and countered by historical experience.[14]

Marxism and Class Struggle

Marx and Engels proclaimed in their *Communist Manifesto*: 'The history of all hitherto existing society is the history of class struggles.'[15] They defined classes in terms of their ownership or non-ownership of means of production. Feudal society was dominated by the nobility, including the king, who owned and controlled the land. Beneath them the vast majority of the population were serfs, working on the land under the control of their lords. In England, serfdom declined rapidly from the fourteenth century. Many serfs became wage labourers. Markets expanded. Two classes—bourgeois and proletarians (employers and workers)—grew in importance. According to Marx and Engels, the development of the productive forces was held back by surviving feudal relations. These fetters included aristocratic 'privilege, the institutions of guilds and corporations' and 'the regulatory system of the Middle Ages'. The rising commercial class progressively undermined these feudal structures and the power of the nobility.[16]

Eventually, according to their account, a social revolution occurred, where one class took supreme power from another. In the transition from feudalism to capitalism the bourgeoisie became dominant. Major constraints on the

---

14. Some varieties of capitalism, such as in the Nordic countries (Kenworthy, 2019; Hodgson, 2019c) are much more progressive and egalitarian than others. On the limitations of socialism, see Hodgson (2019c).

15. Marx (1973a, 67).

16. Marx and Engels (1982, 97).

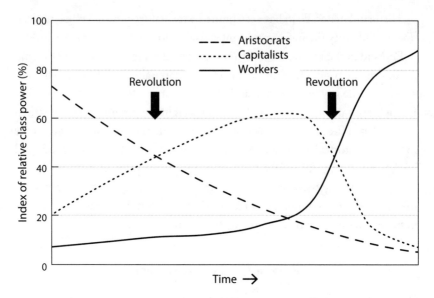

FIGURE 1.1. The Marxist view of history

development of the productive forces were removed. Within capitalism, the working class was eventually brought together in large factories and urban communities. The progressive agglomeration and growing organizational strength of this majority class enables its future seizure of political power. The transition from capitalism to socialism will occur after the workers take overall control from the bourgeoisie.[17] This Marxist historical schema is summarized and simplified in figure 1.1.

Marx described the English transition from feudalism to capitalism as a protracted process. He claimed that an embryonic bourgeoisie and a substantial working class emerged as early as the fifteenth century. In *Capital* he wrote:

> The starting point of the development that gave rise to the wage-labourer and to the capitalist, was . . . the transformation of feudal exploitation into capitalist exploitation. . . . The prelude to the revolution that laid the

---

17. Marx and Engels defined both communism and socialism as common ownership of the means of production. They used communism in their early writings. Engels later favoured the word socialism (Hodgson, 2019c, 27–32).

foundation of the capitalist mode of production was played out in the last third of the fifteenth century and the first few decades of the sixteenth. A mass of 'free' and unattached proletarians was hurled on the labour market . . . the great feudal lords . . . created an incomparably larger proletariat by forcibly driving the peasantry from the land.[18]

Bourgeois commercial interests eroded feudal property relations and, by ejecting peasants from the land, created a mass proletariat. Marx wrote that the 'bourgeois capitalists favoured . . . converting the land into a merely commercial commodity'. An 'alliance' was established between the rising bourgeoisie and big landowners who owned 'not feudal but bourgeois property'. A landed 'capitalist' class developed, allied with capitalist manufacturers and merchants, all making use of waged labour. According to Marx, capitalist production first emerged in England in a rural setting.[19]

Marx and Engels described the English Civil War of 1642–51 as a 'bourgeois revolution' and saw the Glorious Revolution of 1688 as part of the same process of bourgeois ascendancy. Marx wrote that 'two thunderclaps occurred, the revolutions of 1640 and of 1688. In England, all the earlier economic forms, the social relations corresponding to them, and the political system . . . were destroyed.' He drew a parallel between the English Revolution of the 1640s and the French Revolution of 1789. In both of them 'it was a matter of asserting free competition and of abolishing all feudal property relations, such as landed estates, guilds, monopolies, etc., which had been transformed into fetters for . . . industry'. But as shown in chapter 3, Marx exaggerated the destruction of 'feudal property relations' in England in the seventeenth century.[20]

According to Marx, the English Civil War and the Glorious Revolution led to a compromise between commercially minded aristocrats and the rising bourgeoisie. By 'the subordination of the monarchy to Parliament', the Glorious Revolution ensured the king's 'subordination to the rule of a class'. As

18. Marx (1976, 875, 878).

19. Marx (1976, 884–85), Marx and Engels (1978, 254).

20. Hill (1948), Marx and Engels (1982, 97), Marx and Engels (1976b, 322). Marx explained the 'riddle of the conservatism of the English Revolution' by 'the persisting alliance of the bourgeoisie with the majority of then big landowners'. By contrast, the 1789 French Revolution 'eliminated big landed property by parcellation': there was no such class alliance in France (Marx and Engels, 1978, 254). Epstein (1991) placed the decline of English guilds later, mostly in the eighteenth century.

Marx wrote in *Capital*: 'The "glorious Revolution" brought into power, along with William of Orange, the landed and capitalist profit-grubbers.'[21]

A major problem with this account is that the landed aristocracy prospered for more than three further centuries, retaining enormous wealth and power. The aristocracy retains huge wealth and is still a major force in British politics. Although the Parliament Act of 1911 reduced its authority, the House of Lords remains powerful to this day. According to a twenty-first-century estimate of land ownership by Guy Shrubsole, 'the aristocracy and gentry still own about 30 per cent of England'.[22]

The Marxist historian Perry Anderson stressed the survival of aristocratic power in Britain. Following the English Revolution of 1640–51 there was 'no enlarged franchise, no weakening of the principles of heredity and hierarchy. . . . Landed aristocrats, large and small, continued to rule England.' He tried to reconcile this highly pertinent observation with Marxism. He claimed without substantiation that the British aristocracy 'was no longer feudal but essentially capitalist' and there was 'from the start no fundamental antagonistic contradiction between the old aristocracy and the new bourgeoisie'. What does 'essentially capitalist' mean? To keep within Marxism, the aristocracy had to become bourgeois, to cover the awkward failure of the bourgeoisie to gain complete power. Anderson retained the challengeable Marxist view that if a system were capitalist, then a bourgeoisie (of some kind) must be in control. Aristocrats remaining in power had to be relabelled as capitalist. Anderson tried to force the awkward English facts into Marxist class categories. But credit is due to him for underlining the persistence of the landed aristocracy.[23]

As indicated in chapter 4, Veblen provided a robust argument why the rich leisure classes lack the impetus for innovation and development. Instead, change comes largely from those who are most affected by disturbances and have the means to overcome these problems. Consequently, the survival of

21. Marx and Engels (1978, 252–53), Marx (1976, 884). Marx (1976, 884–85) emphasized a bourgeois-landowner alliance. Subsequent scholars have emphasized that the relative degrees to which political systems were dominated by landowners versus (town-based) bourgeois interests were crucial factors in European state formation and the divergence between absolutism and democracy (Moore, 1966; Anderson, 1974; Tilly, 1992; Ertman, 1997; Scott, 2011).

22. Shrubsole (2019, 266).

23. Anderson (1964, 30–31), Marx (1973a, 70). Anderson's essay stimulated a lively debate. See Ingham (1984) for a perceptive critical discussion.

aristocratic power in Britain has been a major brake on economic growth since the eighteenth century.[24]

Factions of the English aristocracy have played historically on different sides. Some aligned with the revolutionaries in both 1642–51 and 1688. Others backed the Royalists in 1642 and King James II in 1688. Many of them would pursue 'profit grubbing' commercial activity. But most also wanted to keep their land within their family, and hence they backed feudal entails that restricted its sale. They might support a revolution, as long as their landed property rights remained secure, for them and for their successors. Class identity was not irrelevant, but it was a weak predictor of an individual's choice of side in these conflicts.

Was the English Civil War a bourgeois revolution? Was there a rural bourgeoisie? The Marxist historian Edward P. Thompson noted sardonically: 'It is a strain on one's semantic patience to imagine a class of *bourgeois* scattered across a countryside and dwelling on their estates.' Anderson noted the odd fit with conventional Marxism: the main protagonists were rural classes, hence 'it was a "bourgeois revolution" only by proxy'. But if the bourgeoisie did not actually come to power themselves, then it is difficult to describe the revolution as bourgeois. Marx emphasized the rise of wage labour and growing production for profit. But if these are the criteria of a 'bourgeois revolution', then it was well under way over a century before the English Civil War. Marx was wrong about timings and outcomes.[25]

The Marxist historian Ellen Meiksins Wood saw much of the social strife in England from the sixteenth century as between landlords and tenants over rents and rights. For her, this 'cast doubt on the characterization of the seventeenth-century English Revolution as a "bourgeois revolution" and, indeed, on the whole concept of "bourgeois revolution"'. It was a struggle between landowners and rural workers, not a primarily a battle involving the bourgeoisie: 'The English Revolution . . . was certainly not a conflict between bourgeoisie and aristocracy.'[26]

Similar difficulties arise with the Marxist account of the French Revolution. Several historians have criticized the idea that it was a triumph of the bourgeoisie. Alfred Cobban noted that the French revolutionaries were typically

---

24. See Veblen (1899, 188–206). Veblen (1906b, 1907) criticized Marxism for its teleological and class-based view of history, but he retained socialist views (Hodgson, 2023).

25. Thompson (1975, 40), Anderson (1964, 28).

26. Meiksins Wood (2002, 118, 121).

lawyers or state officials rather than businesspeople. Capitalists played an insignificant role in the revolution itself. George Taylor and other historians have showed that capitalists in France collaborated with the royalist state before 1789 and that their share of economic activity was then small. The capitalist class did not mount a challenge to the old order. The interpretation of the revolution as a class conflict between the aristocracy and the rising bourgeoisie had to be abandoned. In the light of this evidence, the Marxist historian George Comninel wrote: 'The French Revolution was essentially an *intra-class* conflict. . . . It was a civil war within the ruling class. . . . The Revolution was not fought by capitalists, and did not produce capitalist society. . . . It may be better simply to drop the idea of bourgeois revolution once and for all.'[27]

As indicated in chapter 7, Marxism also has problems with the Meiji Restoration in Japan in 1868. It brought capitalism but was led by powerful members of feudal strata, under the symbolic leadership of an emperor.

'Dropping the idea' of a bourgeois revolution would have major consequences for Marxism. The schema of history unfolding toward a proletarian revolution (as illustrated in figure 1.1) would disappear. If the idea of a bourgeois revolution is questioned, then so too is the future triumph of the proletariat. For Marxists, much is at stake here. If they give up their idea of history creating the possibility of a collective utopia based on proletarian rule, then their ideological lodestone is lost.

Marx pictured the emergence of a rural proletariat and of a landowning bourgeoisie within late feudalism. He dated the beginnings of these developments to the fifteenth century. But there is evidence of wage labour from the late thirteenth century and of the commercial buying and selling of some agricultural land from the twelfth century. Rural wage labour for day wages increased steadily, covering more than half of the population by 1688.[28]

Marx also addressed the rise of industry and the creation of a largely *urban* working class. He wrote: 'Productive capital, or the mode of production corresponding to capital, can be present in only two forms: manufacture and large-scale industry.' In fact, his vision of a large *industrial* proletariat was first realized in England in the nineteenth century.[29]

---

27. Cobban (1964), Taylor (1967) and Doyle (2002, 451–53), Comninel (1987, 200, 202, 205).

28. Marx (1976, 875, 878, 884–85), Postan (1972), Harvey (1984), Epstein (1991), Lindert and Williamson (1982, 393), Allen (1992, 63–63).

29. Marx (1973b, 585), Kitson et al. (2012).

If the rural rise and industrial extension of wage labour are both paramount, then the Marxist account of the rise of capitalism is a hugely elongated process, lasting at least five centuries, from the fourteenth to the nineteenth inclusive. But as Robert C. Allen has argued, the proletarianization of rural labour was not a steady or even process. Neither was it inevitable. It was not a prominent feature of capitalist development in many other countries. Marx was wrong to suggest that other countries would follow England along a similar developmental path. Multiple paths of development are possible.[30]

Much More than Social Class: The State and Finance

Marx acknowledged the existence of non-capitalist elements within capitalism. These impurities include non-market relations, state administration, legal institutions, family units and so on. But Marx oversimplified, by focusing on a capitalism without any impurities. He declared in the preface to the first edition of *Capital* that he was following physicists by studying the capitalist mode of production in its 'most typical form . . . least affected by disturbing influences' and hence closest to its 'pure state'. He did not acknowledge that a pure capitalism could not function. A 100 per cent market system cannot work: not everything can be owned, bought and sold. Contrary to Marx, all capitalisms are enduringly and necessarily impure. Some crucial impurities are essential buttresses to the system.[31]

No single class is ever in control. State power is irreducible to class power. States are complex political and administrative entities with legal and economic functions. Marxists write of the 'relative autonomy' of the state, but their Marxism requires that the state is always connected to a particular social

30. Allen (1992, 1999). Marx (1976, 90–91) claimed in his preface to the first edition of *Capital* that England foretold what would happen in Germany and the 'country that is more developed industrially only shows, to the less developed, the image of its own future'.

31. Marx (1976, 90). Schumpeter (1942, 139) noted that capitalism depended on non-capitalist 'flying buttresses' that acted as 'partners of the capitalist stratum, symbiosis with whom was an essential element of the capitalist schema'. This is similar to the 'impurity principle' in Hodgson (1984, 1988). On Marx's neglect of 'impurities' and his adoption of an Aristotelian 'natural state model', where variation is seen as a temporary deviation from what is natural, see Sober (1980) and Hodgson (2015a, 33; 2016). The 'natural state model' should not be confused with the North et al. (2009) concept of a 'natural state', which is discussed later in this book.

class. But the state has a character of its own. To describe it as simply 'aristo-cratic' or 'bourgeois' is to vastly oversimplify its nature.[32]

Marx and Engels wrote: 'The executive of the modern state is nothing but a committee for managing the common affairs of the whole bourgeoisie.'[33] This is a drastic oversimplification. Elsewhere they put more nuanced views. Marx himself claimed that England was governed for a while by an alliance of the bourgeoisie and the aristocracy. Even with such amendments, Marx un-derestimated the degree of state autonomy, and he gave insufficient acknowl-edgement of counterbalancing subcentres of social and economy power, even within the state itself, including Parliament, the fiscal bureaucracy, the law and the military. Marxism is still committed to a view of the state as ultimately the expression of class interests. Yet organized state agencies have their own agen-das, and these are irreducible to class interests or aims alone. The state too is a social actor, itself made up of multiple interests and agencies.

Another weakness in Marxism is its treatment of financial institutions. Al-though Marx mentioned finance and credit, he did not see them as defining features of capitalism. By contrast, Schumpeter saw finance as central, stressing the importance of modern financial institutions. The definitional inclusion of such financial institutions brings the dating of the birth of English capitalism to sometime in the seventeenth century, with other important developments in financial arrangements stretching into the eighteenth. This is later than Marx suggested.[34]

Partly due to the influence of Marxism, capitalism has frequently been as-sociated principally with profit-seeking and markets, sometimes with the ad-dition of wage labour. Finance is often neglected. Hence Richard Tawney found rising 'capitalists', hiring labour and making profits out of land, as early as the sixteenth century. The Marxist historian Christopher Hill saw 'capitalist farmers' cultivating the land 'along capitalist lines' well before 1640. The non-Marxist John Mackie also saw the employment of waged workers as the defin-ing mark of 'capitalism', dating from before the fifteenth century. The Marxist historian Robert Brenner referred to the 'capitalist class relations' of 'agricul-tural capitalism' emerging after the decline of serfdom, with large landholdings

32. On the relative autonomy of the state, see Evans et al. (1985), Jessop (1990) and Ingham (1984).

33. Marx (1973a, 69).

34. Schumpeter (1934, 1939), Hodgson (2015a, 2021b). On the comparison between ancient and modern finance, see Goldsmith (1987) and later chapters of this book.

'farmed on the basis of capital improvement with wage labour' and 'capitalist tenants who could afford to make capitalist investments'. The non-Marxist historian Robert Allen also highlighted the employment of wage labour and accordingly noted several 'capitalist farms' in England as early as 1279. All these authors followed Marx in seeing profit-seeking 'bourgeois' landowners employing waged labour as manifestations of capitalism. But capitalism, in a Schumpeterian sense that includes modern finance, came much later.[35]

Markets, profit-making, employees and the accumulation of capital goods are insufficient to identify the powerful system that arose in the eighteenth century and spread globally thereafter. Capital goods have existed among humans since they first used spears and stone tools—for millions of years. Markets and profit-making have existed for thousands of years. Trade in land has a long history. Wage labour dominated the English economy after the decline of serfdom in the fourteenth century. Profit-seeking employers become true capitalists when their property is *capital*, not in the misleading sense of capital goods, but in the everyday business and accounting sense of an asset that can be used as security to obtain finance. Marx, Tawney, Hill, Brenner and many others all missed the crucial importance of credit, collateral and the broader growth of financial institutions. Without these, land, buildings and other assets could not be used to finance innovation and expand production. Capitalism is about capital, understood not as physical stuff but as the monetary value of tradeable property rights.[36]

Much More than Social Class: The Role of Law

There are further problems with Marxist class analysis. Engels defined the two main classes of modern capitalism, the bourgeoisie and the proletariat: 'By bourgeoisie is meant the class of modern capitalists, owners of the means of social production and employers of wage labour. By proletariat, the class of modern wage labourers who, having no means of production of their own, are reduced to selling their labour power in order to live.'[37] Engels referred here to *ownership*, the *employment* of waged labourers, and the *selling* of labour power. Marx frequently used terms such as *owner* and *property*. In the third

35. Marx (1976, 884), Tawney (1912, 6–7, 71, 78–97, 136–39, 200–204, 210–30), Hill (1940, 223–24; 1948/49, 37), Mackie (1952, 444, 461), Brenner (1976, 45, 47, 63, 67), Allen (1992, 63).
36. Hodgson (2014, 2015a).
37. Marx (1973a, 67 n.).

volume of *Capital*, in its unfinished chapter on 'Classes', Marx wrote: 'The *owners* of mere labour-power, the *owners* of capital and the land*owners* . . . in other words wage-labourers, capitalists and landowners . . . form the three great classes of modern society based on the capitalist mode of production.' Albeit loosely, Marx and Engels used legal terms to define social classes.[38]

By *ownership* did they simply mean *control*? Take the example of the employment contract. If it were simply a matter of control, then it would be difficult to distinguish wage labour from slavery, except perhaps as a matter of degree. The worker and the slave are both under the control of their masters. On the surface, their circumstances and behaviour can be similar. Yet, probing deeper, Marx himself saw a crucial difference. He wrote in *Capital* of the important 'distinction between . . . a society based on slave-labour and a society based on wage-labour'. He explained that in the employment contract 'the proprietor of labour-power must always sell it for a limited period only, for if he were to sell it in a lump, once and for all, he would be selling himself, converting himself from a free man into a slave, from an owner of a commodity into a commodity.' The wage-labourer, in contrast to a slave, 'manages both to alienate his labour-power and to avoid renouncing his rights of ownership over it'. Marx then added in a note: 'Hence legislation in various countries fixes a maximum length for labour contracts.' When he was analytically careful, Marx was obliged to make use of legal concepts—such as sale, contract and ownership—to define the working class under capitalism. When he probed deeper, he referred to underlying legal relations and not simply appearances.[39]

More broadly, as Robert W. Gordon argued:

> In practice, it is just about impossible to describe any set of 'basic' social practices without describing the legal relations among the people involved— legal relations that don't simply condition how the people relate to each other but to an important extent define the constitutive terms of the relationship, relations such as lord and peasant, master and slave, employer and employee, ratepayer and utility, and taxpayer and municipality.[40]

Gordon pointed out that 'in actual historical societies, the law governing social relations' has been 'a key element in the constitution of productive relations'.

---

38. Marx (1981, 1025, emphasis added).

39. Marx (1976, 271, 325). Unfortunately, Marx in propagandistic mode sometimes contradicted this, by misleadingly describing wage labour as slavery.

40. Gordon (1984, 103).

Consequently, 'it is difficult to see the value (aside from vindicating a wholly abstract commitment to "materialist" world views) of trying of describe those relations apart from law'. He continued: 'Power is a function of one's ability to form and coordinate stable alliances with others that will survive setbacks and the temptations of defection to satisfy opportunistic interests. Such organization and coordination are bound to involve something legal.'[41]

In an early manuscript, Marx addressed 'private property' and claimed that 'an object is only *ours* when we have it . . . when it is directly possessed . . . when it is *used* by us'. Here Marx played down the role of law. But possession and use are two of the aspects of property as legally defined. Cohen insisted that in Marxism 'ownership' signifies power and control 'not relations of legal ownership'. But how are power or control sustained? Owners cannot rely on force alone. Force is often aided and legitimated by law. For thousands of years, legal institutions have defined and protected the powers of property.[42]

Ideologically, Marx and Ludwig Mises are far apart. Mises defended a market economy. But like Marx, Mises saw law as epiphenomenal rather than constitutive. He saw property as neither a matter of legal title nor legitimate ownership. Both Marx and Mises underplayed the roles of the state and law in constituting property rights. Instead they emphasized brute control of assets. Both authors underestimated the importance of legal powers in modern economic systems. This book challenges these positions, stressing the role of law and the state in helping to constitute key institutions and in enabling economic development.[43]

This alternative approach puts institutions before social classes. Analytically, social classes cannot be the elemental building blocks of any social system. Classes are neither separable nor independently constituted entities; they are themselves defined in terms of specific institutional relations of property and power. These relations constitute and precede classes as such. Hence these institutions are more fundamental. The configuration of class power does not

41. Gordon (1984, 105).

42. Marx (1975, 300, emphasis in original), Honoré (1961), Cohen (1978, 63). Cohen (1978, 217–40) admitted (231) that power over productive forces is 'less secure when it is not legal'. But if 'production requires legal expression for stability, it follows that the foundation requires a superstructure. This seems to violate the architectural metaphor, since foundations do not normally need superstructures to be stable'. Cohen unconvincingly tried to circumvent this problem by using an alternative metaphor. In effect he had made the problem in Marxism more apparent. Law itself is foundational.

43. See Mises (1949; 1981, 27) and Hodgson (2015a, 103–11; 2015b; 2016c).

define the system: the system constitutes those social classes and establishes possible configurations of class power. The history of all hitherto existing society is the history of institutional change.[44]

By contrast, Marx insisted that 'legal relations' and 'political forms' were part of the apparatus that sat upon 'the economic structure of society, the real foundation, on which arises a legal and political superstructure'.[45] But Marx had to refer to property and ownership to define the social relations that were part of the basic economic structure. He was unconvincing in his rejection of law from the economic base. Law is constitutive of many important social relations, and it is necessary for the definition of social classes. Law is not an epiphenomenon. It is a central mechanism of social power.

In modern society, the perception and operation of social powers or aspirations is partly framed and constituted through interpretations of rights and laws, as well as by other ideological factors. As discussed in later chapters of this book, the desire and realization of legal change can dramatize the underlying relations and lead to conflict or reform. Hence, as Gordon pointed out: 'Understanding the constitutive role of law in social relationships is often crucial not only in characterizing societies but in accounting for major social change.' This book attempts to show this.[46]

Concluding Remarks on Marxism

Marx saw change as resulting from processes largely internal to a national economic system, through the forces of production or class struggle. He focused on class antagonisms and 'the development of the contradictions' that impelled the system down its historical path. Schumpeter followed Marx in that respect. He defined *development* as 'changes in economic life as are not forced upon it from without but arise by its own initiative, from within'. He saw merit in Marx's theory of capitalism because 'it tries to uncover the mechanism that, by its mere working and without the aid of external factors, turns any given state of society into another'. But Marx and Schumpeter neglected the importance of exogenous shocks by focussing on change 'from within' a

---

44. Earlier statements of this point are in Hodgson (1984, 196–97; 2015a, 63–66).

45. Marx (1971, 20).

46. Gordon (1984, p. 106). Note that Gordon's (rather neglected) argument was similarly a reaction against Marxism, showing that Marx can be useful when he is wrong, as well as when he is right.

politico-economic system. As in the biological world, evolution depends on the environment and rivalry with others, as well as on the development of the organism itself.[47]

The development of individual capitalist systems is important, but capitalism must also be understood as a global, interacting assortment of different national formations, each with their own varied subsystems. Change comes about through both endogenous and exogenous forces. Marx did not deny the importance of exogenous shocks but saw them as disturbances from the normal, endogenous processes of development. On the contrary, an exogenous shock can place a system on a permanently different path. Later chapters of this book will emphasize the importance of some endogenous shocks and pressures in England's economic evolution. Marx paid attention to international trade, and later Marxists explored imperialism and world systems. But they maintained a stages theory of economic development.

Marx identified social classes and the relations between them as fundamental elements in the development of capitalism. But social classes should be considered neither as fundamental elements nor as the exclusive agents of change. The central role of law in modern societies is neglected. Legal changes do not simply reflect economic shifts: law is a constitutive part of the economy. Later chapters of this book demonstrate how struggles in the legal sphere were crucial in shaping England's economic evolution.

Marx's influence on social science has been massive and transformative. His big achievement was to put social relations and systems at the centre of analysis. But we need to go beyond Marx. We need to focus on different kinds of institutions and their interaction, including the organization of work, the property system, finance, and the state. Such an institutional account would cover the conflict and evolution of these institutions, played out by human beings in part on the material register of things. Their interaction would operate on multiple levels, each with a different degree of historical specificity.[48]

47. Marx (1976, 619), Schumpeter (1934, 63; 1954, 391).

48. For a discussion of multiple levels of historical specificity, see Hodgson (2001, 325–29).

2

More Explanations

TECHNOLOGY, RELIGION, IDEAS, CULTURE

> The historians of human culture have . . . commonly dealt with the mutations that have occurred on the higher levels of intellectual enterprise . . . while the lower range of generalizations, which has to do with work-day experience, has in great part been passed over with scant ceremony as lying outside the current of ideas.
>
> —THORSTEIN VEBLEN, 'THE EVOLUTION OF THE SCIENTIFIC POINT OF VIEW' (1908C)

> The decision processes . . . are shaped by a context that includes relative prices, regulatory and other institutional factors. . . . The incorporation of technical change requires the coming together of several pre-existing explicit and tacit knowledge bases and various sources of practical experience. The meaningful space in which technical change needs to be studied, therefore, is that of . . . the economy and the socio-institutional context.
>
> —CARLOTA PEREZ, 'TECHNOLOGICAL REVOLUTIONS AND TECHNO-ECONOMIC PARADIGMS' (2010)

AFTER THE DISCUSSION of Marxism, the aim of this chapter is to review some other prominent explanations of modern economic development. How are the Industrial Revolution and the Great Enrichment to be explained? Four explanatory frameworks are discussed. The first sees technological innovation as the driver of institutional change. The second is Max Weber's claim that Protestantism stimulated capitalism. The third is by Deirdre McCloskey, who has emphasized the causal role of ideas, particularly liberalism. In the fourth framework, Joel Mokyr also stressed the impact of Enlightenment ideas, but he underlined other factors as well. We then draw some conclusions.

Is Technology the Main Driver of Change?

'Technological determinism' has long been debated. A widely recognised problem is that the term has different meanings. Even the word *technology* is difficult to define. Scholars have revealed both strong and weak interpretations of *technological determinism*. Marx suggested a strong version when he wrote in 1847: 'The hand-mill gives you society with the feudal lord; the steam-mill, society with the industrial capitalist.' But his other formulations are more circumspect. A weak interpretation, such as 'technology can influence behaviour, culture or institutions', is hardly controversial. Stronger versions that view technology as the main driver of institutional and social change are debatable. Nathan Rosenberg dismissed that 'crude form of technological determinism, where social, economic, and political changes are explained in terms of antecedent changes in technology'.[1]

We are concerned here not with the whole array of possible meanings of *technological determinism*, but with specific versions that are relevant for our discussion. They suggest that culture and institutions do not lead but follow technology, which is the main driver of economic development. Consider a few examples.

In his theory of 'cultural lag', the American sociologist William Ogburn distinguished between the 'material' and the 'non-material' culture. By material culture he meant technology and the material environment fashioned by humanity. By non-material culture he meant laws, conventions, family arrangements and other social relations. Ogburn argued that the material culture develops before the non-material. The material culture builds cumulatively on its own success. But the non-material culture is governed by habit, inertia and tradition. Hence the non-material culture is slow to adjust to new technological or material conditions. This gave rise to 'cultural lag'. Similarly, Lawrence Kelso Frank saw 'traditional group arrangements of ceremonies, rituals, and symbols' as 'only too frequently acting as impediments and obstacles' to the use of new technology. 'Hence there is an increasing discrepancy between

1. Marx and Engels (1976b, 166), Rosenberg (1969, 3), Smith and Marx (1994), Dafoe (2015).

the needs of the technical processes and . . . the institutional life of the group.'
Technology pushes ahead, while institutions hold it back.[2]

It is likely that both Ogburn and Frank influenced the leading American
heterodox economist Clarence Ayres. For Ayres, 'technological development
forces change upon the institutional structure by changing the material setting
in which it operates'. He argued that 'changes in the alignment of property
rights from feudal to commercial society followed a change in the instruments
of production'. Ayres denied that relevant institutional changes 'preceded the
appearance of machine technology'. Instead, technological change preceded
institutional change. He saw this as confirmed by cases where technology
surged ahead, while accompanied by ancient institutions. With burgeoning
industry and commerce, 'new instruments and materials . . . progressively
overshadowed the products of feudal agriculture and the manorial economy'.
For him, these vestigial survivals showed that institutions were not the drivers
of change.[3]

Some feudal institutions did survive into the twentieth century. Manorial
copyhold tenure, which was an immediate descendent of feudal villeinage, was
not abolished until 1925. The British monarchy and the House of Lords are still
with us today. But these cases do not show that other institutions failed to
change. For example, serfdom declined rapidly in the fourteenth century. Laws
governing land tenure changed significantly in the seventeenth century. Enclosures turned feudal commons and open fields into alienable commercial
property. The financial and administrative revolutions of the seventeenth and
eighteenth centuries helped to enable the Industrial Revolution.[4] Given these
important institutional changes, surviving vestiges of the feudal past do not
show that institutions in general are unimportant. To demonstrate that institutions were generally unimportant, Ayres would have to establish that there was
little institutional change for hundreds of years. Pointing to residual feudal
survivals is not enough.

Ayres typically regarded institutions as constraints. This applied to capitalist as well as feudal institutions. He wrote: 'The productive powers of industrial society have grown not because of the institutions of capitalism but in
spite of them.' He overlooked that some institutions within capitalism facilitated investment, innovation and technological change. Patent laws provided

2. Ogburn (1922), Frank (1925, 184–85).

3. Ayres (1944, 177, 187, 195–96).

4. Wordie (1983), Reid (1995), Bogart and Richardson (2011).

incentives for innovation and invention. The rules of property enhanced business autonomy and were necessary for trade. Financial institutions released
money for research and investment. Generally, institutions can enable as well
as constrain. For example, rules governing road traffic can help to avoid acci-
dents and speed up journeys. The rules of language help communication. Institutional constraints can enable effective action.[5]

In his enthralling study of the role of the state in economic development,
Erik Reinert saw 'technology and increasing returns . . . as the main sources of
economic power'. Technology has been 'fundamentally changing the economy
and society'. He added: 'Human institutions were determined by their mode
of production rather than the other way round.' It is not clear what he meant
precisely by 'mode of production', but he associated it with technology rather
than with institutions. He criticized the new institutional economics of Douglass North and others for 'blaming poverty on the lack of institutions rather
than on a backward mode of production'. Reinert then concluded that 'institutional changes . . . are surely important, but they are ancillary . . . the mode
of production moulds and determines institutions—more than the other way
round'. But it is not possible to separate the system of production from institutions. There must be rules and relations concerning how production is organized, who is in charge, who does what, who gets what, how the workforce
is pressured to work and so on. These systems of social rules and relations
are institutions. Hence, institutions are part and parcel of any properly defined mode of production. Consequently, the argument over whether institutions come before or after the mode of production is fundamentally
misconceived.[6]

Some of the institutions that help to make up the mode of production in
modern society are legal in character. In large and complex societies, legal
enforcement is necessary to make property and other rights function effectively. The 'new institutional economists', to whom Reinert referred, are right
to emphasize institutions and incentives. A problem is that they sometimes
have a narrow view of human motivation, often based on self-interest and util-
ity maximization. This can misinform the analysis of incentives, organizations

5. Ayres (1943, 166). Ayres's generally negative view of institutions contrasts with other original institutionalists (such as Veblen and Commons) who saw them as a vital framework of
economic activity. See McFarland (1985, 1986) and Hodgson (2004, chaps. 16–17) for critical
discussions of Ayres's views.

6. Reinert (2007, 40, 57, 64–65, 222). See Ruttan (2003, 2006).

and enforcement. But incentives—including ethical goals—are still important. To be fair to North, he increasingly emphasized the role of ideology, as well as of material interests. Institutions frame and sustain all these motives.[7]

We take another example from a work on China by the economist Justin Yifu Lin. He claimed that 'technology is the most important' factor in determining economic growth. For him, 'institutional improvement is a passive process . . . as part of the superstructure, institutions must correspond to actual economic conditions. . . . In sum, the potential for economic growth hinges mostly on technological progress.' Lin went on to recognize the importance of 'capital' for economic development, but by 'capital' he seemed to mean capital goods. He neglected the fact that in China today farmers and entrepreneurs need finance to buy equipment or hire labour. Borrowing money requires a complex system of financial institutions based on collateralizable property. In China, the institutions of property, finance and corporate ownership are still relatively underdeveloped. A policy approach focusing on technological innovation will face serious problems unless the needed institutional changes are also addressed.[8]

For sure, technology is a necessary condition of much progress. But what are the conditions for the development and diffusion of new technology? For innovation there has to be a culture of enquiry that values knowledge and human improvement. In a market economy, property rights provide incentives, and finance is required to purchase materials and labour power. There have to be networked communities of scientists and engineers, to scrutinize, share and develop ideas. These communities require political conditions allowing relatively free and open enquiry, with the uncensored publication of much scientific information. The patent system plays an important role. Corporate structures are also useful for the organization of technology and the financing of research. We are back to institutions again. Technological change is a major driver of economic development, but technological innovation itself requires institutions and culture. In turn, new technology often leads to institutional or cultural changes. They interact with one another.[9]

7. Reinert (2007, 65), North (1981, 1990a, 1994, 2005). On motivation and incentives, see Hodgson (2013a, 2021c).

8. Lin (2012, 10, 12, 257), Hodgson and Huang (2013).

9. Polanyi (1962), Rosenberg and Birdzell (1986), Merton (1996), Ruttan (1997, 2003, 2006), Mokyr (2016).

Empirical work by Paul Bouscasse and his colleagues found an important acceleration of productivity growth in England after 1600. How can this be explained? They went for a technological explanation. They considered the delayed impact of the moveable-type printing press that swept across Europe after 1450. But if this important innovation mattered in England, then why also did it not lead to equally rapid productivity growth elsewhere? The wider circulation of printed texts was possible only under political and religious institutions where their publication was tolerated. As early as the seventh century, China developed a printing press. Eleventh-century China had moveable type. But freedom of expression was limited. They had the technology but not the institutions required for mass publishing. As well as technology, other factors matter.[10]

While flawed, the view of technology as the prime mover is understandable, because technology and innovations shape and change our lives in obvious and visible ways. Economics itself is infused with physical metaphors.[11] Institutions, by contrast, are systems of rules. They involve bits of conditional, regulatory information, stored in brains or on documents. Much of the institutional apparatus is beyond immediate sight. For much of the time, institutional rules are latent, awaiting specific triggers and cues. Institutional rules are ingrained in our habitual thoughts and dispositions, and in our culture. They are elemental and unavoidable. But they are covert, and they are sometimes wrongly neglected for that reason.

Max Weber and the Protestant Ethic

Max Weber famously posited a causal link between the spread of Protestantism in Europe and the rise of capitalism. In the English translation of *The Protestant Ethic and the Spirit of Capitalism*, the German word *Geist* became *spirit*. But there is no exact word to represent *Geist* in English. It also connotes mind or erudition. Weber's emphasis on *Geist* followed the German historical school, for whom it was also a key concept. Institutions and economic systems were largely understood in terms of their prevailing *Geist*. Consequently, Weber proposed a causal connection between two mind-centred phenomena: Protestant ethical ideas impelled a capitalist mentality.[12]

10. Bouscasse et al. (2021).

11. Mirowski (1989).

12. Weber (1930), Lessnoff (1994). See Hodgson (2001, 127–29, 149–50, 169–72, 288–95) on the concept of *Geist* in the German historical school.

Against the Catholic focus on ascetic behaviour and their greater toleration of self-indulgence, Protestants claimed that it was our duty to follow God's calling in this life and do good work. Productive activity as well as piety were vital. Labour, profit-seeking and material success became virtues. Weber saw Protestantism as crucial in establishing a capitalist work ethic. He argued that once it had provided material rewards, the capitalist spirit would abandon its Protestant parentage and spread to areas with other religions and cultures.

Weber's theory continues to be debated. Richard Tawney and Fernand Braudel pointed out that the medieval growth of early capitalism in Catholic Northern Italy is inconsistent with Weber's hypothesis. There and elsewhere, systems of banking and credit long preceded the rise of Protestantism. Even at the heart of Italian capitalism, the powerful Medici banking family became protagonists of the Counter Reformation. Another difficulty concerns the direction of causality. Was the rise of Protestantism a cause of economic change or a reflection of it?[13]

Different empirical investigations have drawn contrasting conclusions. Sascha Becker and Ludger Woessmann argued that the effect of Protestantism on economic development was less an outcome of particular doctrines and more a result of its greater encouragement of literacy and education, including among girls. They tested this hypothesis using county-level data from late nineteenth-century Prussia. They found that Protestantism led to better education and higher literacy. In turn, higher literacy among Protestants accounted for most of the local differences in economic prosperity. Davide Cantoni analysed data from 272 cities in the Holy Roman Empire from 1300 to 1900 and found no effect of Protestantism on economic growth.[14]

Weber's argument hinges on the Protestant imperative for individual betterment and dedication to work and commerce. But, as he was aware, there are substantial differences between different strands of Protestantism—such as Lutheranism and Calvinism—on these issues. Tawney noted these variations and pointed out that Martin Luther 'hated commerce and capitalism'. Consequently, both Weber and Tawney put greater stress on Calvinism and Puritanism as enablers of the capitalist spirit. Weber argued that these ideas spread and persisted, even among a more secular population. He quoted Benjamin Franklin on the virtues of frugality and business honesty and on the

13. Tawney (1936), Braudel (1979).

14. Becker and Woessmann (2009), Fukuyama (2011, p. 432), Cantoni (2015). For a survey of additional studies of the economic impact of Protestantism, see Becker et al. (2016).

dangers of indebtedness. According to Weber, Franklin's words expressed 'the spirit of capitalism' in 'almost classical purity'.[15]

Franklin saw rational monetary calculation, guided by honesty and other ethical virtues, as the paramount means of enrichment. But these imperatives would apply in any money-based market economy. Weber's argument focuses on the Protestant stimulus to ethically guided industry and trade, and not necessarily to capitalism as such. If financial institutions are key distinctive features of capitalism, then dealing with credit and debt must be a major part of the doctrinal advice to aspiring capitalists. Franklin is of less help here (although earlier he had advised that American small farmers make use of credit). In Weber's extract, without any mention of the possible economic benefits of borrowing to invest, Franklin warned: 'He who goes a borrowing, goes a sorrowing.' Here he was echoing the ancient prejudice against debt. In Sanskrit, Hebrew and Aramaic, the same word is used to mean *debt, guilt* and *sin*. Both the Old and the New Testament warn against debt. But for capitalism to flourish, the possibility of debt and the probability of its repayment must both be assured. The payment of interest on loans has to be made morally acceptable, contrary to the prohibitions on usury in the Bible and elsewhere. All this meant a break from longstanding cultural and religious taboos.[16]

Overall, it is possible that Weber was partly right, but for the wrong reason. Protestantism stimulated economic development, but more through its emancipatory promotion of literacy and education than anything else. A secondary factor was that when a monarch broke from Rome, as in the English Reformation, papal legitimation of their power was lost, and monarchs had to build support and consent by other means. Jared Rubin has argued that monarchs such as Henry VIII and Elizabeth I made greater use of Parliament for that reason, thus augmenting counterbalancing political powers that were later crucial for economic development. The details of religious doctrines were less relevant.[17]

The Reformation itself was a huge shock to the institutions of sixteenth-century Europe. When Luther nailed his ninety-five theses on the door of a church in Wittenberg in 1517, he started a multinational movement that challenged the ancient ideological foundations of political and ecclesiastical order.

15. Tawney (1936, 92), Weber (1930, chap. 2).

16. Graeber (2011), Calomiris and Harber (2014, 159).

17. Rubin (2017). See Botticini and Eckstein (2012) for evidence that education was a key factor in the economic success of the Jewish people.

These previously depended on one shared religious faith, which served to legitimate monarchical power. Before 1517, all sovereign power in Christian Europe had to be endorsed by papal authority in Rome. The creation of new Christian institutions and creeds, beyond the reach of Rome, cracked open the doctrinal foundations of political and legal authority.

In England, after the brief reign of Henry VIII's Catholic daughter Mary ended in 1558, the break from Rome became permanent. Subsequent English monarchs had to claim that their power was given by God, without papal or other external endorsement. Attempts to unify the nation against external threats encouraged limited tolerance of some religious dissent. While severe religious persecution remained, the liberal notion of freedom of conscience gradually gained ground. But this undermined the monarchical claim of a divine right to rule, which relied on the notion of one true faith. Once the Catholic religious monopoly was ended, the search was on for a secular justification of political and legal authority. There was much that was illiberal about early Protestantism, but it created an opening for liberal ideas.

Deirdre McCloskey and the Role of Liberal Ideas

Deirdre McCloskey highlighted the role liberal ideas in creating the conditions for the Great Enrichment. Liberal ideas, 'not mere trade or investment, did the creating and the releasing. The leading ideas were two: that the liberty to hope was a good idea and that a faithful economic life should give dignity and even honor to ordinary people.'[18]

Given the importance of ideas, we must account for their origins and ascendancies, and for the developments in the social system and culture that allowed them to spread and take hold. Ideas were vital, and their genesis and diffusion must also be explained.

In the third volume of her *Bourgeois* trilogy on the causes of the Great Enrichment, McCloskey developed her argument that spectacular growth after 1800 was caused by 'rhetorical and ethical' developments. Clearly, innovation and change, whether technological or institutional, are inspired and driven by ideas. She wrote of the growth of equality under the law, the removal of tariffs

18. McCloskey (2010, 26). McCloskey saw liberalism as emerging with early Enlightenment thinkers such as John Locke. Bell (2014) and Rosenblatt (2018) pointed out that liberalism was not consolidated as an ideology until the early nineteenth century. When it first emerged, liberals rarely cited Locke.

and other restrictions on trade, the failing grip of conservative institutions and so on. This detailed explanation is much about institutions. Such ideas were important because they led to institutional change.[19]

McCloskey gave reasons for making ideas primary. She pointed out that 'there are literally an infinite number of necessary conditions' for any event 'admittedly more and more remote'. But if this were an excuse for abandoning causal explanation, then all science would redundant. She bemoaned the bad practice of some institutional researchers who proceeded thus: 'Look around for a *necessary* condition that one likes and then elevate it to *sufficient*. But the trouble is that the necessary conditions the neo-institutionalists elevate in explaining the Great Enrichment are commonplace.' She thus rejected explanations such as the rule of law and the security of property rights, because law and secure property were in place long before the Great Enrichment. In this respect, McCloskey's argument is redolent of that of Ayres, discussed earlier. Both pointed to the inertia of longstanding institutions and concluded that they cannot thus be drivers of change. But where Ayers turned to technology as the motor of history, McCloskey embraced ideas.[20]

McCloskey's argument does not rule out other institutional explanations. If we can point to major institutional developments shortly prior to the Great Enrichment, then these novel institutional arrangements might qualify as part of the explanation. Of course, to substantiate these claims we must look much closer at the details. It is argued in this book that there are several important changes, notably in the seventeenth and eighteenth centuries, that helped to lay the institutional foundations for the economic take-off. McCloskey's claim that some institutions were longstanding and 'commonplace' does not mean that there were no major institutional changes in this period. There were important institutional developments in the seventeenth and eighteenth centuries, and some of these may have facilitated economic growth. We need to look further. And we cannot dismiss institutions from the explanation.

McCloskey made a further argument. She narrowed the possible 'causes' to 'the mental states of human individuals'. Indeed, thoughts that motivate actions are crucial. This important insight is obscured by those who focus on behavioural outcomes. She went further, to regard mental states as the primary causes. Other factors, including institutions, were seen as 'intermediate'. With this restrictive, mind-centred notion of *cause*, it is understandable why ideas

---

19. McCloskey (2016b).
20. McCloskey and Silvestri (2021, 725–26).

are highlighted as the drivers of the Great Enrichment. But even if we accept this very limited understanding of a *cause*, institutions and other factors can still be part of the *explanation* of economic development.[21]

It rained heavily during the night before the Battle of Waterloo in 1815, thus soddening the ground and limiting Napoleon Bonaparte's ability to move his heavy artillery. Consequently, he postponed his attack for more than an hour, waiting for the ground to solidify. This delay meant that Gebhard Blücher's Prussian troops would arrive that afternoon before Napoleon had wiped out the British Army. This delay cost Napoleon the battle. Even if we are disallowed from saying that the heavy rain was a *cause* of the French defeat, surely it must be part of its *explanation*?

Similarly for institutions. If I am constrained by an institutional rule, then that rule is part of the explanation of my behaviour. With McCloskey's highly restricted sense of *cause*, it may not *cause* my behaviour. But it is a necessary part of its explanation. Institutions include mechanisms of power. These result in some ideas being ignored and others being followed. Institutions and power help to explain the selection, rise and spread of ideas.

John Gendron's detailed study of the imposition, failure and dismantling of national attempts to regulate the wool trade in England from 1550 to 1640 casts some light on this. The regulatory legislation was eventually abandoned because it restricted employment and production in the wool sector. Several historians, including Christopher Hill and Lawrence Stone, pointed to the rise of free-market ideas as the ideological cause of the eventual deregulation. By contrast, Gendron argued that the government itself promoted deregulation, not primarily because of the growth of free-market ideas, but because of the perceived need to maintain employment for economic and military reasons: 'While it is entirely possible, and indeed likely, that novel attitudes towards the market helped consolidate and sustain the regulatory changes . . . they were not the mainspring of that change.' In that period, high employment levels were seen as providing able-bodied men for national defence and use in war. Expediency came first. Free-market ideology was added later. Of course, we cannot generalize from one case, but it does show that liberal ideas were not the initial drivers of this change.[22]

Liberalism has had an important role in economic development. But we have to explain the rise, spread and hold of liberal ideas. Some liberal notions

21. McCloskey and Silvestri (2021, 725–26).
22. Gendron (2021, esp. 531, 540–41), Hill (1980, 111), Stone (1980, 47).

were expressed in ancient Rome. But they did not spread widely, nor bring material enrichment. Liberalism had to wait until modern times for a context in which it could begin to flourish. Science and technology were important too, and these also required institutional underpinnings.

An exclusive focus on liberal ideas sits awkwardly with some of the facts of British industrialization and enrichment. The economic take-off that started in the closing decades of the eighteenth century entailed brutal colonial conquest, a massive increase in the transport and use of slaves, and harsh working conditions in the factories and fields. The rapidly growing demand for sugar from the seventeenth century onward was largely met by the products of slave labour in the Caribbean sugar plantations. The huge expansion of the British cotton industry after 1780 was based on slave-produced cotton. When it was processed in England, cotton entrepreneurs made the most of the cheap labour of women and children. Slavery also provided profits and collateral for industrial investment. Much of the Great Enrichment did not come from liberal ideas. It came in part from violence and oppression.[23]

McCloskey rightly stressed the importance of innovation. Generally, by innovation we mean the implementation of an invention or modification that leads to new or additional outcomes. Such implementations are organized activities, relying on experiment and interactions with others. There must be networked communities of scientists and engineers, so that fellow experts can scrutinize ideas and proposals. Ideas and innovations always need institutions to become effective.

McCloskey rightly emphasized that the Great Enrichment was massive and unprecedented. She contrasted this innovation and growth with the static and conservative nature of most institutions. But there is no insurmountable problem here. Some static rules are compatible with dynamic effects. 'Drive on the right of the road' is a static rule. But it has enabled growing millions of people to travel from A to B—with countless destinations, routes and speeds. The rule is static, but its usage and effects are dynamic and varied. Similarly, the rules governing markets may be unchanging, but new information can trigger a spectacular boom or a destructive panic. Static institutions can enable dynamic outcomes.

It might be argued that because institutions are systems of rules, and rules had to be formulated from ideas, then institutions should be traced back to the original intentions and ideas of their designers. But many institutions were not

23. Williams (1944), Inikori (1992), Beckert (2015).

designed—they emerged spontaneously out of human interactions. Almost all languages emerged in this way. They evolved by many unintended changes and tacit imitations. Tacit knowledge means that we follow many of the rules of a language without being able to make these rules explicit. Some institutional rules derive originally from instincts, habits or emotions, before they are formed as ideas. Ideas are not generally a first cause.

Joel Mokyr on Culture and Technology

Joel Mokyr has illuminated the explosion of technological innovation and economic growth that began in Britain in the late eighteenth century and then spread around the world, bringing large increases in wealth and average life expectancy. Like the work of McCloskey, central to Mokyr's argument is the role of ideas and culture in driving change. Both authors highlighted the crucial emergence of a culture of progress where humankind can improve its condition through science and reason.[24]

Mokyr defined culture in the following way: *'Culture is a set of beliefs, values, and preferences, capable of affecting behavior, that are socially (not genetically) transmitted and that are shared by some subset of society.'* He distinguished culture from institutions by regarding culture 'as something *entirely of the mind'* which is 'to an extent, a matter of individual *choice'.* By contrast, institutions 'are socially determined conditional incentives and consequences to actions. These incentives are parametrically given to every individual and are beyond their control.'[25]

Some quibbles arise. The extent to which culture is a matter of choice may be highly limited. We do not choose to be born into a particular culture or subculture, yet these contexts engender many of our beliefs. Also, culture must be more than beliefs. If several people believe that it is currently raining, then it would hardly qualify as a cultural trait. Even a shared belief in a God is not enough to constitute something cultural. People must also believe that others share the belief. Culture in this sense is not simply shared beliefs, but the widespread belief that others share them. For Mokyr, like others, cultural transmission is a matter of learning in social networks. But this implies that culture involves social relations as well as beliefs. Culture is relational and not

---

24. Mokyr (1990a, 1990b, 2002, 2009, 2016), McCloskey (2010, 2016b). This section makes use of material from Hodgson (2022a).

25. Mokyr (2016, 8–9), emphasis in original.

entirely a matter of the individual mind. As with institutions, these cultural relations are often beyond individual control.

Mokyr's definition of institutions is close to the near-consensus view that institutions are systems of rules, except he focuses on the incentives and consequences rather than the rules themselves. This is not a persuasive reformulation. Individuals can have different incentives to follow an institutional rule. Sometimes the incentive is simply the expectation and perceived benefit that others will follow it too—as with driving on the same side of the road. In other cases, expected disadvantage or punishment may provide the incentive—as with many laws. But such incentives are different from the laws themselves. And all incentives depend on beliefs. Consequently, Mokyr's distinction between culture and institutions begins to break down.

Mokyr argued that, at a sufficiently abstract level, the Darwinian principles of variation, selection and replication apply to cultural change. Cultural and genetic evolution both involve variation, selection and replication. But of course the detailed mechanisms are very different. Mokyr treated 'culture as genotypical and actions as phenotypical'. Hence culture is distinguished from behaviour. His application of generalized Darwinian principles to cultural evolution is not original. But it is an important milestone, because so far it has not been used widely in economic history.[26]

Mokyr did not dismiss institutions from the explanation of cultural and economic change. As he put it: 'Institutions create the environment in which cultural evolution occurs.' We may add that culture also creates the environment in which institutional evolution occurs. For instance, legal systems were built to a large degree on preceding cultural rules: laws emerged in the light of cultural experience. Mokyr repeatedly stressed the importance of institutions, as well as of culture.[27]

Following Robert Boyd, Peter Richerson and others, Mokyr identified a number of possible biases in the replication of cultural beliefs. Among these he wrote of confirmation bias (where people choose beliefs that are consistent with their already adopted ideas), conformist bias (where people tend to follow the majority) and authority or prestige bias (where the ideas of authoritative or prestigious people are adopted). Mokyr also emphasized the role of

26. Mokyr (2016, 9). Generalized Darwinism goes back to Veblen (1899) and others and is outlined in Hodgson and Knudsen (2010), which Mokyr cited in his 2016 book, along with an article on the topic that he co-authored with me and others (Aldrich et al. 2008).

27. Mokyr (2016, 12).

persuasion in cultural transmission. These and other biases result in different rates of growth of particular ideas. Culture evolves partly through these ongoing processes of differential replication.[28]

Where do new cultural ideas come from, particularly those that lead to the development of knowledge useful to the improvement of the human condition? Mokyr's answer highlights 'cultural entrepreneurs' such as Francis Bacon (1561–1626) and Isaac Newton (1642–1727). Mokyr regarded cultural entrepreneurs 'as the exceptional and unusual specimens who are the sources of evolutionary change: they are the ones who do not take the cultural choices of others as given, but try consciously to change them.'[29]

Bacon developed empirical and experimental methods to underpin modern science. He also understood the importance of an interacting community of scientists who compare and test competing explanations. Furthermore, Bacon reconciled science with religion, claiming that it was virtuous to reveal and respect the laws that God in his wisdom had devised to govern nature. Such religious rhetoric helped to make Bacon's radical ideas more acceptable. For Mokyr, Bacon was the supreme cultural entrepreneur whose ideas contributed to the eventual industrial take-off.

While he sometimes advocated free trade, Bacon was not a political liberal. He supported the use of torture, and he did not emphasise human rights. Mokyr overlooked Bacon's roles as royal legal advisor and attorney general, and his major written contribution to jurisprudence. Bacon was also a legal and institutional entrepreneur. Peter Grajzl and Peter Murrell used a machine-learning (structural topic model) analysis of Bacon's extensive writings to show that his methodological ideas (including inductive reasoning) had their origins in his common law jurisprudence.[30]

Mokyr wrote: 'Cultural entrepreneurs change what people believe, and if enough important people are converted, they will change institutions to conform with the new beliefs and thus the environment in which the next generation of cultural entrepreneurs find themselves.' He concluded: 'What counts for economic history was the beginning of a long and drawn-out rise in the belief in the transformative powers, social prestige, and virtuousness of useful knowledge.'[31]

28. Boyd and Richerson (1985), Mokyr (2016, 20, 33–35, 48–56).

29. Mokyr (2016, 6).

30. Kocher (1957), Hill (1965, 97–98), Langbein (1976, 90), Grajzl and Murrell (2019).

31. Mokyr (2016, 66, 267).

Mokyr showed that the culture of scientific endeavour was empowered by a European community that he dubbed the 'Republic of Letters'. This autonomous organization of scientists began in England and France in the seventeenth century. European scientists in the seventeenth and eighteenth centuries were networked together in a way that promoted critical reflection and synergetic endeavour.

In contrast, while China produced major innovations, after about 1700 it fell behind in terms of economic growth. Mokyr noted a number of important Chinese thinkers that might have helped restore Chinese economic dynamism but failed for a variety of reasons. Strikingly, several of those explanations are political and institutional. At least since 1300, China lacked the plurality and rivalry of states found in late medieval Europe. European political division created economic competition between territories for merchant trade and provided refuges for dissident intellectuals when they were threatened by authoritarian and conservative rulers. By contrast, Chinese geopolitics created a powerful state and bureaucracy, ruling over a large populated area. As Mokyr explained, this state bureaucracy hindered open dialogue and innovation. He also acknowledged the argument of Avner Greif and Guido Tabellini that the enduring absence of a sufficiently developed legal system in China obliged economic actors to rely on extended family or clan networks for contract enforcement and moral authority. By contrast, interstate competition and widening trade helped eventually to generate more effective legal systems in Western Europe. Part of the explanation of the China-Europe divergence hinges on institutions.[32]

Much of Mokyr's argument is forceful and persuasive. His evolutionary framework is highly commendable, but it needs further development. As it stands, his analysis depends too much on successive, fortuitous, cultural mutations in individual beliefs and capabilities. Too much explanatory weight is placed on too few extraordinary people. And there is too little consideration of the circumstances and pressures that led to their prominence.

For Mokyr, the history of technology shows 'totally new options' and the parallel existence of 'discontinuous leaps in culture'. But the point is not only to observe them, but to explain their appearance, and to show why some of them succeeded and proliferated. Mokyr answered with 'mutations' followed by runaway 'positive feedback', particularly between propositional and prescriptive knowledge. But more attention could have been given to environmental

32. Greif and Tabellini (2010), Berman (1983, 2003), Tilly (1992).

changes and exogenous shocks that may themselves trigger new bursts of innovative thought and economic development.[33]

We have ample evidence that external shocks matter. For example, William the Conqueror's invasion in 1066 changed English institutions and culture in fundamental ways. The growth of the British Empire spread English cultural norms and common-law systems to many countries. Napoleon's invasion of much of Europe led to the spread of Napoleonic legal and political institutions. The arrival of American warships in Tokyo Bay in 1853 and 1854 led to the Meiji Restoration of 1868 and to Japan's rapid transition from feudalism to a Western-inspired capitalist society.

Mokyr noted the importance of exogenous shocks in natural evolution, such as 'the spectacular proliferation of new mammalian forms at the beginning of the Cenozoic after the extinction of the dinosaurs' (which was caused by the impact of an asteroid). But shocks on this scale were catastrophic. They led to change because most species were wiped out. In the human world we have to consider lesser exogenous pressures or disturbances that lead to significant but not annihilating internal disruption, thus creating adaptive opportunities for effective cultural entrepreneurship. Mokyr subsequently accepted this point when he amusingly referred to a 'goldilocks view of historical change', based on moderate external shocks—big enough to make a difference but not so big as to destroy too much.[34]

It is no accident that Mokyr's hero Bacon lived during a period of upheaval, following the English Reformation. Tudor and Stuart history saw multiple external and internal shocks. Huge economic disruption followed the Dissolution of the Monasteries. The reign of Elizabeth involved multiple defensive moves against foreign plots and real and threatened incursions. Bacon was deeply involved in major legal and political developments of that time. This turbulent period also produced William Shakespeare, Christopher Marlow, John Donne, Thomas Tallis, William Byrd and numerous other dramatists, poets and composers. Similarly, Newton was born during a century of heightened violence and revolution. In his lifetime, England suffered the devastating Civil War of 1642–51 and the Dutch invasion of 1688. Newton's century also brought Robert Boyle, Robert Hooke, John Locke, Thomas Hobbes, William Petty, John Milton, Henry Purcell and many others of enduring influence.

33. Mokyr (2016, 26–27).

34. Mokyr (2016, 163–64; 2022). On the importance of disturbances for the evolution of populations in biology, see Sousa (1984).

Their combined creativity is testimony to the importance of disruptive (but not devastating) exogenous shocks and disturbances. Periods of disruption and uncertainty created an aesthetic yearning for constancy and security, alongside compulsive attempts to understand and cope with turbulent times. Cultural entrepreneurs do not arise simply as random mutations in a stream of cultural transmission. They become energized, and may gain attention, as a result of the challenging special circumstances in which they appear to offer solutions or understandings. These circumstances evolve, and they too are subject to some kind of evolutionary analysis. Upon culture, evolution occurs on multiple levels.

If the explanation rests mainly on the fortuitous mutation of cultural entrepreneurs, then why didn't successful, modernizing cultural entrepreneurs appear many thousands of years ago? Their emergence may have been prevented by the ubiquitous struggle for subsistence, the lack of a surplus sufficient to sustain a complex division of labour, and of institutions inadequate to support creative thinkers and innovators. If this is correct, then cultural entrepreneurship would have to wait for large-scale sedentary societies with complex institutions, which emerged several thousand years ago. But then the evolution of these institutions becomes a necessary part of the explanation. Cultural mutations and cumulative feedbacks are not enough.

Cultural transmission in a tribal context is much less complex than in large-scale societies. In tribal societies, cultural and technological knowledge is limited. Consequently, any one person can be aware of much of the know-how in the group. By contrast, large-scale societies have more complex divisions of labour and are repositories of more extensive and detailed knowledge. It is impossible for any one person to hold more than a small fraction of this knowledge. Consequently, information transmission depends on the reinforcing and filtering mechanisms of structured authority. Trust and authority are necessary because no one can be an expert on more than a tiny fraction of the relevant knowledge. The organized authority of experts, involving sufficient trust, helps to obtain consensus on basic laws or scientific claims. This applies to modern technology, science and law. These systems of organized, practical and experimental knowledge depend on institutions that build sufficient consensus on key issues and assure the quality of judgement and research.[35]

In short, the cultural transmission of technological and scientific knowledge depends on the higher-level evolution of organized authority. The

35. Polanyi (1958, 1962), Kitcher (1993), Goldman (1999, 2009).

Republic of Letters lacked sufficient organized authority to establish modern science. These considerations bring in institutions as well as culture. Institutions matter, as well as person-to-person persuasion or transmission.

Why didn't enough breakthrough cultural entrepreneurs emerge in (say) ancient Greece or ancient Rome? Why didn't a modern economy begin to emerge much earlier than it did? We can point to innovative and inspiring Greek and Roman thinkers such as Plato, Socrates, Aristotle, Archimedes, Cicero, Aurelius, Hypatia and many others. The absence of printing technology helps to explain their failure to gain traction and produce a critical mass of transformative followers. But, as the example of China shows, printing was not enough. China had printing presses for centuries but lacked laws that protected freedom of expression. Different political circumstances help to explain that when printing was developed in Europe in the fifteenth century, its cultural stimulus was much greater in some European countries than in others. Explanations must involve more than fortuitous cultural mutations and technological breakthroughs alone. We have to consider the evolution of institutions, as well as the evolution of individuals and cultural beliefs.

A major virtue of Mokyr's work is to pose serious questions about the sources of modern economic growth and to develop the analysis further. Among other things, Mokyr is much more explicit than McCloskey and others about the importance of institutions. He also signalled the usefulness of evolutionary thinking—using generalized Darwinian principles.[36]

Expanding Mokyr's Evolutionary Agenda

Much of biological evolution is driven by exogenous changes. This was recognized by Darwin, and it has become a prominent theme in biology.[37] Furthermore, there is not simply a struggle for survival involving individuals, but also rivalry between groups within species, and between different species.

---

36. Note Mokyr's (2016) casual and repetitive use of the phrase 'market for ideas'. This is not a harmless metaphor. Of course, rights to some ideas, as intellectual property, can be owned and sold. But the vast majority of ideas are not traded. There are several other misleading aspects of the non-metaphorical use of the term 'market for ideas' (Hodgson, 2020, 2021c, chap. 8). The ordinary communication or debating of ideas does not involve agreements with the shared intention of creating obligations according to contractual rules. Much day-to-day conversation is not a transfer of specific rights.

37. Darwin (1859), Mayr (1960, 1988), Waddington (1976), Corning (2003, 2005), Weber and Depew (2003).

Politico-economic evolution involves states, networks, companies, families and much else. Rivalry and selection act on multiple levels, between individuals, organizations and nation states. This expands the analysis from merely the 'dual inheritance' of culture and genes.

Rivalry between states remains an important source of exogenous pressure or disruption. Plurality and rivalry of states in late medieval Europe helped to create the conditions for the emergence of capitalism. Water and mountains divided multiple lowland populations, making Europe difficult to unify by military force. The Romans nearly succeeded, but medieval monarchs faced more formidable opponents. Europe remained divided by mountains and water into multiple states. The enduring rivalry of European states was an important stimulus to military and economic development. Growing military strength was necessary for national survival, and somehow it had to be financed. As Charles Tilly put it: "Other states . . . strongly affected the path of change followed by any particular state. From 1066 to 1815, great wars with French monarchs formed the English state, French intervention complicated England's attempts to subdue Scotland and Ireland, and French competition stimulated England's adoption of Dutch fiscal innovations."[38] While war could stimulate some economic activity, devastating defeat could annul any gains. Wars between rival states periodically shattered Europe and checked its development. War can stimulate economic growth, but only under specific conditions. It can destroy more than it builds, and armies and weapons do not feed nations. But England's island location made foreign invasion of home territory less likely, and greater access to the sea helped the deployment of strong naval power. In those special circumstances, war provoked major institutional and technological changes. England's conflicts in the seventeenth and eighteenth centuries promoted state-building, public financial institutions and more efficient administration. Wars in the eighteenth century and early nineteenth prompted the development of more efficient state administrations and reductions in public corruption. English capitalism was forged in war. Werner Sombart and others have described it as 'war capitalism.'[39]

As several authors have recognised, another effect of European political fragmentation was that it allowed dissenting intellectuals to seek refuge from persecution by moving to another regime. Interstate competition also created

---

38. Tilly (1992, 26). See also Kennedy (1988), Diamond (1997, 212–16), Jones (2003).

39. Brewer (1989), Braddick (1996), Ertman (1997), Neild (2002). On war capitalism, see Sombart (1913) and Beckert (2015).

some pressure on relatively enlightened states to develop policies to encourage merchants and trade.[40]

Once a merchant class became well-established in a nation, it became a political lobby to defend its interests, reinforce countervailing power and enable the development of a relatively autonomous system of law. In countries where merchants had greater autonomy (contrast England with Spain), the rewards of global trade made this class more powerful and led to institutional changes that further checked the arbitrary power of the state. Access to emerging cross-Atlantic trade enhanced this process of positive feedback between commerce and power. To be effective, these changed institutions had to bestow a degree of political stability within a complex system with divergent interests. Where they emerged, countervailing powers within pluralist constellations of institutions created spaces for the intelligentsia, the Enlightenment and the advancement of science. They also encouraged growing financial investment.[41]

The selective bankruptcy of business firms is much more common than the elimination of nation states. Changes within states are often stimulated by military rivalry and defence. Much more common than the changing of boundaries and the assimilation of states is the replication via diffusion of legal, technological and administrative structures and ideas from one country to another. This form of development is not solely from within the politico-economic system. Exogenous pressures matter too.

John Maynard Smith and Eörs Szathmáry considered several major transitions in biological evolution, each involving a new way in which information is stored and replicated. They addressed primitive replication, RNA, DNA, animal societies and human language. Each of these introduced a new form of information transmission. With Thorbjørn Knudsen, I have proposed multiple informational levels and transitions in human society, including language, writing, law and science. The expanded hierarchy of objects of selection has included groups, organizations, legal systems, religious institutions, states and scientific institutions.[42]

Sequences of creative disruptions followed by slower change are known in biology as punctuated equilibria. Stephen Jay Gould argued that punctuated equilibria depend upon a hierarchy of evolutionary processes with multiple

---

40. Weber (1968), Pipes (1999), Jones (2003), Mokyr (2016).

41. Acemoglu et al. (2005a, 2005b), Acemoglu and Robinson (2012), Braudel (1984), Cipolla (1965), Ertman (1997), Mokyr (2002, 2016), Moore (1966), Tilly (1992).

42. Maynard Smith and Szathmáry (1995), Hodgson and Knudsen (2010, chap. 8),

levels of selection. Shocks can lead to changes in the articulation of levels and to rapid changes in speciation. Some social scientists have taken up the idea. Mokyr noted that 'the economic history of technology displays a similar dynamic pattern of long periods of stagnation or very slow change, punctuated by sudden outburst like the Industrial Revolution'. Part of his explanation for the uneven development of technology involved 'Cardwell's Law', where technological advances create vested interests that may ally with conservative forces to resist further innovation. The shifting, interacting strata of institutional arrangements may lead to crisis, spur adaptations and result in discontinuous development.[43]

In Conclusion: Taking Stock of Rival Explanations

This chapter and its predecessor have reviewed some prominent explanations of modern economic development. These theories vary over several dimensions. One issue is the extent to which a theoretical approach embraces notions of social structure, including social relations or institutions. This underlines the importance of Marx, for whom social relations and structures were central. But his key concepts are insufficiently grounded on the norms, rules or laws that help make key social structures operational. Here institutional approaches come in, including the original institutional economics of Veblen and Commons and the new institutional economics of Douglass North, Elinor Ostrom and others.

Marx hinted at the driving powers of technology but gave no adequate explanation of how technological change is motivated and enabled. Similar problems apply to other technological explanations of development, including that of Ayres. Weber's emphasis on Protestantism, McCloskey's on liberal ideas, or Mokyr's on cultural mutations by entrepreneurs are all attempts to explain what lies behind technological change. Weber and McCloskey stop there, failing to explain where religious or liberal ideas come from, and what helps them take hold and spread. Mokyr went further by examining the institutional and cultural environment and the mechanisms of change. Mokyr's approach is the closest to the general argument in this book. But there are some differences, as noted earlier and subsequently in this text.

43. Arthur (1990), Baumgartner and Jones (1993), Collins (1988, 34), Eldredge and Gould (1977), Gould (2002, chaps. 8–9), Hodgson (1991, 1993), Mokyr (1990a, 1990b, 1991, 1994, 2002). The quote is from Mokyr (1990b, 351–52).

We have pointed to the importance of institutions in understanding economic development. In the following chapters several kinds of institutions will be highlighted. Among them are legal institutions. In societies under the rule of law, legal institutions impinge on individual choice and action in multiple and often subtle ways. The legal system does not determine all change—far from it. Law is affected by ideas, culture and other socio-economic factors, as well as the other way round. Understanding the role of law in the economy and the causes of legislative change is vital to understand modern economic development.[44]

Changes occur in technology and institutions, and both are expressed in ideas. We need to explain the replacement of one institution or technique by another, and the further development of an institution or technique when it is established. We need to appreciate the motives for advancement and the springs of innovation. Much innovative effort is a result of exogenous disturbances that create practical, technical and legal problems. These problems may be perceived in different ways, leading to a variety of responses. Severe shocks reverberate throughout society, sometimes reaching many spheres of activity, from politics to production.

A paramount example is the need to finance the nation's armed forces in times of war. An external threat can lead to the imposition of taxes or the sequestration of property. As Niall Ferguson put it: 'Military expenditures have been the principal cause of fiscal innovation for most of history.' Such external forces react upon society as a whole, from the highest to the lowest levels.[45]

Both exogenous disturbances and internal developments can lead to crises. People face new perceived problems and are pressured to adapt and find solutions. Some of these are technological. Technological bottlenecks can act as 'focusing devices' that concentrate the attention of multiple engineers and other experts, sometimes leading to a technological breakthrough. There is a similar focusing process with institutional change. The Black Death of 1348 created a massive shortage of agricultural labour, promoting shifts in behaviour by landowners and serfs, which eventually led to major institutional and legal changes and the growth of wage labour. Disruption can stimulate problem-solving experiments and solutions.[46]

44. Fukuyama (2011), Deakin et al. (2017), Hodgson (2015a).

45. Ferguson (2001, 14).

46. Rosenberg (1969).

Exogenous shocks have been of great consequence throughout human evolution. Throughout prehistory, periodic changes in the climate have forced human bands to adapt, both culturally and technologically. More than a century ago, Veblen emphasized that climatic changes, and advances and retreats of ice, played a part in the evolution of human cultures. The idea that climate change is a major factor in long-term human cultural evolution has re-emerged in recent years. Researchers have focused on the last ice age, and on other more recent major changes in the climate, claiming that these disruptions affected human cultures. Disruptive climate change gave the advantage to cultures that were more flexible and adaptable. Major disturbances are often costly and devastating. Instead of advocating these, we should look to the promotion of sustainable socio-economic and institutional adaptability, as briefly discussed in the final chapter of this book.[47]

All this points to a problem-driven, more than a technology-first, ideas-first, culture-first or religion-first, mode of explanation. Of course, understanding and solving any problem involve ideas and they are affected by culture. The need for problem-solving arises in struggles for status, power, reward or recognition. Ideas play a vital part in the communication with others that is essential to all problem solving. Urgent problems focus minds and demand resources to solve them.

47. Veblen (1913, esp. 494–98), Potts (1996), Richerson et al. (2001), Calvin (2002), Staubwasser and Weiss (2006), Dong (2012).

PART II

Explaining England's Economic Development

3

Land, Law and War

Our later Kings granted more freedom to the Gentry than they had presently
after the Conquest; yet under bondage still: for what are prisons, whips and
gallows in the times of peace, but the laws and power of the sword, forcing
and compelling obedience, and so enslaving, as if the sword raged in the
open field? . . . True Religion, and undefiled, is this, To make restitution of
the Earth, which hath been taken and held from the Common people, by the
power of Conquests formerly, and so *set the oppressed free*. Do not All strive to
enjoy the Land? The Gentry strive for Land, the Clergie strive for Land, the
Common people strive for Land.

—GERRARD WINSTANLEY (1650)

Land is the basis of an aristocracy, which clings to the soil that supports it;
for it is not by privileges alone, nor by birth, but by landed property handed
down from generation to generation, that an aristocracy is constituted.
A nation may present immense fortunes and extreme wretchedness; but
unless those fortunes are territorial, there is no aristocracy, but simply the
class of the rich and that of the poor.

—ALEXIS DE TOCQUEVILLE, *DEMOCRACY IN AMERICA* (1835)

IN PRE-INDUSTRIAL ENGLAND, land, law and war were an intimate trinity.
Theories that focus on the internal development of a national system often
neglect the role of war. Marxism, for example, emphasizes the class struggle
between lords and agricultural workers. But the relationship between lord and
worker was not simply about production on the land. The feudal lord inherited
rights over the land from the king, alongside an obligation to raise local troops
for the monarch in war. Similarly, the serf or peasant inherited rights to use the

77

land alongside a duty to fight under his lord. Land was not simply a factor of production. It was the basis of military as well as productive organization. Laws concerning the use and ownership of land also provided troops for war.

After his invasion in 1066, William the Conqueror established a feudal hierarchy with strong monarchical powers. The Crown was the ultimate owner of all land. Various rights over the land were granted to the highest-ranking lords, in return for vassal service, including the provision of troops when needed. Such military obligations, based on land tenure, were described as 'knight service'. These lords, in turn, passed landholding rights to their vassals, in return for labour, military and other services. The manor was a foundational element in the system, with its own courts.[1]

A large proportion of the population were villeins—a form of serf. Villeins were bound to their lord, who were given rights to use some land, with customary rules governing rents, obligations to work and other services to the lord. A lord could fine, beat, imprison or sell his villeins. Villeins had no right to seek justice against their lords in any court, other than the manorial court. But in their relations with others, apart from their lords, they had 'all or nearly all the rights of a freeman', as Frederick Pollock and Frederic Maitland noted in their classic text. There were also slaves, who had more limited rights. Slaves were chattel, controlled by their owners. Like villeins, their status was hereditary. The *Domesday Book* records that in 1086 slaves made up about 10.5 per cent of the English population. Slavery lasted until the twelfth century, when most slaves became serfs and were integrated into the feudal system of fief and vassalage.[2]

Although they later changed their position, North and Robert P. Thomas once claimed that serfdom was 'essentially a contractual arrangement' where the serf 'exchanged' labour services in return for 'the public good of protection and justice' from the lord. But as Arcadius Kahan put it in his study of serfdom, 'Contractual relations are not very meaningful when their adjudication is left to one of the contracting parties'. Robert Brenner saw North's and Thomas's view as 'inconsistent with the realities of serfdom'. The mutual derivation of benefits from a social relationship between two people is insufficient to constitute a contract. Feudal law did not treat serfdom as contractual; instead it ascribed duties, arising from a status acquired at birth, over which both lord

1. Bloch (1962).

2. Pollock and Maitland (1898, 1:397–416), Darby (1977, 338–45), Allen (1992, 61), Pelteret (1995).

and serf had little discretion. Obligations arose out of legally defined structures and duties, not via mutual agreement. There was no legal requirement for voluntary consent.[3]

Some farmers were peasants, holding land by customary or leasehold tenure. Their legal rights strengthened in the twelfth century to the point that they had practical control over their allocated land. Some peasants had the right to lease to others the land they controlled. Other free members of the population worked as land labourers or in trade or manufacturing.[4]

The Nature and Importance of Landed Property

Before the Industrial Revolution, the most important type of wealth was in land. The evolution of landed property rights is central to an understanding of the process of economic development in England. This has been widely recognized, but several influential statements on the evolution of landed property rights are flawed.

Consider the medieval period. Daron Acemoglu, Simon Johnson and James Robinson wrote that in the English Middle Ages there was a 'lack of property rights for landowners, merchants and proto-industrialists'. They cited a work by John Veitch to claim that there were 'numerous financial defaults by medieval kings' in Europe. But Veitch himself gave only four examples of property confiscation or debt default applying to medieval England. In particular, he noted that Edward I expelled the Jews and confiscated their property, and that Edward I, Edward II and Edward III all defaulted on Italian debts. These events occurred from 1290 to 1340 and targeted very few English property owners.[5]

---

3. North and Thomas (1971, 778), Kahan (1973, 91), Brenner (1976, 35 n.). North and Thomas (1973, 29–30) and North (1981, 130–31) later admitted that serfdom was coercive and involuntary. But coercion does not necessarily nullify a contract: all contracts might be coercive to a degree (Hale, 1952; Samuels, 1973). Notwithstanding this correction, North was often disposed to make contracts or markets the universal default position in human interaction (Hodgson, 2020). While Coase (1937) had drawn a distinction between market and non-market arrangements, North found markets in politics and elsewhere. This underpinned his widespread use of the concept of transaction costs. Note that in the antebellum United States, Seabury (1861) imagined that slaves had entered into implicit contracts (for labour in return for protection) with their masters, and hence (for him) slavery was justified.

4. Pollock and Maitland (1898, 1:145–49), Allen (1992, 60).

5. Acemoglu et al. (2005a, 393–94), Veitch (1986, 34).

There were some important property confiscations by Tudor and Stuart kings. They fall into what is generally regarded as the early modern rather than the medieval era and will be discussed later. Although these serious confiscations have to be considered, they occurred when the English legal system was well established, and property was generally under its protection. In their classic account of the Glorious Revolution, Douglass C. North and Barry Weingast argued that it made property more secure, thus preparing the ground for an industrial take-off. But numerous critics have pointed out that property was relatively secure before 1688, and there was still some insecurity thereafter.[6]

Overall, English landed property rights were relatively secure from the thirteenth century. A reformed legal system emerged in the twelfth century, particularly during the reign of Henry II (1133–89), under the influence of the new canon law of the church, and the rediscovery of Justinian Roman law. Systems of adjudication were reformed, as well as some of the laws themselves. Consequently, property rights for the wealthy became quite secure.[7]

Of course, if a landowner committed treason or supported the wrong side in a civil war, then he would likely forfeit his lands. Justice was much less accessible by the poor, and the legal system was often subject to corruption and inefficiencies. The many surviving letters of the Paston family—rising landed gentry in Norfolk in the fifteenth century—illustrate the complications and corruptions of legal processes concerning landownership. Even during the violent disruptions of the Wars of the Roses, they repeatedly used the law to protect their titles to landed property. The main problem for them was not principally the threat of confiscation by a powerful monarch, but the schismatic nobility and the disruption of stable state power and administration, during a struggle between rival dynasties. In these unstable circumstances, they were mostly successful in using the law to protect their property.[8]

Rather than being unsafe, landed property rights before the Industrial Revolution were generally of a different character. What mattered more than changes in the security of landed property was the freeing of land from feudal

---

6. North and Weingast (1989). Critics include Clark (1996, 2007), Sussman and Yafeh (2006), McCloskey (2010), Angeles (2011). Fukuyama (2011, 418–20), Hoppit (2011), Ogilvie and Carus (2014) and Faundez (2016, sec. 2).

7. Berman (1983), Baker (2019).

8. Castor (2006).

encumbrances. Among other conditions of capitalist development, land had to become a saleable commodity.[9]

The influential historical accounts of property rights by North, Acemoglu and others fail to distinguish between multiple types of property right, including the differences between rights to use, rights to sell, inheritance rights and rights to use property as collateral.[10] Long after the decline of classical feudalism in England, enduring and well-defined rights often carried obligations that limited the use of landed wealth as collateral for investment. The growth of markets, finance and capitalism were thus constrained.

In particular, there were enduring restrictions on landed property, known as entails. According to David Hume, they had Anglo-Saxon precedents. In 1285 Edward I encoded entails in statute legislation. Many entails enforced primogeniture, ensuring that a landed estate passed from one generation to another through the eldest son. Consequently, the current landowner could neither sell entailed land nor obtain a mortgage by using it as collateral. Such actions would overturn the lawful inheritance rights of the eldest son. The problem was less the 'security' of property rights than the limited capacity to sell or mortgage land. This issue will be discussed later in this chapter in more detail.[11]

We start our account in the fourteenth century, when the English feudal system was fractured by a huge external shock—the Black Death. The chapter then moves on to consider the struggle between landowners and tenants and the further development of land tenure. This sets the scene for the turbulent events of the sixteenth century, triggered in part by the Reformation. The strife-ridden seventeenth century brought further major changes to English land law and the structure of land tenure. They prompted a century-long revolution in financial institutions, beginning even before the Glorious Revolution of 1688.

The Black Death and the Decline of Serfdom

The fourteenth century was a period of extreme hardship and appalling mortality. The Black Death was preceded by the Great Famine of 1315–17 and another famine in 1321. Climate change and adverse weather were among the

---

9. Fukuyama (2011, 418–20), Hoppit (2011), Ogilvie and Carus (2014).

10. Honoré (1961).

11. Hume (1983 [1778], 1:185, 3:77), Haskins (1977), English and Saville (1983), Spring (1993), Reid (1995), Brewer (1997), Biancalana (2001), Berman (2003, 333–35), North et al. (2009, 89–90), Allen (2012, 65).

causes. Northern Europe was entering what has been dubbed 'The Little Ice Age'. The medieval warm period had come to an end.[12]

The Black Death arrived in the Crimea in about 1345 and then proliferated in Europe. In May 1348 a sailing ship docked at Melcombe, in Weymouth Bay in Dorset. According to the Grey Friars Chronicle: 'One of the sailors had brought with him from Gascony the seeds of the terrible pestilence.' It reached London in autumn. In 1349 it spread northwards and throughout Britain. Estimates of mortality vary, but the consensus is that between 40 and 60 per cent of the population died. In 1361–62 the plague returned to England and caused the death of a further 20 per cent of the population. There were more outbreaks in 1368–69, 1371–75, 1390 and 1405. Overall, the population of England fell from more than four million in 1300 to about two million in 1450. These deadly catastrophes triggered events that changed the structure of English society forever.[13]

While the effects of the Black Death were dramatic, in some respects it accelerated changes that were already under way. Norman feudalism had adapted to growing trade and other changing conditions. In some places, feudal knight services were commuted to cash payments. Many serfs purchased their freedom and established leasehold arrangements with their lords. Others became wage labourers before the pestilence. They were exemplars for the villeins who survived the pandemic.[14]

An immediate economic aftermath of the Black Death was an acute shortage of labour. Serfs saw opportunities for resistance or flight, and contracted workers were put in a stronger bargaining position. King Edward III attempted to fix wages at pre-plague levels. Repressive measures intended to enforce this legislation caused widespread resentment. The levying of a poll tax to fund England's military efforts in the Hundred Years' War led to the Peasants' Revolt of 1381. The insurgents demanded the abolition of serfdom, but they were defeated.[15]

12. Jordan (1996), Fagan (2000), Koyama and Rubin (2022, 26–27). The Little Ice Age lasted until the early nineteenth century, corresponding (by coincidence) to the period covered in this book.

13. Ziegler (1991, 92), Senn (2003), Benedictow (2004, 50–51, 127), Campbell (2010).

14. Duby (1974), Senn (2003, 526).

15. Brenner (1976) argued that high death rates and demographic shifts were not causes of fundamental change. But there is strong evidence that mortality rates mattered. Gingerich and Vogler (2021) showed that the Black Death had different local effects in German-speaking areas in Europe, depending on differing rates of mortality. In areas hit hardest by the disease, surviving

The Black Death dramatized the mortality of unequal social ranks: lords and villeins could all be cut down by death. John Ball, the leader of the revolt, promoted class equality, drawing on biblical authority: 'When Adam delved and Eve span, who was then the gentleman?' John Wycliffe and the Lollards sought an egalitarian Christianity with the drastic reform of the official church. Ideas and religion mattered. But neither collective action, nor ideas, nor religion, nor late fourteenth-century cultural entrepreneurs such as Ball and Wycliffe get us very far in explaining the huge social changes from 1348 to 1400. Something else, very basic and instigated locally, mattered too.

In England, villeins were bound to their own lord. Other lords had no such powers over them. Hence by illegally but successfully fleeing from their lord's domain, villeins could become free. Previously the authorities had been more effective in recapturing runaway serfs and punishing those who harboured them. But among the chaos of death and depopulation, these powers were hugely diminished. Some laws worked in the villeins' favour. After an absence of only four days, the lord had to proceed against any runaway serf in the royal courts. Such litigation was costly and not guaranteed to succeed. Many runaways found areas under lordships with vacant holdings. Others moved to towns for work. A serf also became free after residence for a year and a day on a royal demesne or in a legally chartered town. These migrations, probably aided by covert networks, rapidly undermined villein status.[16]

As an example, there is evidence of several serfs crossing the Tamar Estuary from Cornwall to near what is now Plymouth in Devon, where they obtained their liberty. For a small payment to their new lord, they became customary tenants with additional rights to mill grain, fish and gather oysters. Their liberties were reaffirmed in a charter of 1381.[17]

----

labourers acquired greater power. Subsequently, these areas were more likely to adopt inclusive political institutions and more equitable landownership patterns. Remarkably, these differences persisted in voting behaviour as late as the 1930s. This evidence shows that, contra Brenner, higher mortality rates and consequent labour shortages could have been a major force behind the abolition of serfdom and subsequent social changes.

16. Pollock and Maitland (1898, 1:401, 412), Blum (1957), Bloch (1962, 270–74). On villein flight and mobility, see Bloch (1962, 271), Raftis (1964), Hilton (1969, 32–43), Brenner (1976, 51, 54–55, 61), Ziegler (1991, 199), Allen (1992, 65), Senn (2003, 574–76), Bailey (2016), Peters (2018).

17. Baring-Gould (1906, 153). It is possible that some or all of these fugitive crossings of the Tamar occurred before the Black Death, but the pestilence greatly increased the likelihood of success of serf flight.

Some villeins with money stayed put. They improved their status by buying or leasing lands from lords who had lost their serfs in the pestilence. Stronger peasant bargaining power led to reductions in rents and labour dues to the lords. Were it not for the high rate of mortality, weakened manorial authority, the previously growing practice of leasing land to tenant farmers, and the legal and other peculiarities of its feudal system, English serfdom may have survived the Black Death. After all, in much of Europe east of the River Elbe, serfdom was strengthened after the pandemic. But in England by 1400 it had all but disappeared. Serfdom was in decline before the Black Death, but the pestilence accelerated the process and led to its demise.

The growing power of wage labourers was met by a series of legal attempts to control them. The Statute of Labourers of 1444 set maximum wage rates. The Statute of Artificers in the reign of Elizabeth in 1562 also tried to restrict wages. It limited the movement of labourers and established apprenticeships to raise skill levels. These legal measures had limited effect.

There is some evidence that the general shortage of labour and the growth of employment opportunities had an impact on family structures and norms. Van Zanden and Tine de Moor argued that this offered opportunities for women as well as men to obtain waged employment. This diminished the power of parents over their children, made voluntary marriage more likely and reduced inequality between husbands and wives. Voluntary marriage was to an extent promoted by the church. Women and men tended to marry later, after a period of work and saving, living apart from their parents. Additional skills were acquired, and literacy rates increased. These changes were particularly strong among the poor. This is known as the European Marriage Pattern, and it was prominent (for a while) in England and the Low Countries. The European Marriage Pattern was reinforced in areas where the Black Death led to the end of serfdom. This may help explain an increase in English agricultural productivity in the fourteenth century.[18]

Studies of economic development in the twentieth century show that female empowerment can have strong positive effects on well-being and economic growth. So what role did the European Marriage Pattern play in the English economic take-off? Its resilience and impact seem limited. Van Zanden and de Moor themselves reported that 'the role of women in work and business declined from the sixteenth century onwards'. And 'in the

18. See van Zanden (2009, chap. 4), written jointly with de Moor. See Tylecote (2016) for some expansion of the argument for England.

ideological arena there was also a tendency to stress parental authority again'. To some extent the changes that they highlighted were being reversed from 1500 onwards.[19]

An extensive analysis of data from England and thirty-eight other European counties by Tracy Dennison and Sheilagh Ogilvie found no evidence that delayed marriage had positive effects on economic performance in the period from 1500 to 1900. After reviewing the arguments and evidence, Mark Koyama and Jared Rubin noted that relatively low birth rates in seventeenth- and early eighteenth-century England may have helped to raise per capita incomes and stimulated economic growth. But they found reasons to be sceptical that the European Marriage Pattern was a major explanatory factor. Bigger demographic shifts occurred in the nineteenth century, but these later changes are beyond the historical timespan of this study.[20]

Copyhold and the Rise of the Yeomen

Former villeins became tenants, with legal rights. A typical arrangement was copyhold, which emerged in the later decades of the fifteenth century. The peasant would purchase from the lord the right to use the land and to own and benefit from its outputs. The lord would retain ultimate ownership of the property. The rights to use the land would be certified by a copy of the legal title being passed to the peasant—hence *copyhold*. The rights and duties of copyholders varied from one manor to another, and they were based on custom. The security of copyhold tenure depended partly on the quality of original records and the goodwill of the manorial authorities. Initially, some copyholders were obliged to work for their lords for a few days each year, but these were commuted later to payments of money rents.

There were two main types of copyhold. Copyhold for life existed for the lifetimes of the copyholder or copyholders. More valuable was copyhold of inheritance, which could be passed to heirs in succeeding generations. With inheritable copyhold, the rights could be sold on to others, or the copyhold rights could be used for security for loans. In legal terms, all copyholders had *usus* and *usus fructus* rights. In the case of copyhold of inheritance, some of these rights were *alienable*. Some copyholders acquired the right to lease the

---

19. Sen (1999, chap. 8), van Zanden (2009, 135–36).

20. Bar and Leukhina (2010), Guinanne (2011), Dennison and Ogilvie (2014), Koyama and Rubin (2022, 96–103).

land to others. Copyhold was under the jurisdiction of the local manorial court. Judgements were often biased in favour of the lord of the manor. Complaints about copyhold arrangements were perennial.[21]

Some peasants had rights to land through 'beneficial leases'. Like copyhold, these involved an initial payment and a small annual rent. The lease could be for a specific time period, or for the life of the lessee, or for the lives of multiple lessees. Other peasants held lands under socage tenure. They were virtually freeholders, owning the land with minimal obligations. Socage tenure involved neither military service nor the customary constraints of copyhold tenure. It required 'homage' and an oath of 'fealty' to the lord, often signified by a small gift, such as a flower or a pound of pepper (hence 'peppercorn rent'). Socage evolved into modern freehold. But because of the absence of a land registry and the limitations of the medieval legal system, lords could abuse socage or freeholder rights.

After 1470, partly as a result of Spanish and Portuguese importation of silver and gold from the New World, sustained price inflation emerged in Europe, and England was not exempt. As rents were often fixed in nominal money terms, inflation put strong economic pressure on landlords. Wool prices rose rapidly in the growing domestic and foreign wool markets. Many landowners turned to wool production. To achieve this, land had to be converted from arable to grazing, and some of the peasants had to be persuaded or forced to vacate that land.[22]

The first wave of enclosures was from 1450 to 1525. Common lands were sealed off, and open field systems were reorganized and consolidated. Some lands were 'engrossed', by combining peasant holdings and evicting their tenants. Evictions were obtained by several means. Rents were raised. Manorial authorities put pressure on peasant farmers by enclosing the common grazing lands, thus preventing access by the villagers. Some evictions were carried out by force, with the expectation that the peasants lacked the means to obtain legal remedies through the courts. Some land was enclosed through willing agreement. There were also enclosures after abandonment of the land by their farmers, often because of poor yields.[23]

21. On types of ownership right, see Honoré (1961). On copyhold, see Tawney (1912), Gray (1963), Allen (1992), Reid (1995).

22. Mackie (1952, 448–50).

23. Tawney (1912, 151–52, 187–88, 232–61, 304–5), Allen (1992, 27–28, 37–48). Bogart and Richardson (2011, 247) estimated that at the beginning of the eighteenth century about

This was not simply a class struggle between landlords and peasants. The government and the Crown were involved. Under Richard III, the government had expressed concern about the adverse effects of enclosures, including rural depopulation. Richard was killed at the Battle of Bosworth Field in 1485, and Henry Tudor became King Henry VII. Because depopulation made the Isle of Wight more vulnerable to invasion, an act in 1488 prohibited the engrossing of land on the island. In the following year there was nationwide legislation against depopulating enclosures. This developed into a sustained legal struggle.[24]

Initial legislation against enclosures and rural depopulation was of limited success. More forceful and longstanding efforts began after an anti-enclosure proclamation by Henry VIII in 1514 and acts against enclosures in 1514 and 1515. This legislation ordered the reconversion of pasture to tillage and the rebuilding or repair of dilapidated dwellings. In 1517 Lord Chancellor Thomas Wolsey set up seventeen commissions and allocated the English counties among them. Powers and penalties were issued to deal with breaches of the 1515 act. Proclamations in 1526, 1528 and 1529 ordered the pulling down of illegal hedges to open up enclosed lands. Legislation in this vein continued even after Wolsey's execution in 1530. In the sixteenth century several more acts were passed that prohibited enclosure, the conversion of arable to pasture and the engrossing of farms.[25]

Why did the Crown act to stop enclosures and rural depopulation? It sought the protection of the realm and its privileges within it. Rural depopulation reduced the number of able-bodied men available for shire levies—for military service in case of war. Once again, exogenous pressures were crucial. As Tawney explained, while 'Continental Europe had introduced standing armies . . . England relied mainly on the shire levies, and the shire levies were recruited from the small farmers. . . . One Depopulation Statute after another recites how "the defence of this land against our enemies outward is enfeebled and impaired."' There was also an interest in maintaining a relatively prosperous peasantry to bear a share of the tax burden, particularly to finance wars: 'Political writers from [John] Fortescue [1394–1479] to [Francis] Bacon

one-quarter of arable land in England was still held as commons, where villagers shared rights to the use of pastures, water sources or woods. This common land could not be sold or mortgaged. Enclosures changed this.

24. Tawney (1912, 353–54), Mackie (1952, 451), Allen (1992, 71), Reid (1995, 254).
25. Tawney (1912, 359–60, 397–98), Mackie (1952, 451–53), Allen (1992, 71–72).

emphasise the fact that the ability of the country to bear taxation depends on the maintenance of a high level of prosperity among the yeomanry.' A sizeable and prosperous peasantry was vital for army recruitment and the financing of military power.[26]

Tawney noted that these concerns about military levies persisted into the seventeenth century: 'In 1601 [Secretary of State Robert] Cecil crushed a proposal to repeal the acts then in force against depopulation by pointing out that the majority of the military levies were ploughmen.' Tawney quoted from a document of 1631 in the English state papers where Richard Sandes stressed the 'great hurt done' by enclosures and depopulation. A vibrant rural workforce was necessary for 'musters and all services requirable for the King and country and taxes . . . but the depopulators . . . destroy all means of doing help or service for the King and country what need soever come.' The Crown's desire to arrest enclosure and depopulation stemmed from the needs of war— for the men and the money that were its sinews.[27]

Some of the Tudor legislation against enclosures was of limited effect. Landlords often ignored or got round the regulations. This provoked peasant rebellions against enclosures. The 1530s and 1540s saw dozens of small riots or revolts. Larger insurgencies against enclosures included Kett's Rebellion in Norfolk in 1549 (under Edward VI) and the Midlands Revolt of 1607 (under James I).

In his radical reconstruction of the rural economic history of the period, Robert C. Allen argued that the Tudor legislation had some success in protecting the rights of yeoman farmers against larger landowners and manorial authorities. Consequently, they had incentives to work harder, innovate and increase productivity. Protected copyholds and beneficial leases became more widespread. For well over a century, Tudor policies reduced the rates of enclosure and depopulation. According to Allen, the Tudor legislation led to a revolution in agricultural productivity based on small peasant farms. The needs of war impelled the rise of these yeoman.[28]

James Harrington (1611–77) in his *Oceana* (1656) reported the rising security and prosperity of the yeomanry resulting from Tudor legislation. These measures placed 'a great part of the lands to the hold and possession of the yeomanry or middle people, who living not in a servile or indigent fashion,

---

26. Tawney (1912, 343, 346).
27. Tawney (1912, 343, 416–17, with spelling modernized in the 1631 quote).
28. Allen (1992, 1999).

were much unlinked from dependence upon their lords, and living in a free and plentiful manner, became a more excellent infantry'. Similar remarks appear in his *Art of Lawgiving* (1659). As noted in the following chapter, the yeoman era ended in the second half of the eighteenth century.[29]

English history was not a straightforward development from feudalism to industrial capitalism. The yeomen era intervened. They obtained some legal and economic security from the sixteenth century, resulting from the manpower needs of the state for defence and war. Their influence on events in the seventeenth century will be examined later.

Reformation, Revenue and the Road to Rebellion

The Act of Supremacy in 1534 removed England from papal power and made Henry VIII head of the English church. Although much Catholic ritual was retained, the king lost little time in abolishing forty-nine holy days in 1536. This meant a dramatic increase in the number of working days in a year.[30]

As well as increasing his spiritual authority, the king appropriated all the taxes traditionally paid by churches and monasteries to the pope. Tithes paid by landowners were diverted to the Crown. The severance with Rome increased the likelihood of military threats from foreign Catholic powers, including from nearby France and Scotland. Greater military needs were partly financed by seizing monastic lands and wealth. There were hundreds of religious houses in England, and the church owned about a third of all English land. The break with Rome led to biggest reorganization of landownership in England since William the Conqueror.[31]

The state found legal pretexts for many of these monastic seizures. Some religious houses were given up voluntarily, their incumbents being bribed by offers of a state pension. In other cases, allegations of treason (particularly the refusal to acknowledge Henry as head of the church), corruption or sexual transgression led to legal proceedings and monastic dissolutions. The king manipulated Parliament and legal processes to pursue his objectives.

H. John Habakkuk tracked the impact on the land market as the state sold some of the seized lands. A statistical analysis by Leander Heldring and his colleagues shows that parishes affected by the Dissolution subsequently had

---

29. Harrington (1747, 69, 388–89, with modernized spelling), Tawney (1912, 38).
30. Allen and Weisdorf (2011).
31. Tawney (1941), Habakkuk (1958), Beckett (1984), Heldring et al. (2020).

a greater share of population working outside of agriculture and experienced higher productivity growth. They also provided evidence of the 'rise of the gentry' in the scramble for newly available land.[32]

The Dissolution had a major positive effect on the state's finances. But as well as dealing with internal revolts, Henry VIII was at war with France or Scotland in 1532–33, 1542 and 1544–50. These conflicts ate deeply into Crown funds. Taxes were raised still higher, but heightened revenues remained short of heightened expenditures. The king renewed some feudal laws and obligations to provide him with other sources of revenue. These onerous revivals were to be a source of major complaint for the next hundred years.[33]

The main issue was knight service. This system had its origins in the Norman Conquest. Land was parcelled out to lords with an obligation to provide military services. A century later, knight service was being regularly commuted for a money payment known as scutage. By 1400 scutage itself seems to have disappeared. It was superseded by other forms of taxation, known as relief and wardship. Relief referred to a payment substituting for knight service, particularly on the inheritance of land rights. Wardship addressed the inheritance problem that arose when a tenant on freehold land died, leaving an heir who had not yet reached the age of majority. The minor would be legally unable to pay the relief in substitution for knight service. Under wardship law, the landlord would retain the land and profits until the heir reached his majority. The lord was obliged to fund the maintenance and education of the ward. He was also empowered to arrange his marriage. These laws applied to lands held by knight service. Other landholdings were exempt.[34]

At the beginning of the Tudor period, the laws relating to knight service were falling into disuse. Henry VIII and his advisors saw these withered feudal incidents as an untapped source of funds. Consequently, when seized monastic lands were sold on to new private owners, most of them were traded with the legal requirement of knight service to the Crown. As Charles Reid noted: 'What this meant in practice was that the Crown could claim feudal dues from individual landholders if so little as a single acre of their aggregate holdings was held as knight service.' In 1540 Henry established the Court of Wards and Liveries, which had jurisdiction over these revived feudal laws. This institution

32. Tawney (1912, 380–84), Habakkuk (1958), Beckett (1984), Heldring et al. (2020).
33. Mackie (1952, 400, 410).
34. Reid (1995, 235–36).

continued during the reign of Elizabeth I and reached the apex of its power when Robert Cecil, Lord Burghley, was secretary of state (1596–1612). The Court of Wards and Liveries was a lucrative source of revenue for the Crown, which would not give it up without a fight. Eventually, a fight it got.[35]

Elizabeth died in 1603. The Protestant King James VI of Scotland became King James I of England as well. The first English Parliament of the Stuart dynasty was assembled. After ritual proclamations of loyalty to the king, the House of Commons voiced its grievances. It wanted freedom of speech and election. It demanded the right of Parliament to vet changes in the law. It protested against purveyance, which was an ancient prerogative right of the Crown to seize provisions, horses or vehicles, in return for an imposed price. Bacon explained to James: 'There is no grievance in your kingdom so general . . . and so bitter unto the common subject.' Purveyance was a major source of revenue for the Crown, and James would not abolish it without large compensatory payments to his royal estate. The Commons also complained about the onerous wardship laws, and the Court of Wards and Liveries. Many pressed for their abolition.[36]

Parliament raised these issues again in 1609–10. A compromise was offered to the Crown in the form of an annual tax to replace wardships. This too was turned down. In 1621 Parliament set up a committee to investigate complaints against the Court of Wards. They were kept busy by the high number of pleas. James died in 1625, to be succeeded by his son Charles. Facing financial difficulties exacerbated by the 1624–30 war with Spain, the new king used the Court of Wards to extract even more money from those gentry under knight service. This increased popular resentment even further.[37]

Charles tried other measures to raise funds. By the Act of Revocation of 1625, all gifts of royal or church land since 1540 were annulled. Their occupants were charged a rent. Despite a statute forbidding such action, the king granted manufacturing or trading monopolies to the highest bidders. By late 1627 England was at war with France as well as with Spain. Still short of money to fund his army, Charles inflicted forced loans on his subjects and imprisoned without trial those who refused to pay. He imposed martial law in 1628, forcing his subjects to feed, clothe and accommodate his troops.

35. Wedgwood (1955, 155–56), Reid (1995, 238–39).
36. Davies (1959, 4–6), Hexter (1992), Reid (1995, 241).
37. Reid (1995, 241).

But the House of Commons declared the forced loans and martial law illegal. The Commons presented Charles with the Petition of Right. Drafted by Sir Edward Coke,[38] this historic constitutional document affirmed basic rights, including habeas corpus and protection from taxation unauthorized by Parliament. Eventually it was passed unanimously by the Commons, and then by the Lords. In June 1628 Charles declared that he accepted the Petition of Right. But in the following year he dissolved Parliament and began eleven years of personal rule without it. He resumed his former policies, including unauthorized taxation. Charles revived the ancient tax of Ship Money—originally designed to furnish ships in time of war—imposing it on every county.[39]

In 1630 Charles set up a Crown Commission to investigate enclosures and rural depopulation. Its main purpose was not to prevent enclosures as such, which were accelerating during the seventeenth century, but to extract fines from transgressors of the law, and to raise finances for the Crown in the absence of Parliament. The tide of opinion on enclosures had turned. The rising gentry and other landowners wanted more rights over their landed property, and they saw the decision to enclose, or otherwise, as a matter for them, and not for the state. As early as 1601 Sir Walter Raleigh had argued that prohibitions on enclosures did not work and instead promoted free trade and the free movement of labour. Other thinkers followed his lead. But among the yeoman class, objections to enclosure persisted, and the Levellers took up their grievances in the Civil War. A major division of opinion widened between the yeoman and the gentry. The gentry held sway, and by 1660 the anti-enclosure argument was lost. The gentry and their allies were in favour of 'improvement', including unencumbered individual property rights in land and the conversion of peasants into wage labourers.[40]

In an attempt to obtain more finances for his war in Scotland, Charles I recalled Parliament in the spring of 1640. John Pym spoke for the House of

38. Grajzl and Murrell (2016) argued that Coke and other contemporary lawyers developed a theory of legal evolution that prefigured elements of Darwinism.

39. Gardiner (1906, 65–70), Hexter (1992).

40. Reid (1995, 256–58). On the acceleration of enclosures in the seventeenth century, see Wordie (1983). In his *Intellectual Origins of the English Revolution*, Hill (1965) focused on Bacon, Raleigh and Coke, noting their defences of economic liberalism and of private property rights. Economic liberalism refers to the supremacy of private property and contract, similar to the 'possessive individualism' described by Macpherson (1962). This is not necessarily liberalism in a modern sense, which tends also to emphasize other human rights and democracy (Bell, 2014; Rosenblatt, 2018).

Commons, refusing the king's request for money unless complaints of royal abuse of power were addressed. This Short Parliament lasted three weeks until the king dissolved it. Charles turned elsewhere for funds. He appropriated £200,000 (about £39 million in 2021 purchasing power) in coin and bullion deposited by London merchants in the Royal Mint. After an eruption of protest, the Crown returned the sum on the condition that the depositors loan him £40,000; it became a forced loan. As an unintended consequence, the loss of trust in Crown integrity prompted the further development of private London banks. Money was deemed to be safer in private rather than state hands.[41]

In November 1640 the king was again obliged to recall Parliament. He asked it to tackle the adverse financial position resulting from defeat in the war with the Covenanters in Scotland. The Long Parliament, as it became known, quickly passed a law stipulating that it could not be dissolved except by a vote of its own members. Levying taxes without the consent of Parliament, including forced loans and the contentious Ship Money, were declared illegal. Accused of a failure to grant due legal process to some defendants, the Westminster court of the Star Chamber was abolished. Parliament asserted control over the appointments of royal ministers, and of army and navy commanders. The Court of Wards was criticized for grievously exceeding its jurisdiction. Schism in the state prompted unrest in the country. There were riots in London in 1641. From 1640 to 1644 there were hundreds of anti-enclosure disturbances throughout England.[42]

Tensions between Crown and Parliament were further heightened in October 1641, with the outbreak of rebellion in Ireland. Neither king nor Parliament trusted the other to raise troops to quell the uprising. In January 1642 Charles left London. Parliament decreed that its laws would hold, even without royal assent. In retaliation, Charles declared that Parliament was in rebellion. He amassed his army and raised the royal standard in Nottingham in August 1642. The Civil War began.

---

41. Richards (1929, 35–36); Wedgwood (1955, 335). In Hodgson (2015a, 122; 2017b, 85), I mistakenly put the date of the ling's seizure of the Mint as 1638 (instead of 1640). I may have copied the error from Kim (2014), but the responsibility is entirely my own. A website currency converter was used to calculate the approximate 2021 purchasing power of historical money values, using RPI inflation data: https://www.measuringworth.com/calculators/ukcompare /relativevalue.php, accessed 30 July 2022.

42. Gardiner (1906, 213), Reid (1995, 241), Brailsford (1961, 427).

The First Civil War

The English Civil War is often divided into three phases or wars, from 1642 to 1646, 1648 to 1649 and 1649 to 1651. There were widespread concerns about taxes, tithes, land tenure, enclosures, wardships and arbitrary authority. These economic and legal issues affected many common people and their livelihoods, impelling them to act. How they rationalized these actions was a different manner. Basic feelings were often framed in terms of religion. Catholics and conservative Anglicans generally supported the king and his divine right to rule. Puritans favoured more liberal economic policies and institutions, based on the security of private property and the power of Parliament.

The Royalists made gains in the early months of the war. In 1643 the Parliamentarians obtained military assistance from the Scots. In late 1644 Parliament attempted to reach a treaty with the king and end the war. They listed twenty-seven propositions and put them to Charles in Uxbridge in early 1645. Several addressed the reform of the church. Others concerned future control of the armed forces and the question of a settlement in Ireland. It was proposed that declarations of peace or war must receive the assent of Parliament. There was also the contentious issue of land law. Parliament insisted on an act to abolish the Court of Wards and for ending 'all tenures by homage, and all fines, licences, seizures and pardons for alienation . . . and for turning all tenures by knight service . . . into free and common socage' in return for £100,000 (about £18 million in 2021 purchasing power) per annum to the king in compensation. But the king refused these terms, and there was no treaty.[43]

Led by Oliver Cromwell, the New Model Army was formed in 1645. In the same year it destroyed most of the Royalist army at the battles of Naseby and Langport. The First Civil War ended in 1646 after the Scots captured King Charles and handed him over to Parliament. Some longstanding grievances were addressed. Among them, unilateral legislation by Parliament in early 1646 decreed that all lands held under knight service were 'turned into free and common socage'. The Court of Wards lost its principal function. It was abolished in 1656.

In 1647 about 25 per cent the officers of the New Model Army came from the London area. In terms of social class, 2.6 per cent were aristocracy or greater gentry, 46.1 per cent were from the rest of the gentry, 18.3 per cent were yeoman farmers or husbandmen, 5.2 per cent were professionals or state

43. Gardiner (1906, 277, 290), Wedgwood (1974, 410–11, 418–19).

servants, 12.2 per cent were merchants or large producers, 13.9 per cent were tradesmen or artisans and 1.7 per cent were labourers. Cromwell himself was descended from East Anglian gentry who had prospered after the purchase of dissolved monastic lands in the 1540s. About a half of the officers in the Parliamentarian army came from social classes lower than the gentry.[44]

Peter R. Newman examined the records of 1,630 Royalist officers commissioned by Charles I and Charles II between 1642 and 1659. Of those whose social status could be identified, only 16 per cent were lords or knights. Gentlemen made up 45 per cent and esquires 32 per cent. Some 89 per cent held no honorific title, and esquires and gentry made up 23 per cent of those below the rank of knight. Compared with the Parliamentarian officers, fewer Royalist officers were drawn from London and the Home Counties; more came from the North and West of England. A higher percentage of Royalist officers were Catholics. But the differences in classification and timing make comparison of these Parliamentarian and Royalist officer surveys difficult. It seems that the percentage of aristocrats among the Royalist officers was greater than among those officers who enlisted for Parliament. But otherwise, it is striking how many Royalist officers came from lower social ranks. To staff their army, the Royalists had to recruit extensively from the ranks of ordinary farmers and from all levels of the gentry. We know much less about the social composition of the ordinary soldiery. Both sides widely used conscription.[45]

In his account of the 'rise of the gentry', Tawney saw the resistance of the aristocracy to the rising gentry as a primary cause of the strife. But critics stressed that the actual participants in the conflict did not line up (mostly) as gentry on one side and (mostly) aristocracy on the other. Furthermore, the gentry aspired to aristocratic trappings, including to inherited estates.[46]

Perez Zagorin criticized Tawney's argument, pointing out that among the gentry there were 'plenty of Royalists of prosperous and thriving families. . . . Indeed, the majority of the gentry was probably for the King.' Lawrence Stone cited evidence showing that in 1642 the ruling elite, even in London, had Royalist sympathies: 'This is hardly surprising when it is realized that these patrician elites depended for their political power and economic prosperity on royal charters and monopolies.' He showed that many landlords who had

44. Gentles (1997, 135–36).

45. Newman (1983, esp. pp. 950–2).

46. Tawney (1912, 1941), Trevor-Roper (1957), Hexter (1958), Zagorin (1959), Coleman (1966).

enclosed their lands supported the Royalist cause. These were among Marx's 'capitalist profit-grubbers', fighting for some reason on the 'feudal' side of the revolution. Stone argued 'that the English Revolution was not caused by a clear conflict between feudal and bourgeois ideologies and classes; that the alignment of forces among the rural elites did not correlate with attitudes towards ruthless enclosure; that the Parliamentarian gentry had no conscious intention of destroying feudalism'. The Civil War was an insurrection of neither the gentry nor the bourgeoisie.[47]

The Levellers and Land Reform

In 1647 Parliamentary army units elected 'Agitators' as representatives. The army was fertile ground for radicalism. A group nicknamed the Levellers emphasized popular sovereignty, an extended male franchise, equality before the law, free trade and religious tolerance. Contrary to a widespread myth, the Levellers did not promote common ownership, except when it resulted from the voluntary pooling of the property of everyone involved. Hill pointed out that the Levellers 'sharply differentiated themselves from the Diggers who advocated a communist programme'.[48] The Levellers believed in natural and inalienable rights, bestowed by God. The inalienability of these rights put limits on the legitimate powers of any government. They defended private property and railed against tyranny. The Levellers were the first political movement in Europe to call for the separation of church and state and for a secular democratic republic.

As noted earlier, widespread popular opposition to enclosures erupted from 1640. In 1647 the Leveller Richard Overton wrote an *Appeale* to Sir Thomas Fairfax, the head of the Parliamentary army. Enclosed lands that 'anciently lay in common' should be made accessible for the common use of the poor. A Leveller petition to the House of Commons in 1648 with forty thousand signatures called for recent enclosures of Fens and other common lands

47. Zagorin (1959, 390), Stone (1985, esp. 45, 53). In other respects Tawney's account is more credible. He identified the growing importance of the gentry in social and economic change after the Dissolution of the Monasteries in the 1530s, and their subsequent influence on politics and legislation.

48. The quotation is from Hill (1961, 111). For Leveller statements opposing common ownership (except when agreed by all private owners), see Wolfe (1944, 348, 409) and Robertson (1951, 85–89). See also Brailsford (1961, 315), Macpherson (1962, 152–53), Manning (1976, 295–96) and Hodgson (2018, 18–21).

to be reversed, 'or have enclosed them only and chiefly for the benefit of the poor.' But these pleas were atypical. Some of the Leveller leaders objected to what they regarded as unjust enclosures, but their overall stance on this topic was more muted. As Don Wolfe put it in his commentary on Leveller texts, opposition to enclosures was 'not typical of Leveller propaganda.'[49]

Their attitude to tithes was more forceful. Tithes were paid to the Church of England. Some administrators abused the tithe system, by over-estimating farm outputs. There are documented cases where goods or animals were seized to pay tithes, with value far in excess of the amount due. Nonconformists and Catholics opposed tithes in principle. Quakers refused to pay them, and hence any Quaker farmer had to take up another trade. A Leveller petition of March 1647 called for the total abolition of all tithes. This plea was repeated in many Leveller publications. It provoked a response from those with vested interests in the existing system. 'Nine thousand clergymen, one in every parish, were now provoked to denounce the Levellers as the enemies of God and for their angry sermons they could draw on an inexhaustible armoury of scriptural texts.'[50]

Leveller leaders engaged with Cromwell, Henry Ireton and other grandees in the Putney Debates of late 1647. They argued over the extent of the suffrage and the future powers of the Crown and the two Houses of Parliament. Tithes and land tenure reform do not figure much in the surviving records of these meetings. Cromwell and Ireton opposed the Leveller idea of a near-universal male franchise: it might threaten the security of landed property.[51]

The Levellers argued that copyhold tenure should be converted into freehold. In principle, copyhold was still bound by the custom of the manor. This had been an unreliable legal safeguard for the tenant, especially after a century of growing commercialization of agriculture. In June 1647, in the name of the Hertfordshire peasantry, a petition was presented to the Parliamentary army at its headquarters in St Albans. It complained that the copyholders 'may now be left finable at the will of the lords, in regard the generality of them have been very malignant . . . and from whom they cannot but expect very severe dealing'. The Levellers took up their cause. The *Army Petition* of May 1648 proposed 'that the ancient . . . badge of slavery, viz. all base tenures by copies, oaths of

49. Wolfe (1944, 155, 195, 288). On Leveller attitudes to enclosures, see Brailsford (1961, 233, 431–33, 449–50, 526) and Hill (1975, 119).
50. Brailsford (1962, 133–35), Wolfe (1944, 140, 193–94, 200, 205, 207, 216, 288, 376, 408).
51. Woodhouse (1951, 1–124).

fealty, homage, fines at the will of the lord, etc. (being the Conqueror's marks upon the people) may be taken away; and . . . all possessors of land may purchase themselves freeholders'. In December of the same year, a few weeks after the end of the Putney Debates, the Leveller leader John Lilburne called for the abolition of all 'base tenures'. In 1652 a Leveller petition asked that 'copyholds and the like . . . may be taken away'. A Leveller publication in 1653 demanded: 'All servile tenures of lands, as by copyholds and the like, to be abolished and holden for naught.' But the Leveller campaign for the replacement of copyhold by freehold came to nothing. In 1656 Cromwell's Parliament threw out lingering attempts to limit enclosures and rebutted efforts to convert copyhold into freehold tenures. These actions served the larger landlords, not the yeoman farmers.[52]

The Levellers promoted a fair contractual system based largely on freehold, with an open market for land based on an accurate land registry. They stressed the importance of land registration for the security of landed property and land market transparency. An edition of the Leveller *Agreement of the People* in 1659 insisted: 'That for the preventing of Fraud, Thefts and Deceits, there be forthwith in every County or Shire in England and the Dominion of Wales, erected a County Record for the perfect registering of all Conveyances, Bills, Bonds, &c. upon a severe and strict penalty.' But this far-sighted proposal failed. As with the full abolition of copyhold, substantial progress on land registration was not made until the twentieth century.[53]

Leveller publications spoke for the poor and against abuses of power by the rich and powerful. But they rarely made a case for a more egalitarian distribution of landed wealth. An exception is a local Leveller pamphlet entitled *Light Shining in Buckinghamshire* from 1648, which called for a complete redistribution of wealth among the population, 'without property one more than the other'. But national Leveller leaders such as Lilburne explicitly rejected such 'levelling' of income or wealth. They accepted the term *leveller* only in regard to equality under the law. At that time, this was a radical position. Lilburne and others argued that it was important to retain private ownership and incentives to improve land.[54]

52. Brailsford (1962, 449, 454).

53. Wolfe (1944, 303) and Shrubsole (2019, 41) stated that around the beginning of the twenty-first century 17 per of English land was still unregistered.

54. Quote from Hill (1975, 117), Wolfe (1944, 316). On Lilburne on economic incentives and equality, see Robertson (1951, 3, 85–89) and Hodgson (2018, 20–21).

A more nuanced proposal would be to limit landed wealth, rather than to redistribute it equally. This idea did not appear in Leveller writings. The promotion of such an 'agrarian law' (as it came to be known) had to wait until 1656 with Harrington in his *Oceana*, where he proposed that there should be no landholding with revenue in excess of £2,000 (about £360,000 in 2021 purchasing power). This would not have generally reduced incentives to increase efficiency or output. Instead it would mean that when output reached the threshold, then the landholding would be divided, and part sold. Given that the economies of scale in agriculture were generally small or non-existent, the adverse effects of limiting farm size would be slight at worst, and they would be countered by the benefits of maintaining rural employment.[55]

The Protectorate and the Restoration

The Second Civil War started with a series of Royalist revolts in 1648. The Royalists were defeated, and Charles I was tried and executed in January 1649. Cromwell also suppressed rebellions in Ireland and Scotland. By 1651 his victory was complete. The Levellers had been crushed and had little remaining influence. Cromwell became Lord Protector in 1653, taking up the twin roles of head of state and head of government. The radical impetus of the revolution was lost.[56]

In the civil wars of 1640–51 about 85,000 died in combat and a further 100,000 perished from war-related disease and famine, out of a total population of about five million. From 1638 to 1651 about 15 to 20 per cent of all adult males in England and Wales served in the military. It was a huge upheaval, affecting the entire population of the British Isles.[57]

Britain was briefly a republic. Marxists describe this as a 'bourgeois revolution'—a major turning point in history. But compared with the French Revolution of 1789, the lasting institutional effects in England were much less

55. On an agrarian law, see Harrington (1747) and Allen (1992, 305–7). Allen (1992, 212–31) showed that agricultural economies of scale in the seventeenth and eighteenth centuries were moderate at best.

56. One can imagine an alternative or 'what if?' (Ferguson, 1998) future where the Levellers triumphed after the Putney Debates of 1647, and English capitalism took a different evolutionary path. In this alternative history, it might have required a Bonapartist military coup to check the powers of the landowners and the aristocrats, despite the democratic sentiments of the Levellers.

57. Carlton (1992).

significant. The radical upsurges of the 1640s contrast with the political conservatism of the Protectorate from 1653 to 1660.

Although the new republic confiscated Royalist lands, there was no discernible effect on the concentration or control of landed wealth. Confiscated properties were put up for sale. Even under the eye of the Cromwellian government, many Royalists won back their lost lands through trustees acting on their behalf. The aristocracy and the gentry were allowed to regain their wealth and rebuild their power.[58]

Cromwell died in 1658 and was succeeded by his son Richard, who lacked the experience, authority and popular support enjoyed by his father. The regime descended into disorder. In 1659 George Monck, the Protectorate's governor of Scotland, marched south with his army and seized control of London. He restored the Long Parliament, thus including members who had been removed in Pride's Purge in 1648. Parliament began negotiations with Charles II, the son of the executed king, who made several promises in the Declaration of Breda in April 1660. Charles returned to England and was crowned in the same year.

The Restoration Parliament annulled almost all the legislation that had been enacted without the king's assent in the 1640s and 1650s. But it also solidified the commitments that Charles had made at Breda before his return to England. The interests of the landed gentry had been foremost under the Protectorate, and they kept up the pressure to preserve their welfare. The Tenures Abolition Act of 1660, otherwise known as the Statute of Tenures, confirmed the Protectorate's abolition of military tenures, knight service and the Court of Wards. As Hill put it: 'Confirmation of the abolition of feudal tenures was the first concern of the convention parliament after hearing the declaration of Breda.'[59]

Against the appeals of yeoman farmers, the act of 1660 made clear that existing copyhold would be retained. But all future tenures created by the king were to be under 'free and common socage'. As a minority voice, Sir Roger North called for the abolition of copyhold. He argued that it had become too expensive for the poorer sorts to pay the fees required to retain it. His efforts were unsuccessful. The Protectorate had done little to protect the yeoman

58. Hill (1940), Thirsk (1952), Allen (1992, 104). In marked contrast to the Civil War, relatively little has been written on the history of the Protectorate. Lay (2020) gives a useful account of the Protectorate's imperial ambitions in the West Indies and elsewhere.

59. Hill (1940, 250), Reid (1995, 241–42, 250–51, 301).

LAND, LAW AND WAR   101

farmer, and the Restoration Parliament did no more. Both regimes favoured the gentry instead.[60]

At the time, peasant farmers occupied as much as two-thirds of the land. Their interests had been abandoned after the defeat of the Levellers in about 1650. Perez Zagorin noted that after the Restoration 'nothing was done to relieve the insecurity of small occupants of the soil or to satisfy the agitation against copyhold tenures, and the conditions that were to make England a country of concentrated landownership went on apace'. England became a realm of big landowners. Other countries differed. Capitalism in nineteenth-century France had a rural peasantry and fewer large, landed estates. Capitalism is not predestined to develop along one path. Britain took one road. France took another. In Britain, the turbulent political events of 1640–60 were ultimately decisive. The powerful landowning families remained.[61]

Keeping Land within the Family: Entails and Strict Settlements

Growing trade and commercialization put pressure on restrictive entails. Entailed land could be leased but not fully alienated. The legal device of 'common recovery' was developed from 1440 to 1502 to provide a means of undoing entails, so that land could be sold or mortgaged. But this did not abolish entails themselves. Legal disputes over entails and other 'perpetuities' endured for centuries. As late as the seventeenth century much land was not under freehold tenure and entails were still widespread.[62]

In 1595 Bacon made a case against 'perpetuities'. Although the two men disagreed on other points, Coke took a similar view on this issue. The arguments against entails and for the free alienability of land intensified. Economic liberals such as Bacon and Coke wanted to enhance the possibilities for trade, including in land. They argued that it would be better for economic development to remove restrictions on the possible sale of land. But the law in this area was complex, and the assault on perpetuities was not easy. Progress against entails was incremental. A succession of test cases removed some

60. Reid (1995, 250–51, 301).

61. Zagorin (1959, 399), Allen (1992 85), O'Brien (1996).

62. Haskins (1977), English and Saville (1983), Spring (1993), Reid (1995), Brewer (1997), Biancalana (2001), Berman (2003, 333–35), North et al. (2009, 89), Allen (2012, 65).

barriers to free alienability. For example, restrictions on land sales by uniden-
tifiable descendants of the current owners were nullified.[63]

But feudal entails endured, largely because the wealthy elite endorsed them.
Owners were disinclined to sell or mortgage buildings or land that had been
in their family for generations. Loss of land meant loss of status, influence, titles and privileges. Much of the larger gentry wished to emulate—or even
become part of—the landed aristocracy. They too desired power and status.
They were not content with being mere country capitalists. The aristocracy
and the higher gentry, while pursuing land enclosures and commercial agriculture, wanted enhanced power and prestige for their families, partly by ensuring that their landed estates would be passed on to their family heirs. In the
higher echelons of English society, and for those who aspired to reach them,
aristocratic norms held sway. They wanted a land-based lineage of prestige
and power.

The aristocracy and gentry welcomed the abolition of knight service and
the Court of Wards in the Statute of Tenures of 1660. They also supported
enclosures. But it was not full speed ahead with expanding markets and economic liberalism. Much of the gentry allied with the aristocracy, not to jointly
promote trade as Marx opined, but to counter the assault on entails that had
started with Bacon, Coke and other economic liberals.

Influential accounts of the rise of capitalism in England, including those of
the two Karls—Marx and Polanyi—emphasise the growing commercialization of the economy, expanding markets, and the creation of a class of wage
labourers.[64] The actual story is more complex. The preservation of entails was
not a profit-maximizing strategy, and it did not promote economic development. But in the layer cake of English society, it meant that the upper tiers
could ensure their survival and prosperity. The impulse to keep land in families
often prevailed over commercial gain. While the big landowners otherwise
welcomed commerce, family trumped profit when it came to the inheritance of
their estates. As Charles Reid pointed out: 'These two rival interests—the
need to allow for economic development and the requirement that family estates be preserved and handed down to the next generation—were the subject
of an enduring compromise worked out by the common lawyers in the years

63. Stone (1967), Haskins (1977), Reid (1995). Grajzl and Murrell (2022a) showed that
1660–1750 case law refinements pertinent to land tended to inhibit, rather than promote, economic development.

64. Marx (1976), K. Polanyi (1944).

after 1660.'[65] This compromise followed the failure of the English Revolution of 1640–60 to challenge the interests of the landed aristocracy and the higher gentry. While the common law had chipped away at the security of entails, the possibilities for keeping land within the family would remain.

An urgent problem focused minds and brought a solution. Sir Orlando Bridgman was a prominent lawyer who had participated in the trial of the surviving regicides of Charles I in 1660. Before his death in 1674, Bridgman devised a scheme that complied with the letter of the common law but allowed landed estates to be passed down indefinitely through succeeding generations, as entails had done before. This new device was called a *strict settlement*. Strict settlements were also described as entails because they performed a similar function. With a strict settlement, a trust would be set up to take legal control of the estate while giving the son (or another male heir) full use of it. The trust ensured that the son could not sell the property. When the son himself had an heir who had reached the age of maturity, the younger man would be asked to sign papers that replicated the same arrangement that had been agreed by his father. With a modicum of ceremony and a few glasses of claret, the wealth and power of the landed family would be handed down in the family for yet another generation. Family wealth and power were thus secured.[66]

The strict settlement was a protective reaction by the landowning class to legislative pressures that were driven by an ideology of economic liberalism. Many in the gentry and aristocracy opposed legislative efforts to stimulate land markets and to make more land alienable. Strict settlements endured for centuries.[67]

But strict settlements did not comply with the Marxist picture of a rising bourgeoisie (or 'capitalist' landowners) tearing down the bastions of feudalism. On the contrary, much of the rising gentry wanted to emulate the aristocracy and adopt some of its feudal encumbrances. Britain consolidated a Janus-faced ruling elite, relying on ancient privileges and tentatively looking forward for commercial and consumption opportunities.

The novelist Jane Austen mentioned strict settlements. In her *Pride and Prejudice* (1813), Mr Bennet's land is 'entailed' to his second cousin. On Mr Bennet's death his estate would pass by legal agreement to this heir, thus depriving the Bennet daughters, including the central character Elizabeth, of

65. Reid (1995, 305).
66. Berman (2003, 333–35).
67. Underhill (1901, 282), Reid (1995, 277), Shrubsole (2019, 38, 281–82).

home and inheritance. Hence Mrs Bennet's rush to get at least one of her daughters married to a rich suitor.

As with other entails, strict settlements could break down for several reasons, and they sometimes did. They typically depended on an unbroken succession of male heirs. Some kind of legal rectification had to take place to deal with these mishaps. But otherwise they were extraordinarily persistent and successful. As Reid put it: 'Historians in recent decades have come to understand the strict settlement as a device that had the utmost importance for the functioning of elite social structures in England for a period that runs roughly from the Restoration of Charles II to the outbreak of World War I.'[68] But to economic liberals, these arrangements were anomalous. More than a century after the Restoration, Adam Smith mocked entails and strict settlements in his *Wealth of Nations*:

> They are founded upon the most absurd of all suppositions, the supposition that every successive generation of men have not an equal right to the earth, and to all that it possesses; but that the property of the present generation should be restrained and regulated according to the fancy of those who died, perhaps five hundred years ago. . . . Entails are thought necessary for maintaining this exclusive privilege of the nobility to the great offices and honours of their country; and that order having usurped one unjust advantage over the rest of their fellow-citizens, lest their poverty should render it ridiculous, it is thought reasonable that they should have another.[69]

Having the benefit of this legal protection that could keep their estates in the hands of their families, the aristocracy continued the process of consolidating and expanding their holdings. The more landed property they had, the more wealth and influence they and their descendants would enjoy. Estates were merged, partly by buying up or running out copyholds and leases. But to maximize this expansion, they needed to borrow money. To acquire loans, especially from people outside their extended families, they would consider a

68. Reid (1995, 277). On the growth of large estates after the restoration, see Beckett (1984), Habakkuk (1940, 1950, 1960, 1979, 1980, 1981).

69. Smith (1976 [1776], 384–85). Other prominent critics of entails included Blackstone (1765–69, 2:chap. 7) and de Tocqueville (1838, 30–33). Hume (1983 [1778], 3:77) welcomed the legislation of Henry VII that helped landowners to break entails, but he greatly exaggerated its impact. Thomas Jefferson and others identified the survival of entails in the English law adopted by the American revolutionaries as a major problem, and this led to important legal changes in the United States (Brewer, 1997).

mortgage, where portions of freehold land, which were not under entails or strict settlements, could be used as collateral. As Habakkuk noted, marriage dowries were also used to aggrandize estates, where often the bride's parents mortgaged land to raise funds to pay the groom's family.[70]

Reforms to Mortgage Laws

Before the seventeenth century, even non-entailed and tradeable lands could not easily be used as collateral for loans. Land mortgages were rare. When mortgages did occur, they relied on crude and restrictive financial arrangements, almost always between geographically proximate lenders and borrowers. Institutional rules for mortgaging generally favoured the lenders: the borrowers ran severe risks of losing their wealth.[71]

Loans were sometimes obtained by mortgaging of expected crops or assets apart from land and buildings. Some mortgages involved the transfer of both *usufructuary* rights and legal title to the lender, for the period of the loan. One reason for this arrangement was to circumvent the usury laws. Rather than interest payments, the lender received the fruits of the land. Sixteenth century legislation made limited interest payments legal, but mortgages remained rare.[72]

In the seventeenth century the mortgaging of inheritable copyhold lands became more common. The lord of the manor owned the land but passed lifetime or inheritable copyhold to a tenant, who paid a nominal rent. If the copyhold were inheritable, then the *usus* and *usus fructus* rights were assets that the tenant could sell or mortgage, under the jurisdiction of the manorial court. The manorial court registered the land and the transactions upon it. In contrast, most freeholder mortgages lacked any land registry or assembled public record.

Juliet Gayton ascribed the absence of copyhold mortgages before 1600 to the strict usury laws in the Elizabethan period. These laws were subsequently modified, making mortgaging slightly easier. Using a sample of manorial

70. Habakkuk (1950).

71. The essays in Harvey (1984) provide evidence of growing trade in freehold land from the twelfth century. But there is no mention of any mortgage. Neither 'mortgage', 'collateral' nor 'security' appear in the index of the volume. The studies in Briggs and Zuijderduijn (2018) confirm that mortgaging in medieval England was rare.

72. Briggs and Zuijderduijn (2018). Usufructuary mortgages are still used today (especially by Muslims) in the Indian subcontinent.

records, Gayton found a pronounced rise in the number of copyhold mortgages from 1606 to the time of the Restoration. She noted that most borrowers
and lenders lived within fifteen miles of each other. There was little recorded
use of financial intermediaries. Debts had to be settled on a face-to-face,
borrower-to-lender basis, generally no longer than a day's travel away. In Gayton's sample there is a decline of copyhold mortgages after 1660. But other
studies do not show a similarly timed decline in copyhold mortgages.[73]

Generally, copyholders were small farmers. The higher gentry and aristocracy needed bigger money to satisfy their aspirations. From the seventeenth
century, forms of mortgaging evolved in attempts to get around the legal
encumbrances tied up with landed property. One option was to obtain a mortgage on leasehold rights as collateral, rather than on the legal title to the property. But such transactions were fraught with difficulties. Before 1670, obtaining
a mortgage on freehold land was prohibitively risky and expensive.[74] As
Allen explained:

> It was possible to mortgage freehold land, but the arrangements were so
> unsatisfactory that money was raised by a mortgage only in dire circum-
> stances. In such mortgages the freehold in the property was conveyed to
> the mortgagee, who advanced all the money. Repayment was normally
> to be made in six months. If default occurred by even so much as one day,
> the title remained permanently with the mortgagee. Moreover, the mort-
> gagor was still indebted to the mortgagee for the repayment of the loan. The
> mortgage was thus not a device for long-term finance and was at best a risky
> procedure for raising long-term funds.[75]

The seventeenth century saw the first steps in developing modern mortgage
law. The common law courts were slow to adapt. The Court of Chancery intervened in 1625 but then to little effect. The new balance of power after the
Restoration put the initiative in the hands of the large landowners, including
Royalists who had lost their lands under the Protectorate. They petitioned the
courts for more favourable legislation. The Crown backed its longstanding and
more powerful supporters.

This time Chancery played a major role. Chancery was a high court in
England that had power to deal with limitations in the system of common law.

73. Gayton (2018), French and Hoyle (1999).
74. Anderson (1969a), Neal (1994, 163), Clark (1998a, 60).
75. Allen (1992, pp. 102–3).

It dealt with problems of delay, imprecision, contradiction or 'inequity' (harshness) in the common law. For much of its existence the Lord Chancellor presided over it. In highlighting the English system of common law, many historians have underestimated the role of Chancery in the evolution of the legal foundations of English capitalism.[76]

Allen explained how Chancery addressed the grievances of the Royalist landowners: 'The mortgaged lands of many of the Royalists were in the hands of their creditors. To aid their recovery, Chancery was allowed to elaborate its doctrine of the equity of redemption. The law, however, remained confused at least into the 1670s.' Equity of redemption would make mortgages extendable as long as the interest was paid. Allen continued: 'It was not until the end of the [seventeenth] century that mortgages became automatically and indefinitely extendable, as long as the mortgagor regularly paid interest. Only then did the mortgage become a routine device for using land to raise long-term finance.'[77] Empirical research by Peter Grajzl and Peter Murrell into English case law shows that the rules of mortgaging became an object of elevated court attention from about 1640, and the pace of case law development on mortgages increased until 1690. Subsequently, the intensity of legal development, remained at around that level, until about 1720, when it began to fall. This is illustrated in figure 4.4 in the following chapter. This research shows that mortgage law had become largely settled before the middle of the eighteenth century.[78]

Gregory Clark gathered data on land sales from 1500 to 1910, but these show no instance of a mortgage before 1680. Then the volume of finance raised by mortgages grew rapidly. In 1696 Charles Davenant estimated that loans secured on land amounted to £20 million (about £3.0 billion in 2021 purchasing power), which equalled about 8 per cent of the value of English and Welsh property.[79]

An enduring problem with mortgaging was the lack of land registration. In its absence, it was difficult to establish clear boundaries for any land owned or

76. Grajzl and Murrell (2022d) showed the relative importance before the Industrial Revolution of financial legislation of rules of equity, which were developed by the Lord Chancellor and Chancery rather than by the common-law courts.

77. Allen (1992, 104). See also Simpson (1961, 226–29), Mingay, (1963, 36), Sugarman and Warrington (1995) and van Bochove et al. (2015).

78. Grajzl and Murrell (2021a, 2021b, 2022a).

79. Clark (1998a, 74–76), Allen (1992, 104), Habakkuk (1980, 206).

transacted. The issue had been raised before. In 1522, with an eye to tax revenues, Cardinal Wolsey planned an extensive land survey known as the General
Proscription. The landowners strongly opposed this project, and it had to be
abandoned. When he was governor of the Channel Island of Jersey in 1600–
1602, Walter Raleigh established land registration over the territory. As noted
earlier, the 1649 edition of the Leveller *Agreement of the People* called for land
registration throughout England and Wales. The draining of the Fenland became the occasion for the first significant documentation of land title. By 1663
a land registry was in operation called the Bedford Level, covering 703 square
miles, including the whole of the Isle of Ely and adjacent areas within Huntingdonshire, Norfolk and Suffolk. But in England before 1704, this was the sole
operative exception. Generally, land titles were often unclear. This inhibited
land sales and mortgaging.

The economist William Petty had been inspired by Bacon. For a while,
Petty was personal secretary to Thomas Hobbes—another major influence.
Under the Protectorate in 1654, Petty was awarded the contract to survey
confiscated Catholic lands in Ireland that could be allocated to soldiers and
financiers who had backed the Cromwellian invasion. In 1661, despite his
former Cromwellian sympathies, he was knighted by King Charles II. Petty
proposed that his and other surveys of Ireland should be developed into a
functioning registry, so that legal title to the land should be 'always clear',
making land transactions 'less tedious, confused, intricate, numerous, and
changeable'. Consequently, landed property would also act as 'security' in
trade and hence serve as a source of money. Petty argued that levying taxes on
land would be easier, yet clear ownership title would increase the value of land.
In 1686, under the reign of King James II, Petty proposed a registry of land
titles for England that would in effect 'coin lands into money.' The phrasing
is significant. Institutions establishing clear landownership, the possibility
of mortgaging, and a system of credit would indeed make landed property
a source of money. But Petty died in the following year. His dream of an English
land registry did not progress until the late twentieth century. His argument
that registration of legal title to land would facilitate economic development
did not become prominent again until the year 2000, with the work of
Hernando de Soto.[80]

---

80. Petty (1927, 1:77–79, 256–57), de Soto (2000). See also Pipes (1999), Steiger (2006, 2008)
and Heinsohn and Steiger (2013).

Conclusion: England in 1688

Prompted by growing domestic and international commerce, new financial institutions had been developed. An act under Elizabeth I in 1571 had established banks in London, York, Coventry, Chester, Bristol and Exeter. The earliest known English cheque appeared ninety-nine years later. During the seventeenth century some of the early goldsmith exchanges and depositories took on enhanced banking functions. There were forty-four goldsmith bankers in London in 1677.[81]

England's involvement in global trade increased hugely in the second half of the seventeenth century. The East India Company was formed in 1600. The English colonization of North America began around the same time. The British Empire had expanded into India and the Caribbean. In 1651, 1663 and 1673 Navigation Acts had been passed to help protect England's global trade from its competitors. English exports increased by more than 50 per cent between the 1660s and about 1700.[82]

By 1688 England had the largest merchant marine fleet in Europe, which had increased from 2 million tonnes in 1660 to 3.4 million in 1686. During the seventeenth century the slave trade had expanded massively. In the quarter century from 1676 to 1700 inclusive, English traders transported 243,300 slaves from Africa to the Caribbean and North America. Some of the profits of slavery were invested in the British economy.[83]

Legal changes were crucial for the expansion of the slave trade. Property rights in slaves had sometimes proved insecure. Insufficient clarity and protection in the laws concerning slave property had contributed to the bankruptcy of the Royal African Company in 1671. Its governor and major shareholders all belonged to the royal family. Holly Brewer has explained how the Crown reacted: 'Charles II helped to make the buying and selling of people as slaves both fully legal and enforceable across the empire.' The Crown used the common law courts to circumvent Parliament. It relied on the retrieval and reinterpretation of ancient laws concerning villeinage. These feudal laws had fallen

---

81. Muldrew (1998), Richards (1929, 93), Powell (1915, 57–64), Grossman (2010, 170).

82. Davis (1954, 160).

83. Williams (1944), Cipolla (1965), Braudel (1984), Inikori (1992), O'Gorman (1997, chap. 1), Eltis (2001, 43), Acemoglu et al. (2005b), Beckert (2015), Whately (2018).

into disuse, but they remained on the statutes. The legal basis for British Imperial slavery was built on surviving fragments of feudal law.[84]

Increasing overseas and domestic trade may help to explain the increase in productivity after 1600 noted by Paul Bouscasse and his colleagues. Prior to that date, overall productivity growth was near zero. But according to their estimates, productivity in England rose by 48 per cent from 1600 to 1680. This averaged about 5 per cent per decade. They also estimate an average growth rate of productivity of 4 per cent per decade between 1600 and 1810.[85]

Figure 0.1 in the introduction, which uses data calculated by Broadberry and his colleagues, shows clear rising trends in GDP per capita and industrial output from the seventeenth century. The Civil War of 1642–51 disrupted economic activity. But economic growth in industry and services was well under way for decades before the Glorious Revolution of 1688. The data provided by Broadberry and his colleagues show that overall GDP per capita grew from 1650 to 1700 at an average rate of 0.74 per cent per annum. From 1700 to 1760 growth was slightly lower at 0.67 per cent. No data suggest that the Glorious Revolution had an immediate and substantial positive effect on economic growth.[86]

Commercially driven development strengthened the political power of merchants, financiers and other traders and eventually stimulated a process of institutional reform. These changes coincided with economically liberal ideas that appeared with Bacon, Coke, Raleigh and others from the 1590s. But as we have seen, other powerful interests restricted the growth of internal trade and markets by insisting on provisions to restrict the alienability of landed property, so that it could be passed intact to descendants in future generations. This challenges the Marxist view that the British landed aristocracy had become archetypical 'profit-grubbers' and were 'essentially capitalist'. The big landowners had motives additional to profit. They used their land to sustain status and power. These motives did not spring from a peculiar 'English culture' that favoured country living, but from the survival of feudal institutions in politics and law that channelled behaviour in familial landowning directions.

---

84. Brewer (2021, with quote from 766). In 1732 Parliament ratified the laws governing slavery, at least for the English colonies. The slavery laws from Charles II's reign survived in the southern states of the United States until emancipation after the Civil War.

85. Bouscasse et al. (2021, 20, 35).

86. Hoskins (1968), Broadberry at al. (2015, 194, 199, 227–44, 404). Crafts and Harley (1992) and other data series for this period paint slightly different pictures, but they concur in finding no discernible acceleration of growth after 1689. Ogilvie and Carus (2014) and Murrell (2017) reviewed evidence on growth in Britain in the seventeenth and eighteenth centuries.

This tension between rising commercial interests and enduringly powerful landed families was to characterize English economic development well into the twentieth century.[87]

Gregory King's survey gave a picture of England and Wales in 1688. Peter Lindert and Jeffrey Williamson have since revised King's data in the light of additional evidence. They found that the major landowners, consisting of 'lords, esquires and gentlemen' made up 1.4 per cent of all families and received 16.2 per cent of all national income. They were already exceeded in total numbers and aggregate income by 'merchants, tradesmen, manufacturers, builders and miners', who accounted for 27.7 per cent of all families and received 37.6 per cent of the national income. Hence in 1688 there was already a sizeable commercial and industrial sector. The bourgeoisie was then of economic significance, but with much less power and influence than the nobility. The supreme social strata were the nobility and other large landowners. And they remained so for centuries thereafter.[88]

J. V. Becket estimated that in 1690 in England and Wales the 'great owners' and other gentry owned between 60 and 70 per cent of the land, with 'small owners' holding between 25 and 33 per cent. Allen wrote: 'In 1688, the peasantry of England occupied not a third of the country, but closer to two-thirds.' The two claims would be compatible if about half of Allen's 'peasants' were tenant farmers. It has also been estimated that around 1700, about one-quarter of arable land in England was still held as commons, despite the progress of enclosures in the preceding one hundred years. [89]

England in 1685 was a growing economy, with increasing productivity and expanding trade. In that year, on the death of Charles II, his brother James came to the throne. The new King and his Queen made no secret of their Catholic devotions. The Protestant Establishment feared a reversion to the old religion and the removal of their liberties, hard-won since the Petition of Right in 1628. In 1685 the exiled Duke of Monmouth returned to England to lead an armed rebellion. His army, mainly made up of poor labourers, cloth workers and farmhands, was routed at the Battle of Sedgemoor in Somerset. James then prorogued Parliament and assumed personal rule for the remainder of his reign. Protestant fears were heightened when the queen bore a son in June 1688—a possible Catholic successor to the throne. The British political system was plunged into another crisis.

87. Marx (1976, 884–85), Anderson (1964, 31), Weiner (2004).
88. Lindert and Williamson (1982, 393–401)
89. Beckett (1984, 5), Allen (1992, 85), Bogart and Richardson (2011, 247), Wordie (1983).

4

From the Glorious to the Industrial Revolution

The late seventeenth and eighteenth centuries saw an astonishing transformation in British government, one which put muscle on the bones of the British body politic, increasing its endurance, strength and reach. Britain was able to shoulder an ever-more ponderous burden of military commitments thanks to a radical increase in taxation, the development of public deficit finance (a national debt) on an unprecedented scale, and the growth of a sizable public administration devoted to organizing the fiscal and military activities of the state As a result the state cut a substantial figure, becoming the largest single actor in the economy.

—JOHN BREWER, *THE SINEWS OF POWER* (1989)

Over the course of a century, a country accumulates towering debts, mainly to finance foreign wars—it is fighting abroad in two years out of three. Could such a country transition from centuries of stagnation to sustained growth? Surprisingly, the answer is yes—the Industrial Revolution in Britain occurred under such circumstances.

—JAUME VENTURA AND HANS-JOACHIM VOTH (2015)

WILLIAM OF ORANGE was married to his first cousin Mary, a daughter of James II.[1] William had multiple family connections with Stuart dynasty. But why did he organize a risky and massively expensive military expedition to England in 1688? Crucially, the survival of the Dutch Republic was at stake.

1. This chapter uses material from Hodgson (2017b, 2021b).

France had nearly overrun the United Provinces in 1672. Catholics had become influential in James II's Court, and he had admitted Catholic officers into the English armed forces. Papal diplomats were trying to get France and England to join in a military alliance against the Dutch. Powerful Catholics wanted to rid Europe of Protestantism. If the Protestant United Provinces were crushed, there would be the added booty of substantial Dutch colonial territories around the world. William's venture in 1688 was a bold move to defend Protestantism and to protect and extend Dutch influence and power.

In 1688 the French armies were tied down in campaigns in Italy and Germany. William saw an opportunity to send Dutch forces to England. The aim was not to make Britain a Dutch colony, but to bolster Protestantism and to turn Britain from a French into a Dutch ally. His purpose was regime change, not colonisation. To give this expedition a veneer of legitimacy, William asked for some leading English nobles to declare their backing. Two signatories were land magnates—one Whig and one Tory. Two more came from the army and two from the navy. A bishop completed the carefully selected list. The seven nobles wrote in their letter of their current 'worse condition', being 'less able to defend ourselves' and asking for William's help. They also advised William on the needed size and likely popular support for his invading army. Important as it was, too much has been made of this document by some historians. The letter did not invite William or Mary to take the throne from James II. Although all were well-connected, none of the signatories was a legitimate representative of any political party or other organization.[2]

The Dutch States General declined to formally declare its support, but it allowed William to use its army and fleet. In October 1688 the English ambassador in The Hague reported that 'an absolute conquest' of England was under preparation. The invasion force comprised 463 ships, 10,692 regular infantry, 3,660 regular cavalry with horses, artillery gunners and about 5,000 volunteers. It included many English and Scottish exiles, plus mercenaries from Germany, Switzerland, Sweden and elsewhere. There were 9,142 crew members and approximately a further 10,000 men on board. The original plan was to land on the East Coast of England. Easterly winds forced the decision to land in the Southwest. When the Dutch fleet arrived at the Dover Strait, it was

2. Ashley (1966, 120–24), Jardine (2008, 4). We may speculate that if Napoleon had invaded Britain in 1805 or Hitler in 1940, then in each case several prominent members of the Establishment could have been found in advance to sign a letter of invitation. The existence of such letters would not have absolved Napoleon or Hitler from the charge of invasion.

in lines twenty-five deep, taking several hours to pass through. It was larger than the ill-fated Spanish Armada of a century earlier.[3]

Blessed by favourable winds, they anchored at Torbay and disembarked at the port of Brixham in Devon in November 1688. After consolidating his position at Exeter, William moved east towards James II's even larger army, which was camped near Salisbury. Some of the king's forces defected to William, and James II was obliged to retreat. As William advanced, he received widespread support from a predominantly Protestant population. Orangist rebels seized York, Nottingham and Bristol. There were a few skirmishes and fatalities. Facing certain defeat, James left London for France. William and his army entered and occupied the capital. London and its surrounding area were placed under Dutch military occupation until the spring of 1690. Until then, no English regiment was allowed within twenty miles of the city.[4]

New elections were held in January 1689, and Parliament was recalled for the first time since 1685. Its negotiations with William were not straightforward. Some politicians wanted his wife Mary to rule alone, thus preserving the Stuart succession. But insurrection in Ireland and a renewed French military threat against the United Provinces helped to focus minds. Parliament agreed that by fleeing Britain, James II had lost the right to govern. In April 1689 William and Mary were crowned as joint monarchs. Crucially, unlike preceding laws of hereditary succession, this new arrangement was an outcome of negotiation with Parliament. The acceptance of Parliament's role in endorsing the monarch was a powerful rebuttal of the Stuart ideology of divine right.[5]

In 1689 Parliament published its *Declaration of Right*. As well as listing James II's transgressions, it asserted the right of Parliament to dispense, suspend and execute laws, and to approve or veto taxes. It declared standing armies in peacetime illegal, except by parliamentary consent. It declared unlawful the seizure of the property of law-abiding people. It supported freedom of speech and condemned 'cruel and unusual' punishments. These rights were not new. Most of them had appeared before, including in the Petition of Right of 1628. The Bill of Rights, incorporating the *Declaration*, received royal assent in December 1689.[6]

3. Ashley (1966, 157), Israel (1991, 335–63), Jardine (2008, 6, 8).
4. Israel (1991, 128), Jardine (2008, 23).
5. Trevelyan (1938), Harris (2006), Pincus (2009).
6. Cox (2012, 2016), Pincus (2009).

Given the propensity of the Stuart kings to prorogue Parliaments, legislation was contrived to make it difficult for the Crown to dismiss that assembly without its own approval. Among the measures was the Mutiny Act of 1689, which allowed the sovereign to maintain a standing army in war or peace for one year, but no longer. Consequently, if the country were to be kept on a war footing, Parliament had to meet annually and renew the Act. A new Mutiny Act was passed each year until 1879. Financial legislation in 1690 ended most lifetime grants for the king and replaced them by time-limited stipends. By such arrangements the Crown became more dependent on Parliament.[7]

The legislation of 1689–90 established no new right or additional security for property that had not been passed before. But the details of some legislation, plus the circumstances under which William and Mary came to the throne, shifted the balance of power towards Parliament, thus reducing the likelihood of despotic monarchy.

Did the Glorious Revolution Increase the Security of Property Rights?

In a famous article, Douglass C. North and Barry Weingast claimed that property rights in England were insecure before the Glorious Revolution. They argued that the development of Britain's economy depended on 'secure property rights' and the 'elimination of confiscatory government'. The constitutional settlement of 1689 between the Crown and Parliament, which made the king subject to Parliament on important matters of legislation and taxation, was allegedly crucial in this process. And 'the credible commitment by the government to honor its financial agreements was part of a larger commitment to secure private rights'. Similarly, Daron Acemoglu, Simon Johnson and James Robinson highlighted the settlement of 1689, which allegedly limited the power of the monarch and facilitated 'the development of property rights'.[8]

There is an element of truth here. But, as noted in the preceding chapter, it is misleading to suggest that property rights were insecure throughout the medieval period. Landed property rights were quite robust from the thirteenth century, as several authors have noted. Some serious confiscations of property occurred under the Tudors and Stuarts. Henry VIII seized monastic lands.

---

7. Winthrop (1920, 19–20), Roberts (1977), Ertman (1997, 210).

8. North and Weingast (1989, 803, 816, 824), Acemoglu et al. (2005a, 393–94).

North and Weingast pointed out that from 1604 to 1628 James I and Charles I extracted forced loans from English lenders, that Charles I raided the London Mint in 1640 to finance a war, and that Charles II defaulted on his debts in 1672, suspending interest payments to lenders for a year, in the so-called Stop on the Exchequer. There was some threat of property confiscation by the Crown. But it should not be exaggerated. Neither should it be assumed that 1689 greatly reduced the possibility of state confiscation of property.[9]

North and Weingast did not mention property in the form of slaves. By the end of the eighteenth century, slaves amounted to about a third of the capital value of all owned assets in the British Empire. Here there is some additional difficulty in the claim that 1689 significantly increased the security of property rights, through a reduction of monarchical and an increase of parliamentary powers. As noted in the previous chapter, the security of slave property was established before the Glorious Revolution, and Parliament had little to do with it, although much later it ratified the legal arrangements. Instead, secure rights to own slaves flowed from the initiative of Charles II in the 1670s, using the common law courts to avoid parliamentary scrutiny or resistance. Slave property was made more secure by a Stuart king, and without Parliament.[10]

North and Weingast pointed to a number of changes in the financial system after 1689, including the formation of the Bank of England in 1694, reductions in interest rates, rising trade in stocks and in securities, and the growth and development of banks. They cited these developments as confirmation that the settlement of 1689 helped to secure property rights and laid the foundations of eighteenth-century economic growth.[11]

The settlement of 1689 did reinforce the power of Parliament against the monarchy, but there was little rewriting of the rules. Although Parliament met more regularly thereafter, the Declaration of Right was vague on this matter. Other legislation calling for frequent parliaments had been passed as early as the fourteenth century but had been ignored. Prominent historians have stressed the 'conservative' nature of the constitutional settlement of 1689: it

9. North and Weingast (1989, 819–20), Richards (1929, 35–36), Wedgwood (1955, 335).
10. Edwards (1806, 3:244), Brewer (2021).
11. North and Weingast (1989, 825–28). Olson (1993, 574; 2000, 37–38) imagined that the Glorious Revolution marked 'the initial emergence of democracy' and brought 'representative government in Britain', with an 'independent judiciary', while it 'increased the security of property rights and the reliability of contract enforcement'—none of which is true. Before 1832 only landowning males could vote—less than 3 per cent of the adult population.

was aimed at the restoration of established rights, it salvaged previous constitutional arrangements after the turmoil under the Stuarts, and it was 'defensive' rather than innovative.[12]

The settlement involved no legal changes in property rights. Steven Pincus
and James Robinson wrote: 'There was also no new legislation enjoining the
supremacy of the common law' in 1689. They pointed out that the 1689 settlement was preceded in 1624, 1644 and 1677 by similar legislation attempting
parliamentary oversight of state finances. Pincus and Robinson concluded:
'While North and Weingast were right to insist on a radical change in English
political behaviour after 1688 . . . the mechanisms they have highlighted cannot
have been the cause. . . . The causes of England's revolutionary transformation
must be sought elsewhere.'[13]

Anne Murphy argued that 'the financial promises of the post–Glorious
Revolution were no more credible than those of previous Stuart monarchs'.
Consider the *Case of the Bankers* of 1690–1700. Shortly after the *Declaration of
Right* in 1689, Parliament decided to appropriate the revenue it had previously
dedicated to its creditors. This was similar to Charles II's Stop on the Exchequer of 1672. It led to a long legal case with several bankers as litigants. In 1700
the case went to the House of Lords, where the bankers won, overturning the
notion that Parliament or Sovereign could decline to repay debts at their discretion and break a legal contract. Then the credibility of commitment was
enhanced less by Crown or Commons and more by the highest court.[14]

Sheilagh Ogilvie and André Carus likewise argued that property was no
more secure *after* the Glorious Revolution. The very fact that Parliament
met more often posed greater legislative risks to property. Julian Hoppit noted
some items of property that became more insecure after 1689: 'Heritable jurisdictions were courts and offices granted by the Crown to individuals and
effectively owned as freeholds to be passed on by inheritance, gift or sale as
they chose.' Although jealously guarded as sources of revenue and prestige, heritable jurisdictions began to be phased out in the eighteenth century, leaving
such offices to be filled by salaried appointments. As another example,

12. Western (1972), Scott (1991), Jones (1992), Morrill (1992), Trevor-Roper (1992), Nenner
(1997), Pincus (2009), Fukuyama (2011), Ogilvie and Carus (2014), Murrell (2017).

13. Quotes are from Pincus and Robinson (2014, 197, 198, 201). On property rights, see Clark
(1996, 2007), Sussman and Yafeh (2006), McCloskey (2010), Angeles (2011). Fukuyama (2011,
418–20), Hoppit (2011), Ogilvie and Carus (2014) and Faundez (2016, sec. 2).

14. Murphy (2009, 5; 2013), Desan (2014, 281–87).

enclosures by act of Parliament meant the removal the property rights of tenants and others, sometimes against their wishes. The British Parliament's abolition of property in slaves in 1833 is a dramatic later example of property made insecure.[15]

North and Weingast concentrated on threats to the security of property that came from the Crown. They disregarded the possibility of parliamentary interference in such rights. They also overlooked that the general security of property and contract depends on a legal system with low levels of corruption and a relatively independent judiciary, both of which were lacking for a long time after 1689. As noted later, serious and sustained attempts to tackle state corruption began only after Britain's catastrophic defeat in the American War of Independence in 1783. The Act of Settlement of 1701 granted judges life tenure, with the aim of moving toward an independent judiciary. But progress was painfully slow, and the bribing of judges remained commonplace, including in commercial cases, throughout the eighteenth century. As Robert Neild put it: 'Radical reform of the courts, sufficient to end corrupt behaviour by the judiciary, came only after 1832, that turning point of the political tide in England.' Events in 1689 had little additional effect on making the legal system fit to support trade.[16]

Whatever its causes, Britain's industrial development gathered pace much later. Gregory Clark noted: 'Institutionalists were stretching a point when forging the link between the institutional changes of 1688 and the Industrial Revolution beginning in 1760.' Robert Allen questioned similarly: If the outcome of the Glorious Revolution was so crucial for property and business, then why did England have to wait nearly a century for the surges in innovation and productivity in the Industrial Revolution?[17]

There are several reasons for this long gap between 1689 and the Industrial Revolution, and they will be explored shortly. Much of the discussion concerning the economic consequences of the Glorious Revolution has been guided by an unsatisfactory notion of property rights, with a failure to distinguish between multiple types of property right, including the differences between rights to use, rights to sell, inheritance rights and rights to use property as collateral. The importance and detail of the links between property and

15. Hoppit (2011, 108), Ogilvie and Carus (2014). British slaveholders did receive compensation. Much of this capital was invested in the railway boom of the 1840s.

16. Neild (2002, 62–67, 108–19).

17. Clark (1996, 588), Allen (2009).

finance are also neglected, thus downplaying the major role of finance in the development of capitalism. Secure property rights were not enough. More wealth had to become alienable and usable as collateral for borrowing and financing investment.[18]

In summary, the North-Weingast 'secure property rights' argument has four major flaws—historical, analytical, motivational and distributional. Historically, property rights were mostly secure for the landed nobility in England from the thirteenth century, with relatively few debt defaults or confiscations of wealth by medieval monarchs. Furthermore, after 1689, particular kinds of property right were made less secure by increasing parliamentary powers, including the enforced removal of entails and heritable jurisdictions, and (much later) the abolition of slavery in the nineteenth century. North and Weingast treated the security of property rights as largely a matter of eliminating confiscatory actions by monarchs. But that is only part of the story. Security of property depends on restraining confiscation by Parliament as well, which in turn depends on an effective and relatively autonomous legal system. The security of landed property also depends on clear and undisputed deeds or title. Corruption too must be reduced.

Analytically, to enable the rise of capitalism, a major problem with older property rights was not their insecurity, but their entangled, feudal nature. In particular, the property rights of an heir to his father's estate prevented the sale of such property or its use as collateral for loans. In a sense, the problem was not that there were too few property rights, but too many.[19]

Motivationally, it is overlooked that strong vested interests protected the feudal nature of landed property rights. The aristocracy enjoyed huge wealth and power. Much of the nobility and landed gentry resisted the reforms to landed property rights, including the removal of entails or strict settlements. These vested interests were undiminished by the 1689 settlement. Major institutional changes were required to provide incentives for the commercialization of land and to enhance a money-making culture that was less inhibited by matters of lineage and status based on landed property. These shifts are ongoing today.

18. Honoré (1961), de Soto (2000), Cole and Grossman (2002), Steiger (2006, 2008), Besley and Ghatak (2008), Heinsohn and Steiger (2013), Hodgson (2014, 2015a, 2015b, 2015c), Cole (2015).

19. Thickets of property claims were the feudal version of the 'anti-commons' problem of multiple entangled rights in modern capitalism (Heller, 2008).

Distributionally, the development of capitalism required the extension of real and enforceable legal rights, from a narrow elite to a larger segment of the population. Such extensions often compromised the rights of existing property owners and were often resisted for that reason. Nineteenth-century examples of ending property rights for some, in favour of the rights of many others, included the abolition of slavery and the removal of the right of a husband to the property of his wife upon marriage.[20]

Some accounts of 'secure property rights' suggest that, once these were in place, institutions would largely be ready to support investment and entrepreneurship. This is mistaken. At least in the English case, a major problem was to reform well-established and secure property rights, not to inaugurate them. The evidence (discussed later) suggests that several of the more dramatic changes in the nature and allocation of property rights came after 1750.

Gary W. Cox, Dan Bogart and Gary Richardson pointed out that the new concord between Crown and Parliament created greater possibilities for the purchase of development rights. The King could no longer sell these rights on his own account. Accordingly, there is evidence from 1690 to 1730 of an increase in infrastructural investment such as turnpikes and river improvements. But this upturn in economic activity was minor compared to later developments. The overall impact on the economy of these 1690–1730 infrastructural improvements was relatively small.[21]

Going Dutch and Fighting Wars

The term 'Glorious Revolution' suggests a largely internal affair. Scholars from Marx to North have focussed on internal reconfigurations of relative power—the rising bourgeoisie, the subjugation of Crown to Parliament and so on. External pressures and shocks have been downplayed. But in 1688 external factors mattered in several ways. First, there followed an influx of Dutch merchants and financiers, extending networks and bringing new ideas. Second, the Dutch invasion and the accession of King William III meant that France

20. Hoppit (2011), Hodgson (2015a, 120–22).

21. Bogart and Richardson (2011), Cox (2012, 587–90). Pincus and Robinson (2014, 203) and Bogart (2011) give evidence of improvements from about 1690 to 1730. But Bogart's (2005) own data show that this early activity was minor compared with later infrastructural developments after 1730. Expenditure on turnpike roads alone tripled from 1730 to 1760, and they grew impressively thereafter.

and Spain were no longer its allies but its enemies. Britain was plunged into a century replete with major wars.

In the seventeenth century the United Provinces had developed a relatively sophisticated system of public and private finance. The state was able to raise a steady supply of funds through taxation. The Dutch contrived a range of innovative institutional devices for investment in trade, industry and infrastructure. Among these were public bonds and shares in publicly traded companies such as the Dutch East India Company. Financial markets, including the Amsterdam stock exchange, facilitated capital mobility and investment. Stock markets permitted smaller fractional shareholdings in mercantile and manufacturing enterprises. Fractional reserve banking was developed. During the seventeenth century about half of all ocean-going vessels worldwide were Dutch. This tiny country dominated the international capital market until the collapse of the Dutch Republic in 1795.[22]

Dutch financiers brought knowledge of Dutch financial institutions and helped to establish London as the world's leading financial centre. Dutch innovations in public finance included the systematic dedication of revenues to service and amortize the public debt. Unsuccessful opponents of the formation of the Bank of England reportedly said that 'this project came from Holland and therefore would not hear of it, since we had too many Dutch things already'. Although England had made important changes before 1688, including major Treasury reforms from the 1660s and the reconfiguration of mortgage law from the 1670s, the impact of the Glorious Revolution on financial institutions was dramatic. Stephan R. Epstein argued that the constitutional restrictions on the power of the monarch in 1689 were less significant than England's 'belated catch up' with continental Europe's most developed financial systems: 'the result of the country's financial revolution rather than a revolution in political freedom and rights'. The new financial practices transplanted from the United Provinces were crucial. In the decades after 1688, partly as a result of the Dutch invasion and the escalation of war, the institutional infrastructure of British finance was revolutionized.[23]

22. Israel (1989), de Vries and van der Woude (1997).

23. Quotes from Bank of England (1970, 6), Epstein (2000, 211). See also Powell (1915), Bagehot (1919), Dickson (1967), Kindleberger (1984), Neal (1990), Hart (1991), Roseveare (1991), Carruthers (1996), Murphy (2009), Wennerlind (2011), Grajzl and Murrell (2021a, 2021b, 2022a).

Set up to fund the war effort and financed by London merchants, the Bank of England institutionalized the national debt. It issued loans to the royal treasury at 8 percent interest, the payments of which were in turn funded by taxes and custom duties. For the Bank of England, these royal debts were among its monetary assets, which were buttressed by a renewed public faith in sovereign integrity. These assets became the bases of a further loan issues by the bank. The government borrowed extensively, cementing together the monied interests of aristocrats, gentry, manufacturers and merchants. As Larry Neal put it, the Bank of England helped to develop a 'web of credit . . . anchored securely in the City of London'.[24]

Several other London banks were established, reaching about twenty-five in number in the 1720s. Stephen Quinn's study of the accounts of a prominent London banker showed how from 1680 to 1705 'the mechanics of private debt were transformed by the dual revolutions in England's systems of constitutional power and public finance. Bankers and their customers began to use the improved financial instruments of the government to facilitate private lending.' After 1688 'came a flurry of joint-stock company formations. . . . By 1695 100 new companies had been formed with a capital of £4.5 million in all' (about £730 million in 2021 purchasing power). By 1698, stock price quotes were regularly published in London. The state continued to play an important role in stimulating corporate activity overseas. The Crown organized groups of creditors into companies, including the New East India Company (1698), the United East India Company (1708) and the South Sea Company (1711). Business and finance were transformed.[25]

The Glorious Revolution dramatically upturned Britain's foreign alliances. Before 1688, Britain was allied with France and Spain against the Dutch. After 1688, Britain was allied with the Dutch against France and Spain. Consequently, England was plunged into a long period of war, requiring major reform of its fiscal and administrative arrangements. The Nine Years' War (1688–97) was quickly followed by the War of Spanish Succession (1701–13). The overthrow of the Stuart king in 1688 led within Britain to the Jacobite Rebellions of 1715 and 1745. There was the War of the Quadruple Alliance (1718–20), the Anglo-Spanish War (1727–29), the War of the Austrian Succession (1740–48), the global Seven Years' War (1756–63), the War of American Independence

24. Murphy (2009), Neal (1994, 180–81).

25. Morgan and Thomas (1962), Kindleberger (1984, 196), North and Weingast (1989, 826), Quinn (2001, 613).

(1775–83), the French Revolutionary Wars (1792–1802) and the Napoleonic Wars (1803–15). Britain was involved in major military conflicts in 86 of the 127 years from 1689 to 1815 inclusive. Much of the impetus for the heavy involvement of the state in the development of the British financial system in the eighteenth century was the need to finance the army and navy. Repeated wars brought constant pressures to adapt and innovate both institutions and technology. This was the era of war capitalism.[26]

Contrary to the claim of North and Weingast that 1689 made government more stable, Pincus and Robinson wrote: 'Far from making government more predictable, the Revolution of 1688 instantiated one of the most intensely polarized and unstable periods in English and British history.' The litany of conflict from 1688 to 1815 underlines this.[27]

Of course, there were many wars before 1688. After the Restoration, there were the Second (1665–67) and Third (1672–74) Anglo-Dutch Wars. But the sovereign often had difficulty raising money to finance these conflicts. Part of what changed in 1689 was the practical accord between the sovereign and Parliament, which ultimately locked them together in common cause, especially when dealing with enemies abroad, despite no shortage of internal disputes in those difficult times. The year 1689 secured the compliance of both king and Commons in meeting the needs of war.

Niall Ferguson has ranked the twelve 'biggest wars in history' by war dead as a percentage of world population. Six of these wars were in the 1688–1815 period, namely, the Nine Years' War, the War of the Spanish Succession, the War of Austrian Succession, the Seven Years' War, the French Revolutionary Wars and the Napoleonic Wars. All these wars involved England.[28]

Figure 4.1 focuses on England, using a roughly similar measure of war intensity, but a database different from that used by Ferguson. It shows the recurrence of war and revolt during the fifteenth, sixteenth and seventeenth centuries. But the intensity of conflict after 1688 was unprecedented. There were three extraordinary eruptions of conflict during the eighteenth century, the third lasting until the end of the Napoleonic Wars in 1815.

Sustained war after 1688 had many immediate impacts. For example, from 1687 to 1703 the number of workers employed in naval yards more than quadrupled. Daniel Defoe remarked at the time that 'in some respects the navy is

26. Mann (1986, 485–86), Bowen (1995, 5), Carruthers (1996).

27. North and Weingast (1989), Pincus and Robinson (2014, 199).

28. Ferguson (2001, 37, 426).

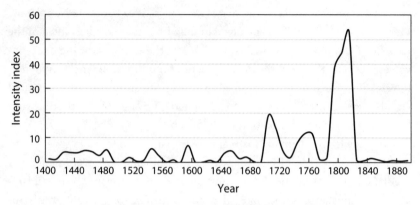

FIGURE 4.1. Intensity of violent conflicts involving England, 1400–1900
For each (external or internal) conflict involving England, the total number of estimated casualties (civilian and military, on all sides) was divided by the number of organized belligerents in the conflict (with a minimum divisor of 2 and a maximum of 6). The intensity index was then constructed by summing the results for each decade and dividing by the contemporary population (in thousands) of England (before 1700) or of Britain (after 1700). Data from Centre for Global Economic History (2021), plus calculations by the present author.

the largest industry in the country'. More people were required to administer the growing war machine and to raise taxes to finance it.[29]

Sinews of War: The Growth of State Fiscal Capacity

The needs of war and the combined pressures of global and domestic commerce were major forces behind the development and reform of financial institutions and state administration. The Glorious Revolution and subsequent international conflicts led to major transformations of the state apparatus, including the Act of Union with Scotland in 1707. As Henry G. Roseveare pointed out, accompanying the political and fiscal changes after 1688 there was 'an administrative revolution—or, at least, a striking growth in the power and effectiveness of the state which manifested itself not merely in war but in the subtler tasks of peace'.[30] Figure 4.2 shows the growth of the number of full-time employees involved in the fiscal bureaucracy, including those in customs,

29. Hill (1961, 230).
30. O'Brien (2011), Roseveare (1991, p. 4).

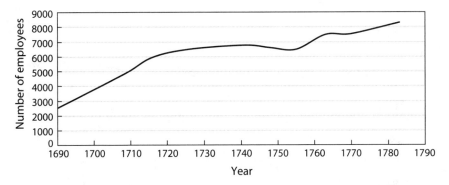

FIGURE 4.2. Full-time employees in the state fiscal bureaucracy, 1690–1783
Data from Brewer (1988, 66).

excise, the post office and the Treasury. It depicts a remarkable rise from 1690
to the 1720s, when the bureaucracy more than doubled in size. The settlement
of 1689 strengthened the political consensus, making possible a more effective
fiscal state. A stronger fiscal base enabled a growth in tax revenues, particularly
to finance wars.

In 1692 Parliament instigated a national land tax. Set at one-fifth of land
income, it was introduced explicitly to fund 'a vigorous war against France'. In
1696 this tax accounted for 52 per cent of all state revenues. It was administered
by local gentry, with county revenue quotas. In the absence of a national land
registry and of adequate central monitoring, one can imagine how the richer
and more influential gentry might lighten their own tax burdens. Given the
possibility of influence over the process, appointments to the local land tax
administrations were often vigorously contested. The tax was not withdrawn
after the 1688–97 war, but it became less significant as a source of state revenue.
The land tax of 1692 lasted until 1832. It has been blamed for encouraging yeoman farmers to sell their land to larger and richer landowners.[31]

Excise taxes had been significant since Charles I. A window tax was introduced in 1696. From 1693 onwards, a major part of state revenue was from
customs and excise charges, which increased with the growth of Britain's
power and trade abroad. There were numerous additional taxes, which extended to consumption goods, including food and clothing.[32]

31. Ruffhead (1763, 483–99), Ward (1953), Mathias (1983, 462), Turner and Mills (1986),
Brewer (1989, 95–101), Roseveare (1991), Allen (1992, 101).
32. Braddick (1996), Ferguson (2001, 60–67), Neild (2002, 61).

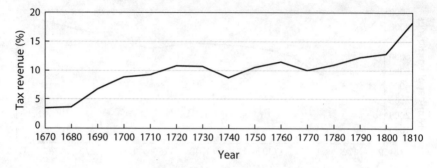

FIGURE 4.3. Total tax revenue as a percentage of national income, 1670–1810
Data from O'Brien (1988, 3). See also O'Brien (2011, 428) and Cox (2012, 576).

Figure 4.3 shows the total tax revenue as a proportion of national income from 1670 to 1810. There is a marked rise from 1680 to 1690, and thereafter to 1700. Impelled by the outbreak of war in 1688, and as a result of the settlement of 1689, the government was able to ramp up tax revenues, more than doubling the tax-take as a percentage of national income. Ironically, the most obvious and immediate effects of 1688 were not a growth in free enterprise, but a considerable expansion in state bureaucracy and taxation.

The rises in taxation and credit were closely connected. When the government borrowed, its creditors demanded regular and reliable payment. Taxation was necessary for the credibility and expansion of the credit system.[33]

Modern Financial Institutions

Financial institutions have a very long history. Bank depositories existed in Babylonian temples and in India almost four thousand years ago. They were also found more than two thousand years ago in ancient Greece, the Roman Empire and Qin dynasty China. These ancient banks stored gold and other portable wealth for clients, provided credit and kept records. Their lending function was constrained, partly because only portable wealth could readily serve as collateral. From the twelfth century, banks in Italy acted as money changers and provided credit using future agricultural outputs or mercantile profits as security.

33. Brewer (1989, 89–91), Desan (2014, 386).

In the basis of such historical reflections, McCloskey argued: 'Finance and saving and investment cannot have been crucial' for modern development, as places such as Florence, Athens or Beijing 'would have innovated us into the modern world.' But this overlooks the primitive state of banking, by eighteenth-century standards, in ancient China, ancient Greece and even medieval Florence. Raymond W. Goldsmith claimed that in Augustan Rome the value of financial assets 'was very small compared with that of tangible assets'. This was 'substantially lower' than in England in 1688, where the value of financial assets was about one eighth that of tangible assets. Compared with ancient Rome, Medici Florence had a higher ratio of financial to tangible assets (i.e., a higher 'financial interrelations ratio'). But Medici Florence had 'a still relatively low degree of institutionalization of the financial structure' compared with Britain during the Industrial Revolution. The ratio of claims against financial institutions to all financial assets (the 'financial intermediation ratio') was significantly lower in the Italian case. The evidence shows that earlier financial systems, from ancient Rome to medieval Florence, were well behind eighteenth-century London in their financing capacities. The relative value of financial assets in these earlier economies was lower than it was in England during the Industrial Revolution.[34]

Although ancient financial institutions foreshadowed several of the features of modern banking, there was no developed system of public debt, and the capacities for credit creation in ancient Greece or Rome were limited. There was no general issue of secure paper money. Neal saw the beginnings of 'modern finance', with stable currencies and long-term public debt, in Genoa in the fifteenth century. But political fragmentation and wars prevented the full development of a modern financial system in medieval Italy. While paper money emerged before, it was not until the eighteenth century in England that it became relatively secure and widely used.[35]

From the fourteenth century a growing number of commercial banks operated by keeping only a fraction of their deposits in reserve as cash or gold. Depositors of gold, silver or other coin received notes of deposit from the bank. With sufficient confidence in their validity and in the viability of the banking institutions involved, these notes could then in turn be exchanged as money. Hence fractional reserve banking can expand the money supply

---

34. McCloskey (2010, 138), Goldsmith (1987, 57, 169). Goldsmith provided no data for China.

35. Neal (2015). See Desan (2014, chap. 8) on the development of paper money in eighteenth-century England.

beyond the scale of the deposits alone. But recurrent crises of confidence in these institutions led to bank failures. Central banks were eventually seen as a means of reducing such risks.

Modern, finance-driven economies typically involve central banks that issue money, including token money. There is a national debt and markets for debt. There were no equivalent institutions in ancient Greece or Rome. These ancient civilizations had well-established financial institutions, but financial markets were not the primary drivers of their economies.

A system capable of sustaining and servicing public debt emerged in Britain in the eighteenth century. It involved private banks, financial markets and the Bank of England. Other countries created central banks. The Bank of Amsterdam was founded in 1609 and assumed some of the functions of a central bank. The Swedish Riksbank was founded in 1668 as a central bank. The Bank of Scotland was set up in 1695. Central banks were founded in France in 1800, Belgium in 1850, Germany in 1876 and Japan in 1882. As Charles W. Calomiris and Stephen H. Haber have shown, modern banking systems are partly political creations, conditioned and guided by political structures and circumstances.[36]

A major laggard here is the United States, which, after the closure of the Second Bank of the United States in 1836 (which was followed by a major financial panic in 1837 and a long recession), had no central bank until the Federal Reserve in 1913. Nevertheless, studies suggest that the general development of financial institutions was vital for the early expansion of the US economy. Throughout the nineteenth century the US financial system was dominated by small, state-chartered banks. But this did not stop greater economic growth after the Civil War of 1861–65. Other factors help to explain this, but they are beyond the scope of the present work.[37]

---

36. Grossman (2010), Calomiris and Haber (2014). The Bank of Scotland was not set up to finance war or to service the national debt. It had no fiscal connection with government, and it had a greater orientation toward business. This may help to explain Scotland's important role in the Industrial Revolution, despite its prior economic backwardness.

37. On the role of finance in US economic development, see Sylla (1969) and Rousseau (2003). According to Goldsmith's (1985, 45) data, the financial interrelations ratio (ratio of financial to tangible assets) was higher in the United Kingdom than the United States for the entire 1850–1913 period. Nevertheless, at least by this measure, the United States was still in the top league in terms of financial development. The US financial interrelations ratio was higher than in Belgium for the 1850–95 period, and higher than in France and Germany for the 1850–75 period. From 1850 to 1880 the total value of US tangible assets increased by a factor of 5.3. In the

With the formation of the Bank of England, control over the money issue and the national debt was denied to the Crown and placed under parliamentary control. The modernization of public finance involved standardized debt contracts and the development of the tax system. Arrangements were needed to sustain both short-term and long-term borrowing to finance the national debt. Chartered companies provided credit to the central bank as part of the deal for obtaining or renewing their charters. Debtor obligations had to be reliably monetized, with risks parcelled out via legally viable markets for debt.

Some institutional reforms in the financial system were resisted. As Peter Dickson noted, there was widespread public hostility to the London market for financial securities: 'It was denounced as inherently wicked and against the public interest.' Once again, financial development went against longstanding cultural norms. But the needs of war surmounted these moralistic sentiments. Exogenous pressures overcame popular resistance and provoked institutional change. Progress was sometimes slower in times of peace.[38]

The English Financial Revolution had a major impact. In 1672, as Bruce Carruthers noted, although there were trading in stocks, there was no organized stock market in London. 'England was a weak nation-state and a second-rate military power. In 1712, only forty years later, the shares of many joint-stock companies were traded on an active and highly organized capital market that had emerged in London. Furthermore, Great Britain had become one of the major military powers in Europe and had successfully checked French expansion.'[39]

The Uneven Evolution of English Banking and Finance

The development of a modern financial system involved experimentation in a novel and uncertain context. Not all institutional innovations were successful. In 1690 the economist Nicholas Barbon helped to develop the National Land Bank, which would make mortgaging easier. But, opposed by the Treasury and

---

same period the total value of US financial assets increased by a factor of 7.4 (Goldsmith, 1985, 297). Despite the unique limitations of the US financial system, it increased in scale and remained as effective as those in several other developed countries. While the United States was behind in the sophistication of its financial institutions, it forged ahead in terms of the relative efficiency of its management and work organization (Chandler, 1977).

38. Dickson (1967, 32–33), Brewer (1989), Braddick (1996), Ingham (2008, 70–74), Cox (2012, 576–80), Calomiris and Haber (2014).

39. Carruthers (1996, 8).

Parliament, this scheme foundered in 1697. As Richard Richards commented: 'Any attempt to issue incontrovertible "bills of credit" based on variable land securities in an age of financial instability when the negotiability of various other forms of paper credit already in use had not yet been settled by Act of Parliament was foredoomed to failure.' Much land in the 1690s could not yet be used as collateral. The economic disruption following the Great Recoinage of 1696 ended the project. It took several decades to build up financial institutions under which alienable land could be readily mortgaged.[40]

Ordered by King William III and administered by Isaac Newton, the Great Recoinage of 1696 was an attempt to end forgery. It severely disrupted coin issue, leading to a contraction of the amount of money in circulation, high interest rates, and a run on both silver and the paper money issued by the Bank of England. Several legislative and institutional changes, spreading over decades, were required to rectify the problems. These included the development of a sound paper currency. The use of paper money expanded during the eighteenth century, but it was not until 1758 that bank notes were legally recognized as currency.[41]

Another major setback occurred during a brief period of peace. The government was eager to reduce the size of the national debt, which had resulted from the wars of 1688–97 and 1701–13. The Bank of England encouraged holders of its fixed-term annuities to exchange them for stocks in one of the big three English companies, including the South Sea Company. The South Sea Company made the biggest bids, providing incentives for the annuitants to sell. This created a huge bubble in South Sea stocks. But when the bubble burst in the autumn of 1720, the buyers incurred serious losses. The government reacted to the crash by trying to ensure a greater dispersion of debt in future. The Bubble Act of 1720 put severe restrictions on the formation of joint stock companies. It hindered the development of industrial and mercantile corporations for more than a hundred years.[42]

There was much resistance to the idea that the state could issue paper money by fiat, and build up credit and debt, in part to serve the cause of war. The Irish philosopher Bishop George Berkeley first published *The Querist* in the 1730s. Among other topics, he used the form of the query to challenge

40. Chamberlain (1695), Richards (1929, 130), Clapham (1966, 33–34), Rubini (1970), Habakkuk (1980, 207), Pincus and Wolfram (2013), Desan (2014, 327, 367–69).

41. Desan (2014, 327–29, 361–69).

42. Dickson (1967, 134–39), Brewer (1989, 125–26).

conventional intuitions about money and credit, and to hint that the value of money was not necessarily based on an association with valuable metals. He asked: 'Whether the true Idea of Money, as such, be not altogether that of a Ticket or Counter?' And whether 'there can be no greater Mistake in Politics, than to measure the Wealth of the Nation by its Gold and Silver'. He suggested that money is a socially constructed sign and a social tool, denoting value and its measure in a monetary production economy. Paper money was viable. Its efficacy and value were grounded on institutionalized social practices. From this standpoint he highlighted the benefits of credit and of the national debt. Under these conditions, the supply of money is expandable by fiat.[43]

Berkeley argued that the creation of credit increased the national stock and enhanced trade. Could 'the Credit of the publick Funds be not a Mine of Gold to *England*'? He also asked: 'Whether such Credit be not the principal Advantage that *England* hath over *France*? I may add, over every other country in *Europe*?' He noted that as domestic credit might grow, industry and trade would grow likewise. He thus pinpointed Britain's crucial advantage over its European adversaries. It had developed a set of financial and political institutions that enabled credit creation and the financing of industry, trade and war.[44]

The British financial system needed institutions that ensured the 'negotiability' or saleability of debt. A key problem was effective legal enforceability. For general negotiability, the transfer of obligations also had to be recognized and enforced by the legal system. Contracts ordinarily involve legal obligations to deliver goods or services in exchange for money. By contrast, deals with promissory notes involve sales of promises, not goods or services. Originally, the purchase of a promise was not recognized as a valid contract in law. What happened, for example, if the lender had stolen the money that was passed to the borrower? Did that mean that the contract between them was invalid? Or was the borrower still obliged to repay? Major legislative changes were necessary to make debt markets work. A promise to pay could then be sold to another, who would then take on the legal obligation of payment.

43. Berkeley (1750, 3, 60).

44. Berkeley (1750, 25–26). See Kelly (1985) and Murray (1985). Note that Berkeley concurred 'with Mercantilism in opposing economic liberalism and giving strong powers to the state'. Berkeley promoted the regulation of financial institutions, enhanced education and training of the workforce, and moral direction of economic activity, rather than the promotion of economic self-interest (Murray, 1985, 156).

All this depends on a legal structure of enforceability, a banking system backed by private and state assurances, and sufficient confidence that debt can be redeemed. Despite repeated attempts, it took a while to put the required institutions in place. In the seventeenth century, commercial cases had shifted from the law merchant courts to common law courts. But the 'blundering attempts' by common law courts to deal with the negotiability of debt led businessmen to press Parliament for robust legislation. In 1694 the Bank of England made an ineffective attempt to deal with the problem. In 1704, during the reign of William's successor Queen Anne, Parliament passed 'An Act for giving like Remedy upon Promissory Notes, as is now used upon Bills of Exchange, and for the better Payment of Inland Bills of Exchange'. But this act had relatively little traction. Significant further legislation was required to consolidate negotiability. Crucial in this effort was the work of William Murray, the Earl of Mansfield. Born in Scotland in 1705, he was English Lord Chief Justice from 1756 to 1788, and he is credited as the founder of English commercial law. In judgements in 1758 and after, he made paper money legal tender and harmonized the rules relating to inland and foreign bills of exchange and to promissory notes. He insisted on the rights of the innocent buyer to the value of what debt he had purchased. He reiterated that negotiable instruments were a form of currency. Just as Francis Bacon and Edward Coke were legal entrepreneurs for the seventeenth century, Lord Mansfield was perhaps the most important for the eighteenth. The clarification of operative rules for markets trading in debt was one of his crowning achievements. He and Chancery stepped in where the common law courts had failed to provide satisfactory solutions. Lord Mansfield turbocharged British capitalism and incidentally, in later judgements, began the process of dismantling British slavery.[45]

Once the negotiability of debt was more firmly established in law, financial markets expanded. As Henry Dunning MacLeod wrote: 'If we were asked— Who made the discovery which has most deeply affected the fortunes of the human race? We think, after full consideration, we might safely answer— The man who first discovered that a Debt is a Saleable Commodity.'[46] The use

45. Beutel (1938, esp. 840), Shientag (1941), Baker (1979), Lawrence (2002), Desan (2014, 390, 393). In 1772 in the Somerset Case Lord Mansfield judged that there was no sound legal basis for slavery on English soil, and in 1783 in the Zong Insurance Case he ruled against slave traders that had massacred slaves (Walvin, 2011; Scanlan, 2020, 162–64; Brewer, 2021, 787, 829–30).

46. MacLeod (1872, 481). MacLeod (1858, 476–78) coined the term 'Gresham's Law'. Mitchell Innes (1914, 9) credited him as the originator of the state theory of money. Commons (1934, 394) described him as 'the first lawyer-economist'. Schumpeter (1954, 718) judged him the only contemporary of Marx to make a systematic advance towards a credit theory of money.

of this 'discovery' required firm legal foundations and consolidation through multiple acts of Parliament and several case judgements. But eventually, through these means, the emerging capitalist financial system empowered economic development on a massive scale. When legal institutions supporting collateralizable property, credit money, and the sale of debt were in place, a new dynamic was unleashed. The capitalist genie was out of the bottle.

Modern banks do not act simply as intermediaries. Banks themselves create money by making loans. The bank issues a loan and receives the debtor's obligation to repay. The loan entry (in the name of the customer) appears on the asset side of the bank's balance sheet, and the bank simultaneously creates a new and equal-sized deposit entry (in the name of customer) on the liability side of its balance sheet. Hence the bank simultaneously expands both sides of its balance sheet by equal amounts. If the loan is used for investment, then investment is not a result of saving, but of finance. By these devices, commercial bank money is created endogenously. In modern monetary systems, banks can create money, subject to their own solvency and credibility, which depend on institutional supports.[47]

These provisions include the role of a central bank as lender of last resort. The Bank of England did not become established as the institutional lender of last resort until about 1760, after a series of financial panics. Michael C. Lovell put it: 'On the eve of the industrial revolution it took its first step towards the assumption of the powers and responsibilities of central banking. . . . The lender of last resort [was] a function of much greater significance than its former role as a fiscal arm of the crown'. Notably, in the eighteenth century the Bank of England had little to do with mortgages. The foundations of modern state banking and private finance were slowly built.[48]

The Dating of the Financial Revolution

Writers vary on the dates they give for the Financial Revolution, and on whether it began before 1688. Peter Dickson put it as from 1688 to 1756; Henry Roseveare, from 1660 to 1760 and Carl Wennerlind, from 1620 (dating from when Baconian and other scientific thinking influenced understandings of credit and risk) to 1720. From an institutional point of view, it is vital that we

47. Robertson (1928), Moore (1988), Minsky (1991), Ingham (2004), Goodhart (2009), Wray (2012), Desan (2014), McLeay et al. (2014), Werner (2014), Jakab and Kumhof (2015), Pistor (2019), Kelton (2020), Keen (2022).

48. Lovell (1957, 15–17), Joslin (1954, 175–77).

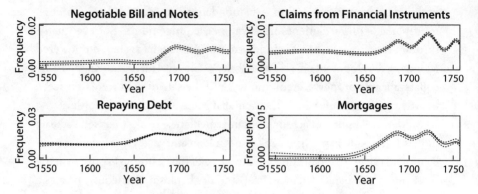

FIGURE 4.4. The development of case law on some financial issues
From Grajzl and Murrell (2021b, 209).

recognize the importance of early reforms to public finances and the issue of
public bonds under Sir George Downing from 1667, mortgage law reform in
the 1670s, the crucial institution-building period following the Glorious Revolution of 1688, and the vital importance of the development of markets for debt
with the Bank of England as lender of last resort, especially around 1758–60
under Lord Mansfield.[49]

Figure 4.4 gives further information on timing. It illustrates some key developments in case law relating to finance. The graphs are selected from empirical work on the development of English case law by Peter Grajzl and Peter
Murrell. Their graphs show that case law pertaining to negotiable bills and
notes, and to claims from financial instruments, both began to develop significantly around 1670, before the Glorious Revolution. From the 1690s the development of case law in these areas reached higher levels, which endured until
about 1750. Attention to case law pertaining to the repayment of debt and to
mortgages increased earlier, starting from about 1640 in both cases. The pace
of development of case law concerning mortgaging was very slow before 1640,
reflecting the much lower frequency of mortgaging before that date. The development of mortgaging case law increased from about 1640 and reached
high levels of deliberation from about 1680 onwards. The Glorious Revolution gave these developments further impetus. But these legal and financial
processes were underway before 1688. Overall, these data confirm a dating

49. Dickson (1967), Hart (1991), Roseveare (1991), Wennerlind (2011), Desan (2014,
246–54).

for the Financial Revolution from about 1660 to about 1760. This is in line with Roseveare's periodization and also concurs with several other authors who emphasised important developments in financial institutions in the years before 1688.

In another large-scale study of English case law, Grajzl and Murrell found that the reform of laws concerning families and inheritance after the Restoration had a positive effect on English economic development, particularly by affecting birth rates and incomes. For example, some legal reforms made it possible for women to shelter their own wealth in trusts before they were married, when, under the common law of coverture, their other assets became the property of their husband. Developments in English case law from 1660 to 1760 opened up new ways of distributing and bequeathing family property. Some of these helped to spur commercial activity.[50]

This dating from 1660 to 1760 places some importance on the Civil War, the Protectorate and the Restoration, as well as on the Glorious Revolution. The turbulent events from 1640 to 1660 determined that English capitalism would be headed by the landed gentry and aristocracy, rather than by industrial capitalists, merchants or small farmers. Once the Restoration stabilized this balance of class power, the aristocrats and the gentry could then lobby for arrangements that favoured their landed interests and their family lineages. The large landowners were politically dominant and held together under the real and ceremonial authority of the Crown. They lobbied not simply for entails or strict settlements, but also for easier access to mortgages. After difficulties under James II, the Glorious Revolution consolidated the role of Parliament and the Protestant nature of the ceremonial authority. Intensified war after 1688 provided further impetus for institutional and industrial transformations. These wars accelerated the Financial Revolution and led to a massive expansion of state capacity.

More War, More Finance, More Debt

In 1751 a new financial product was launched to help fund the national debt. Consolidated annuities, known as Consols, were devised by the Jewish banker Sampson Gideon. Cromwell had allowed Jews back into Britain in the 1656, after their expulsion by Edward I in 1290. Gideon had helped to finance the suppression of the Jacobite Rising of 1745–46, and he gained some influence

---

50. Grajzl and Murrell (2022b).

within the British government. He persuaded Prime Minister Henry Pelham to convert much of the outstanding British government debt into consolidated annuities. These Consols were a form of sovereign perpetual bond. They paid interest at 3.5 per cent a year, reduced to 3.0 per cent in 1757. (In 1888 their interest yields were further reduced.) During times of war, investors could buy these bonds by paying only 60 per cent of their value but still receive 3 per cent interest on their nominal value. Consequently, an up-front investment would yield 5 per cent per year. There would be buyers for Consols as long as there was sufficient confidence that the government would redeem them if desired. There was a strong demand for them, and they were traded as liquid assets. They paid a major part in financing UK state expenditures, including on wars.[51]

From 1749 to 1754 Britain was at war in India against France. Conflict between Britain and France over their North American colonies renewed in 1754. In 1756 this struggle expanded to Europe and elsewhere and became part of what is described in Britain as the Seven Years' War (1756–63) (known as the French and Indian War in the United States). This was one of the largest and most significant conflicts in Britain's history. Britain again faced the problem of financing its war machine. The government borrowed by issuing more Consols. As the war expanded in scale and intensity, the national debt soared upwards.

Figure 4.5 shows the progressive rise of public debt, which was largely due to war. Such debt was made possible by institutional changes during the Financial Revolution. Even the low levels in the early 1700s were historically unprecedented. In 1712 public debt exceeded 50 per cent of GDP for the first time. It rose further in the 1740s. The Seven Years' War pushed it above 100 per cent. It was ratcheted upwards by further conflicts, reaching a peak of 194 per cent, just seven years after Waterloo. The following eighty-five years of limited war, relative peace and economic growth saw the national debt decline slowly towards its levels in the early 1700s.[52]

Figures 4.1 and 4.5 are worthy of some joint reflection. It is striking how debt accumulated as a result of war. The unprecedented surges of military activity that followed 1688, combined with the new accord between Parliament and the Crown from 1689, joined them in common cause against foreign

51. On Cromwell's re-admission of the Jews, see Lay (2020, 30–32). On Consols, see Dickson (1967), Ventura and Voth (2015), Hutchinson and Dowd (2018).

52. UK public debt began to rise again from 1914. Two World Wars brought it to the twentieth-century peak of 259 per cent of GDP in 1946.

FIGURE 4.5. UK public debt as a percentage of annual GDP, 1700–1900
Data from Bank of England (2021).

enemies and enabled a massive buildup in state administrative capacity, taxation potential and debt expansion. The Industrial Revolution from 1760 to 1820
coincided with high levels of public debt.

Did ballooning public debt cause inflation to rise? During the 1751–1822
period, when UK public debt was consistently over 60 per cent of GDP and
rose to a peak of 194 per cent in 1822, price inflation averaged only 1.14 per cent
per annum, albeit with large variations, with years of price deflation and of
inflation. There is no discernible upward trend in inflation over these years.
While the use of gold and silver coins in this period may have helped to prevent runaway inflation, it did not ensure price stability.[53]

Did state borrowing stimulate industrial advance? Or did public debt crowd
out private borrowing and industrial investment, meaning that industrial
growth would have been much faster if the state had borrowed less? In fact,
industrial growth was surprisingly slow. Both sides to this argument depend
on counterfactuals, involving possible outcomes that did not actually happen.
This makes the issue difficult to resolve empirically.

David Hume and Adam Smith took a negative view of public debt. But
against Hume in particular, his contemporary Isaac de Pinto had argued at
length that public debt could have positive effects, by fostering credit and increasing the circulation of money and goods. The effects of public debt have

53. Data from the UK Office of National Statistics, https://www.in2013dollars.com/UK
-inflation, accessed 29 June 2022. For an analysis of monetary stability in Europe from 1300 to
1814, see Karaman et al. (2020).

been controversial ever since. The debate has been going on for well over two hundred years.[54]

It is important to disentangle possible short-term and long-term effects. In a paper subtitled 'How Sovereign Debt Accelerated the First Industrial Revolution', Jaume Ventura and Hans-Joachim Voth constructed a model showing how government debt could first restrict and then stimulate growth. In the end, according to their analysis, sovereign debt 'accelerated the Industrial Revolution'. This line of argument would suggest that Britain's industrial take-off was stimulated by Keynesian-style deficit financing that raised effective demand on a massive scale.[55]

Crucial to the argument, from de Pinto to John Maynard Keynes, is that modern monetary systems, which depend on a symbiosis of state and private banking and markets for debt, have a greater capacity to generate credit, and hence to create money. While gold and silver are in permanently limited global supply, credit and paper money make the supply of money more expandable. The transition from commodity money to state money was part of Britain's Financial Revolution. This long process was one of intricate legislation and institution building, including the creation of effective markets for debt. Even when the currency was tied to a metallic standard, extensive credit creation was still possible. The supply of money could expand well beyond the physical reserves of gold or silver.[56]

Contrary to the view of some writers, interest rates do not help us ascertain whether crowding out was occurring. Low rates do not necessarily indicate a surplus of finance capital, nor high rates a shortage. As Sidney Pollard pointed out, even at the end of the eighteenth century, British financial markets were fractured and poorly integrated. Stressing the restraints of usury laws, Peter Temin and Hans-Joachim Voth also argued that interest rates were a poor indication of financial supply or demand. Fluctuations in interest rates were often related to political crises or wars. Interest rates tell us little about the money supply.[57]

Carol E. Heim and Philip Mirowski critiqued the historical claims of Jeffrey Williamson and others that war spending crowded out private investment.

54. De Pinto (1774), Popkin (1970), Kelton (2020), Keen (2022).

55. On crowding out, see Williamson (1984), Clark (2001), Temin and Voth (2013), Ventura and Voth (2015).

56. Keynes (1930, 1936), Ingham (2004), Wray (2012). During the eighteenth century there was a bimetallic currency system, with both gold and silver coins being minted. A formal gold specie standard was first established in 1821 (Narsey, 2016).

57. Pressnell (1960), Clark (1996), Quinn (2001). Pollard (1958, 221–22), Temin and Voth (2013).

Heim and Mirowski argued that it was important to focus on net receipts from borrowing, rather than changes in government debt. Crowding-out effects depend on near-full employment of limited physical resources, including labour. This was not generally the case. Heim and Mirowski also raised deeper questions concerning the usefulness of standard neoclassical, supply-constrained models to understand capital accumulation in capitalist economies where money can be generated by issuing bonds.[58]

There is now a large literature supporting the view that extensive money creation is possible in modern capitalist economies. It builds on state and credit theories of money. Once the financial system emerges with state currency issue, a state lender of last resort, within a relatively stable political framework, buttressed by networks of private finance and markets for debt, then money can be created to reflate the economy up to the point of full employment or resources, at which point inflation may pose a greater risk. The British experience in the eighteenth century suggests that it was unnecessary to reduce the national debt through austerity. It was gradually eroded through economic growth in the nineteenth century and increased taxation made possible by rising prosperity.[59]

Estate Consolidation and Rising Inequality

The launch of Consols in 1751 and the financial legislation under Lord Mansfield made the 1750s a watershed in Britain's financial development. The Financial Revolution served landed as well as industrial interests. Sovereign bonds such as Consols were an attractive option for wealthy landowners because they offered higher rates of return than landed property. Access to status and power were still strong reasons for holding onto land. The growing debt market after the 1750s created additional borrowing opportunities. Land enclosures continued, not simply because of expected rises in agricultural productivity—which were generally tiny at best—but because landed capital would preserve status and could be used to make still more money.[60]

58. Williamson (1984), Heim and Mirowski (1987).

59. Mitchell Innes (1914), Knapp (1924), Keynes (1930), Lerner (1947), Schumpeter (1954), Davidson (1972), Moore (1988), Wray (1998, 2004, 2012), Goodhart (1998, 2009), Mehrling (2000), Smithin (2000), Bell (2001), Ingham (2004), Goodhart (2009), Heinsohn and Steiger (2013), Desan (2014), Kelton (2020), Keen (2022).

60. Habakkuk (1994), Clark (1998a, 1998b, 1998c). On the productivity of enclosure, see Turner (1986) and Allen (1992, 1999).

Arbitrarily imposed enclosures risked litigation or protest. Voluntary enclosures, often initiated by local interest groups, involved the appointment of commissioners and surveyors, the holding of village meetings and adjudication in cases of dispute. Parliamentary enclosures were different. Parliament could impose enclosures against the will of tenants or other villagers. But many property owners and users received some compensation. Parliamentary enclosures took off in the 1750s, making still more land alienable.[61]

Parliamentary enclosures had a big impact. As Hoppit noted, 'between 1750 and 1830' parliamentary legislation on landed property 'not only redistributed some property rights, but redefined or clarified the meaning of others in ways which many villagers disputed. Over 5,200 acts were passed, involving up to 6.8 million acres, some 21 per cent of England's surface area.' By 1830 very little agricultural land in England was unenclosed. In the early years of the nineteenth century, large-scale rural unemployment re-emerged.[62]

Bogart and Richardson gathered parliamentary data on the numbers of estate, statutory authority and enclosure acts from 1700 to 1830. Estate acts undid entails or strict settlements. Statutory authority acts were used to develop infrastructure, including improvements to roads and rivers and the construction of canals (and railways in the nineteenth century). Bogart and Richardson showed that legislative reform of landed property rights was sluggish from 1700 until about 1750 and then took off rapidly, with the strongest growth trends coming from enclosure and statutory authority acts. These trends are shown in figure 4.6.[63]

By contrast, the erosion of entails or strict settlements was a modest and steady process, lasting into the twentieth century. In 1901 the lawyer Sir Arthur Underhill estimated that 'nearly all the great estates, comprising perhaps the greater part of the land of England, are held in strict settlement'. Even in the early twenty-first century, substantial tracts of English land were still held by trusts that enforced male primogeniture. These measures constrained the use of land as collateral for finance.[64]

Enclosures made more land usable as security in mortgages. As yet, we have insufficient information to assess the extent of mortgaging in this period, or the different uses to which the funds might have been put. Much of it might

61. Allen (1992), Tawney (1912, 343).
62. Hoppit (2011, 100).
63. Bogart and Richardson (2011, 248–50)
64. Underhill (1901, 282), Reid (1995, 277), Shrubsole (2019, 38, 281–82).

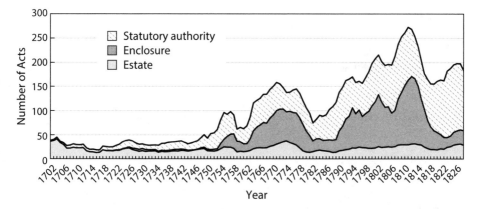

FIGURE 4.6. Parliamentary acts reorganizing landed property rights, 1700–1830
Five-year moving averages, in a vertically cumulative presentation, using annual
data from Bogart and Richardson (2011, 250).

have been used to fund improvements after enclosure. Mokyr wrote: 'A substantial demand for capital was generated by the enclosures: the fences and
hedges that enclosures required were costly, and paid for by taking out mortgages.' As the historian Leslie Pressnell had noted over half a century earlier:

> Most enclosure Acts contained a clause which permitted the commission-
> ers to mortgage the land in order to finance the work of enclosure. . . . No
> trace of bankers' having lent on mortgage for this purpose, or indeed of
> anyone else having done so, has been found in the course of this study; but,
> in view of the monotonous recurrence of this clause in private Acts, it is
> surely likely that such lending occurred. The evidence doubtless awaits dis-
> interment from the piles of mortgage agreements in county record offices
> and solicitors' offices. [65]

But Michael Turner pointed out that the extensive use of enclosed land to raise
funds by mortgage 'has yet to be demonstrated' and 'yet to be investigated.'

65. Pressnell (1958, 350), Blum (1981), Mokyr (2009, 266). Mingay (1963, 97–98), Blum (1981,
491) and Brunt (2006, 87) also noted the option of mortgaging enclosed land. But relatively few
academic articles on enclosures mention mortgages. A search on 29 August 2022 of JSTOR's
economics journals found 3,941 articles with mentions of histor* AND (enclos* OR inclos*) in
their text (where * is a wildcard). Only 7.2 per cent of these articles on enclosures in economics
and economic history mentioned mortgages or mortgaging.

TABLE 4.1. Landownership in England and Wales,
1690–1873

Percentage of land owned	1690	1790	1873
Great owners	15–20%	20–25%	24%
Gentry	45–50%	50%	55%
Small owners	25–33%	15%	10%

Source: Beckett (1984, 5).

Sadly, this is still largely the case, despite the issue of enclosures being an enduring hot topic for economic historians.[66]

As well as agricultural improvements, the funds obtained through mortgages could also have been used to invest in growing industry, or to buy Consols. Ventura and Voth suggested that the latter option was more prominent. The more secure returns on Consols typically exceeded those from the land. On the other hand, investing in Consols would have had a much lower return than a highly successful industrial venture. But Consols were less risky and were often the preferred option.[67]

Enclosure, agglomeration and consolidation meant that more land was in fewer hands. Table 4.1 shows the growing concentration of landownership as estimated by J. V. Beckett. The most dramatic outcome was the decline of the share of the small landowners, decreasing from about 30 per cent of the land in 1690 to 15 per cent in 1790 and 10 per cent in 1873. This is evidence of the 'decline of the yeoman'. Allen's figures place the small owners' share in 1690 as higher, and hence its decline would be even more dramatic. Both authors agree that the beneficiaries of this sizeable reallocation of land were the gentry and the 'great owners'.[68]

According to the estimates of Stephen Broadberry and his colleagues, agricultural productivity rose very slowly during the sixteenth and seventeenth centuries. Its growth then increased from 1700 to 1759, reaching a peak

66. Turner (1981, 236–37).

67. Ventura and Voth (2015). In Jane Austen's *Pride and Prejudice* (1813), Consols are described as 'four per cents', which was their expected annual return at the time. Consols are also mentioned in *David Copperfield* (1849) by Charles Dickens.

68. Beckett (1984), Allen (1992). For other estimates of land distribution, see Mingay (1963, 25–26) and Thompson (1966).

of 0.57 per cent per annum in that period. But from 1759 to 1801, when parliamentary enclosures were increasing, average annual agricultural productivity growth dropped to 0.41 per cent. From 1801 to 1851 average annual agricultural productivity growth fell to only 0.10 per cent. While productivity growth slowed, the post-1750 wave of parliamentary encloses increased the number and scale of large, landed estates and helped to finish the era of the yeomen. In addition, sample data suggest that average working days in the year for farm workers increased massively from 1750 to 1818, when they peaked and began to fall. By 1790 yeomen husbandry was largely replaced by poor rural labourers working many hours for big landowners.[69]

The rich landowners gained more access to borrowed cash as more of their land became alienable. The increasing opportunities for using land as collateral fed further economic inequality. In general, while capitalism is typically unequal at its outset, much (but not all) of the additional inequality generated within capitalism results from the unequal distribution of collateralizable property. Capitalist arrangements involve alienable productive assets that can be used to borrow still more money and thus generate additional wealth. Any concentration of ownership of these assets creates the possibility of still further inequality.[70]

Other factors increased economic inequality. Taxes on consumption were largely regressive, taking a larger proportion of the income of the poor. By about 1815, as Ashton wrote, 'perhaps about one-eleventh . . . of the money income of the people of the United Kingdom consisted of sums raised from the taxpayers, including the poor, and transferred to the relatively rich holders of government bonds.' The lucrative returns on Consuls and other bonds increased economic inequality still further.[71]

69. Broadberry et al. (2015, 365). Labour productivity (output per worker) is different from the output per capita (output per member of the population). Compare Broadberry et al. (2015, 226–44). See also Allen (1992, 1999). This evidence undermines the Marxist analysis of Brenner (1976, 42, 63), who saw increases in agricultural productivity as resulting from 'larger and larger' consolidated units, many rented out to 'large tenant farmers' who hired waged labourers. According to him, the creation of these larger 'capitalist' units 'was the indispensable precondition for significant agrarian advance'. Rebutted also are the claims of Overton (1996) and others than a 'revolution' in agricultural productivity occurred after 1750. On the increase in the working year, see Allen and Weisdorf (2011).

70. Piketty (2014), Hodgson (2015a, 361–62).

71. Ashton (1968, 6–7).

TABLE 4.2. Shares of household net worth in England and Wales, 1670–1875

Percentage share of total household net worth	1670	1700	1740	1810	1875
Top 1 per cent of households	49%	39%	44%	55%	61%
Top 5 per cent of households	73%	71%	74%	74%	74%
Top 10 per cent of households	83%	81%	86%	83%	84%

Source: Lindert (1986, 1145, table 4, quoting his 'preferred' estimates).

TABLE 4.3. Ratios of average real household incomes to bottom 40 per cent in England and Wales, 1688–1867

Ratio of average real household incomes to the bottom 40 per cent	1688	1759	1802	1867
Top 5 per cent of households	29.0	22.0	43.2	22.3
Top 10 per cent of households	18.4	14.0	26.4	13.3
Top 20 per cent of households	11.8	8.8	16.8	7.6

Source: Hoffman et al. (2002, 342).

Peter Lindert provided a range of estimates of wealth inequality in England and Wales from 1670 to 1875, using probate records. His 'preferred' estimates of percentage shares in total household net worth are shown in table 4.2. For most of this period, land was by far the largest owned asset. Note that wealth inequality decreased from 1670 to 1700, with the top 1 per cent, top 5 per cent and top 10 per cent all losing out on their shares. But from 1700 to 1740 there was a turnaround, with all three wealthier groups increasing their slices of the pie. From 1700 to 1875 the share of the top 1 per cent increased steadily and dramatically from 39 per cent to 61 per cent of all net wealth. The Great Enrichment favoured a few, much more than most others, even though by 1875 there was much more wealth overall.[72]

Income inequality also rose during the eighteenth century. Philip T. Hoffman and his colleagues provided estimates for the period from 1688 to 1867. Table 4.3 shows that the top three income groups all experienced a decrease in relative income (compared with the bottom 40 per cent) from 1688 to 1759, followed by a large increase in relative income from 1759 to 1802. But there was

72. Lindert (1986, 1145, table 4). Lindert (1986, 1146–57) also noted that trends were reversed in the twentieth century, with wealth distribution becoming more equal.

a substantial decrease in relative income from 1802 to 1867. Income inequality was still great in 1867, but its dramatic widening from 1759 to 1802 had been reversed.[73]

Taking these figures for changes in inequality of income and wealth as whole, it is clear that landed property and other wealth became increasingly concentrated in the hands of the top 1 per cent. Income inequality increased strongly from 1759 to 1802. These were the opening years of the Industrial Revolution. England's path to riches was unique. It was based on surviving aristocratic power and growing inequality. In his poem *The Deserted Village* (1770), Oliver Goldsmith may have exaggerated rural depopulation. But these selected lines ring true:

> Ill fares the land, to hastening ills a prey,
> Where wealth accumulates, and men decay. . . .
> One only master grasps the whole domain, . . .
> Usurp the land, and dispossess the swain;
> Along the lawn, where scatter'd hamlets rose,
> Unwieldy wealth and cumbrous pomp repose;[74]

Innovation, Class and the Expansion of Industry and Trade

These were turbulent times. But, as Veblen noted, the rich 'leisure class' has been relatively 'sheltered from the action of the environment', including external shocks and disruptions. Consequently, it 'will adapt its views and its scheme of life more tardily to the altered general situation; it will in so far tend to retard the process of social transformation. The wealthy leisure class is in such a sheltered position with respect to the economic forces that make for change and readjustment. . . . [They] do not yield to the demand for innovation as readily as other men because they are not constrained to do so.'[75] This remark is relevant for England in the eighteenth and nineteenth centuries. Relatively little technological innovation and industrial investment came from the rich and powerful, who held much of their wealth in land. Land might have been used to raise capital for industrial or infrastructural investment, but often

73. Hoffman et al. (2002, 342).
74. Lines 51–52, 39, 64–66, respectively.
75. Veblen (1899, 193, 199).

it was not. Many of the English upper classes preferred conspicuous luxuries and social status to investment in enterprise. Of course there were exceptions, like Francis Egerton, the Duke of Bridgewater, who borrowed money and invested in a major canal in Lancashire. But rich or aristocratic entrepreneurs were relatively rare.

The fathers of Boulton and Watt were businessmen, and their sons were often short of finance. Other notable entrepreneurs were drawn from lower classes. The pioneers of mechanized cotton spinning—James Hargreaves, Richard Arkwright and Samuel Crompton—all came from poor families. All three were intimately involved in the processing of cotton in Lancashire. Each found ways in which spinning could be improved. John Kay, the inventor of the flying shuttle, was born in Lancashire as the son of a yeoman farmer. The foundry owner Abraham Darby was the son of a locksmith and a yeoman farmer. Like Darby, many eighteenth- and nineteenth-century entrepreneurs were Quakers or other religious nonconformists, who suffered exclusion from the higher ranks of society because of their religion. Many Quakers refused to pay tithes and hence could not own land. The main impetus for innovation and industrialization came not from the landowning rich, but from those most impelled to improve their condition, and with the aptitude, means, social connections and luck to do so.

Many scholars date the Industrial Revolution from about 1760. But several important developments were earlier. In Coalbrookdale in Shropshire in 1709, Darby successfully cast pig iron, using coke rather than charcoal. This made larger castings possible. Coke-smelted cast iron was then used to construct steam engines, bridges and much else. Thomas Newcomen invented a steam engine in about 1710. In his comprehensive tour of the 1720s, Daniel Defoe noted pockets of manufacturing activity all over Britain. Expanding global activity by the British Navy prompted a search for accurate chronometers to measure longitude. Following Parliament's offer of a £20,000 prize in 1714 (about £3.1 million in 2021 purchasing power), John Harrison designed navigational clocks for the British Navy from 1730 until his death in 1776. Much manufacturing innovation happened before 1760. But some of the subsequent industrial growth was dramatic. Ashton noted that 'whereas in 1792 there had been only two cotton mills in and about Manchester, in 1802 the number had reached fifty-two'. In such places the Industrial Revolution had massive effects.[76]

76. Defoe (1727). Ashton (1968, 60), Allen and Weisdorf (2011).

Several other innovations were in textiles, such as the flying shuttle invented in 1733 by Kay, the spinning jenny invented by Hargreaves in 1764, the water frame patented in 1769 by Arkwright, and the spinning mule invented in about 1779 by Crompton (which combined features of the spinning jenny and the water frame). These machines were used to process imported cotton in the expanding numbers of (then mostly water powered) textile mills that became a common feature of the British industrial landscape.

Increased textile production was driven initially by economic demand from the upper classes, including rich consumers overseas. Trevor Griffiths and his co-authors showed that textile production in the 1760s concentrated on the luxury end of the market—the silk and hosiery trades: 'Production remained geared to the demands of polite society—primarily the established landed gentry and the rising professional and middle classes of Hanoverian towns.' The rapidly rising incomes of the upper classes powered much of the early innovation and enlargement of the textile industry. But as factory production expanded, productivity increased and prices fell, then textiles became affordable for lower classes and additional buyers abroad.[77]

The take-off of the British textile industry has been dated to about 1783, after a period of slow growth and the end of the American War of Independence. To supply the growing number of cotton mills, there were spectacular increases in raw cotton imports. From 1770 to 1815 the output of the British cotton industry increased by twenty times or more. Between 1785 and 1830 the value of British cotton exports increased by a factor of about thirty. With mass factory production, cheaper products reached lower-income groups.[78]

The products of Matthew Boulton and James Fothergill's partnership near Birmingham also served the luxury market. From 1765 they made objects of silver plate and vases partly covered in milled gold. From 1763 Boulton's friend Josiah Wedgwood produced delicate ceramics for the high-end market. Rising income inequality skewed early industrial production towards luxuries.[79]

Developments in financial institutions in the 1750s created waves of enclosing, consolidating, borrowing and spending that initially stimulated the

77. Griffiths et al. (1992, 897–98). On the products of the Boulton-Fothergill partnership, see Mason (2009). Humphries and Schneider (2019) argued that the machinery often substituted less skilled (female and child) labour for that of skilled males. Savings were thus made in both hours and wage rates.
78. Williams (1944, 128), Chapman (1972, 63), Harley (1982, 272), Beckert (2015, 72–76, 86).
79. Hoffman et al. (2002, 330–32), Mason (2009).

production of high-end textiles and other luxury goods. They prompted the
landed class to enclose lands and borrow money on the newly accessible collateral. Much land was mortgaged to pay for conspicuous consumption, buildings, marriage settlements and idle pleasures. This was an eighteenth-century
version of Veblen's leisure class.[80]

Pleasure-seeking and conspicuous wealth were combined with nepotism
and corruption among the British elite. As Robert Neild pointed out, 'corruption was rife in the eighteenth century'. For much of that time, public offices
could be bought and sold. Elections were rigged and officials were bribed. But
a delayed effect of a century dominated by major wars was a substantial decrease
in public corruption. Eventually, these things 'came to be seriously attacked only
towards the end of the century at the time of the American and French Wars'.
Defeat in the American War of Independence left Britain with burdensome
taxes and towering debt. Public debt as a percentage of GDP increased from
83 per cent in 1775 to 137 percent in 1784—a massive leap in only nine years, to
an unprecedented peak. Edmund Burke and others mounted a campaign
against patronage, sinecures and corruption. The Commissioners for Examining
the Public Accounts made recommendations for the reform of government
finances and administration from 1780 to 1787. Further impetus for reform came
in response to increased debt during the French Revolutionary (1792–1802) and
Napoleonic Wars (1803–15). Substantial reforms paved the way for a more efficient and less corrupt civil service in the nineteenth century.[81]

The eighteenth century revolutionized Britain's relations with the outside world. It was a century of war, state-building, financial development and
expanding empire. Before 1688 England had colonies in North America, the
Caribbean and West Africa. By 1763 Britain had gained much more territory,
particularly in India and North America, and had established a strategic Medi-
terranean base in Gibraltar. When the Industrial Revolution began, Britain
had become a trading nation second to none.

In the first three quarters of the eighteenth century, the British slave trade
tripled in size. The numbers of slaves transported by British traders from Africa
to the Caribbean and North America reached an all-time peak of 859,100 in
1751–75. This transatlantic human cargo was much greater than that carried by
France, Netherlands, Portugal or any other nation at that time. The profits of
slavery financed ports such as Bristol, Liverpool and London. In his classic
study of *Capitalism and Slavery*, Eric Williams explained in detail how bankers

80. Joslin (1960, 176), Cannadine (1977, 1980).
81. Neild (2002, 62–67)

and industrial entrepreneurs (including Boulton and Watt and several Lancashire mill owners) sometimes made use of finance obtained from the slave trade. Sven Beckert charted the crucial role of the cotton trade in the Industrial Revolution, showing how slave produced cotton from North America fed expanding mills in Lancashire. Throughout the seventeenth and eighteenth centuries, sugar made up the largest share of slave-produced imports. Caribbean slave plantations produced sugar to satisfy the awakened taste for sweetened food and drink. Slaves also produced coffee, tobacco and rice. Slavery was a major factor in Britain's industrial expansion and consumer enrichment, but it was contingent rather than essential. The Industrial Revolution could still have happened if there had been no slavery.[82]

That does undermine its importance. In 1788 it was estimated that the capital value of all owned assets in the British Empire was about £70 million, of which about £47.5 million (about £6.4 billion in 2021 purchasing power) consisted of land, buildings, animals, ships, equipment and other non-human assets, and about £22.5 million (about £3.0 billion in 2021 purchasing power) was the value of about 450,000 slaves. Capitalism had expanded the value of capital (defined properly as money, or the money value of alienable assets) in the British Empire. Almost a third of that capital consisted of slaves.[83]

Capitalism is defined, in part, by widespread markets, private entrepreneurship and production based on wage labour. At least in the English case, capitalism also depended on quite different additional arrangements, including the colonial production of raw materials by slaves and strong state intervention in the economic and financial system. No system is ever pure. And English capitalism had specific characteristics and admixtures of its own.

Conclusion: Explaining the Long
Eighteenth Century (1688–1815)

Although it draws insights from all the authors involved, the analysis here differs from that of Marx, Weber, North, McCloskey, Mokyr and several others. It addresses crucial developments in English capitalism from 1688 until the

82. Williams (1944), Solow (1987), Eltis (2001, 43), Inikori (1992), Draper (2008), Beckert (2015), Whately (2018).

83. Edwards (1806, 3:244). In 1788 the young United States was independent of the United Kingdom, and hence US slaves are not included in these figures, although they continued to produce cotton and other commodities that were exported to the UK. The overwhelming majority of UK slaves were then in the Caribbean.

beginnings of the Industrial Revolution. This concluding section compares the account just presented with some other explanations of key developments in the eighteenth century.

Marx was right to stress growing commercialization and markets, and the rise of merchants, manufacturers and wage labourers. But he paid little attention to the institutional preconditions of capitalist finance, including markets for debt and a central bank able to act as lender of last resort. Instead, he underlined class power. He depicted the Glorious Revolution as the ascendancy of the bourgeoisie, in 'alliance' with 'capitalist' landowners. He missed the point that Britain remained an aristocratic society, where power and privilege were often related to the ownership of land. Capitalists had landed aspirations too. As Adam Smith remarked in 1776: 'Merchants are commonly ambitious of becoming country gentlemen'. In 1892 Engels noted the enduring anomaly: 'In England, the bourgeoisie never held undivided sway. Even the victory of 1832 left the landed aristocracy in almost exclusive possession of all the leading Government offices.' He complained that 'the English bourgeoisie are . . . deeply penetrated by a sense of inferiority'. Engels was grappling with English developments that did not fit readily into the Marxist class analysis. Marx downplayed these key peculiarities of British capitalism. His analytical framework obliged him to assume that capitalism meant bourgeois hegemony. Also, by subscribing to a perspective of evolution largely 'from within' the system, he missed the crucial shocks of repeated war.[84]

Max Weber's *Protestant Ethic* does not give an adequate explanation of the development of financial institutions. Weber's argument that markets lead to meaningful prices and enable rational calculation has some force, but markets are thousands of years old. Financial markets were among the key developments in the eighteenth century, and the *Protestant Ethic* neglects these. Like Marx and Schumpeter, Weber spoke the language of Hegel. This helps explain their shared emphasis on the internal evolution (or unfolding) of the immanent within, rather than on external shocks leading to problems and needs to adapt.

North and Weingast's assessment of the impact of the Glorious Revolution, published on the tercentenary of the crowning of William and Mary, has some important strengths. They rightly emphasized that the events of 1688 led to a new rapprochement between the Crown and Parliament, which constrained the power of the monarch to tax and spend. But they hugely exaggerated the

84. Smith (1976, 411), Marx and Engels (1962, 2:111–12).

changes to law and property rights. The Glorious Revolution was explicitly concerned with restoring lost rights, rather than making new ones. It made no laws concerning property and few edicts on the role of Parliament. It did not increase the security of property rights—they had been relatively secure for centuries. Furthermore, Parliament proved itself just as capable of taxing or even appropriating property as the Crown.[85]

North and Weingast missed the point that a major problem was not so much the security of landed property, but the fact that much of it could not be used readily as collateral for loans to invest in agricultural improvements, infrastructure or industrial entrepreneurship. Possibilities for collateralization were limited by widespread entails or strict settlements that greatly limited the alienability and mortgageability of land. The Glorious Revolution did not lead to an immediate acceleration in the pace of economic growth. The Industrial Revolution started about seventy years later.

Rather than changes in the security of property rights, the account here underlines how 1688 ruptured England's preceding international alliances and thrust the country into a series of wide-ranging wars against France or Spain, ending with the defeat of Napoleon in 1815 at Waterloo. These wars prompted the Financial and Administrative Revolutions. The need to protect and maintain a growing trading empire pressured the British state to reform its finances, gather more taxes and purchase industrial, agricultural and service outputs destined for its armed forces. The development of the financial system created new incentives and possibilities for the use of landed property as collateral to finance investments, infrastructure and industry.

North and Weingast developed their ideas further in their book with John Wallis entitled *Violence and Social Orders*. They used the broad term 'natural state' to describe large states where control of resources is limited to armed coalitions of elite groups, who exert their power over the majority of the population. Much of their argument focuses on the transition from the 'natural state' to the 'open access order'. In the latter, armed elites are replaced by a state with a monopoly of violence, operating under the rule of law, where legal rights extend more broadly into the population. 'Open access orders' involve a polity and economy with 'open entry and competition in many markets, free movement of goods and individuals over space and time, the ability to create organizations that pursue economic opportunities, protection of property rights, and prohibitions on the use of violence'. Apart from the state monopoly of

85. North and Weingast (1989).

violence, the rest of the 'open access order' operates under market-like principles. Market competition in the economy restricts rent-seeking and spurs productivity. Market-like competition in the political sphere provides opportunities to replace inefficient, corrupt or self-serving governments. The authors stressed the importance of organizations such as corporations and political parties, which have some permanence and can outlive their individual members.[86]

Their terminology and their chronology can be questioned. As well as being extremely broad in its application, the 'natural state' label is rather odd. It suggests that preceding and succeeding forms of society were unnatural. It describes autocratic states as 'natural', but these have existed for only a tiny fraction of human history. They described eighteenth-century Britain as a 'natural state' in the process of transition to an open access order in the final decades of that century. But there was little that was natural about Britain at that time. It was an era of heightened war, political uncertainty, ballooning public debt and unprecedented state-building.

The use of the term 'open access order' is also questionable. According to North and his co-authors, Britain and the United States 'made the transition to open access between 1800 and 1850'. But in Britain in 1850, married women had no right to own property, and no woman could vote. The franchise was con-fined to about 10 per cent of adult males. Access to power and wealth was largely restricted to a small, property-owning, white, Christian, male minority. In practice, with few exceptions, the general population had no access to the corridors of political power. Furthermore, economic opportunities were highly limited, even for men. Employment prospects for women were narrow and servile. Turning to the United States, in 1850 the franchise was also con-fined to a fraction of males, and slavery was still prominent in the South. How can countries with slavery, markedly inferior legal rights for women and a majority of largely disempowered males be described as 'open access'? Access to markets was highly limited at the time, by poverty as well as by slavery and other legal discrimination.[87]

Previously criticized notions concerning the 'security' of property rights were repeated in their 2009 study. North and his co-authors continued to

---

86. North, Wallis and Weingast (2009, 2). North (1990a, 1990b) elsewhere wrote (seemingly non-metaphorically) of 'political markets'. In Hodgson (2020, 2021c, chap. 8) I criticize North's inappropriate over-extension of the market concept to the political sphere.

87. North, Wallis and Weingast (2009, 27, 240).

downplay the multi-faceted nature of legal ownership. They wrote that land-ownership in England 'was not completely secure from political manipulation until 1660.' But the parliamentary enclosures from 1750 abolished land-use, copyhold and leasehold rights for many. If this was not political manipula-tion, then what was? Political 'manipulation' of property rights endured long after 1660.

North, Wallis and Weingast cited the arguments of Tilly and others on how war motivated states to strengthen themselves militarily and to develop ad-ministratively. But they did not give exogenous pressures much additional significance. Redolent of Marx, they focussed instead on a stages model, un-folding largely from within. Missing is any discussion of the development of the national financial institutions, financial markets and mortgages. Despite their emphasis on markets, the words 'debt', 'finance', 'money' and 'mortgage' are absent from the index of their book. Their depiction of historical stages (from 'natural state' to 'open access') does not invoke these crucial institutional developments. The major dynamic interaction of war and financial develop-ment is largely absent.[88]

Turning to McCloskey, she rightly stressed the importance of ideas, mentioning liberal ideology in particular. But there must be some explanation of the rise of these ideas and for the features of the social system and culture that allowed them to spread and take hold. Rhetoric and persuasion were essen-tial, but their mention is insufficient to explain why some ideas proved more persuasive than others, and why they spread in some circumstances and not elsewhere. McCloskey's contention that institutions are less relevant for the explanation of the Great Enrichment is based on her false claim that institu-tions did not change. She rightly criticized North's and Weingast's claim that the Glorious Revolution made property rights much more secure. But this does not mean that there were no other major institutional developments be-tween 1660 and 1760.

Several major institutional changes have been listed in this chapter and its predecessor. For example, Chancery radically reformed mortgage law in the 1670s, elaborating its doctrine of 'equity of redemption'. Liberal ideas played their part in this legislation. But probably more important under Charles II were the landed interests of Royalists, who had suffered losses during the Pro-tectorate. Moving into the eighteenth century, many politicians at that time favoured a small state and worried about the growth of bureaucracy, but the

88. North, Wallis and Weingast (2009, 174–80, 218–19, 240–41).

needs of war overrode these ideas. State bureaucracy expanded and public debt soared upwards. Other major institutional changes in the eighteenth century include legislation to consolidate markets for debt, the evolution of the Bank of England as lender of last resort, and the parliamentary enclosures that reallocated landed property rights and increased the extent of land alienability. These are part of the explanation of the Great Enrichment.

Especially when threats to vested interests were perceived, reactions would be fired by emotion and sentiment. Appeals would be made to religion and commonplace notions of justice. Some agents would focus on the problems and try to find a solution. Ideas were vital. But they are never the sole drivers of change. Ideas and reasons are often driven by emotions, which in their turn were generated by shocks and perceived threats. There are struggles for power and recognition. Change comes through disruption, followed by angst, recovery and effective problem solving.

Like McCloskey, Mokyr emphasized culture and ideas. But Mokyr created a stronger evolutionary narrative, using concepts such as mutation and selection. He considered the circumstances in which people are obliged to focus on particular problems. Mokyr's primary concern has been with technology, to the study of which he brings great insight. But he also mentioned several key institutional changes, including the development of financial institutions. It is argued in this book that Mokyr's evolutionary perspective can be expanded, to provide more detailed explanations of why mutations and other changes occur.[89]

Two other authors developed approaches that in some respects are close to the one adopted here. In his *Origins of Political Order*, Francis Fukuyama addressed questions that are very similar to those posed in the book by North, Wallis and Weingast. But the explanations are different. Fukuyama argued that modern liberal democracies combine three sets of institutions in stable balance: '1. the state, 2. the rule of law, 3. accountable government'.[90] He considered the possibilities of autocracy or political collapse. He did not take a liberal democratic outcome as inevitable or eternal. Politico-economic development in different countries will follow different routes. Emphasizing the importance of political and legal institutions, he saw them as irreducible to economic factors. This contrasts with the North-Wallis-Weingast framework, which stresses markets in the economy and market-like competition in the polity,

89. Mokyr (2009; 2016, 163–64; 2022).
90. Fukuyama (2011, 16).

and it gives less precedence to law.[91] By contrast, Fukuyama devoted many pages to the evolution of legal systems, charting their relations to state authority and religion. This deeper appreciation of the evolution of law informed Fukuyama's statements on 1688: 'The significance of the Glorious Revolution is not that it marked the onset of secure property rights in England, as some have argued. Strong property rights had been established centuries earlier.'[92] Consonant with the arguments of Dickson, Brewer and others, Fukuyama stressed that 1688 led to unprecedented outbreaks of intensive war. The need to finance the war machine and its state administration prompted major institutional advances in the financial system, higher taxes, increased borrowing and enlarged markets for debt.[93] 'The Glorious Revolution and the fiscal and banking reforms undertaken in its wake, such as the establishment of the Bank of England in 1694, did indeed revolutionize public finance. They allowed the government to borrow on transparent public debt markets in ways unavailable to France or Spain.'[94] Fukuyama referred favourably to the works of Charles Tilly and Thomas Ertman on how external military threats can prompt state development and enlarged tax capacity.[95]

Tilly has written a great deal on how rivalries between European countries promoted the development of national states with enhanced military capacities. He stressed external pressures, particularly war: 'Within limits set by the demands and rewards of other states, extraction and struggle over the means of war created the central organizational structures of states.' He emphasized the importance of cities as centres of wealth accumulation and loci of power. 'Over the centuries, tribute-taking empires have dominated the world history of states.' He focused on at least two paths for state development in these

---

91. Faundez (2016, sec. 4) argued convincingly that North and his co-authors typically treated law as an epiphenomenal expression of economic and political forces, with little or no power itself to bring about institutional change, and with no internal institutional dynamics worthy of analysis. In this respect, North followed Marx and much of the 'economics of property rights' in treating property principally as a matter of de facto control rather than of legal title (Cole and Grossman, 2002; Hodgson, 2015c).

92. Fukuyama (2011, 418–20).

93. Fukuyama (2011, 419), Dickson (1967), Brewer (1989).

94. Fukuyama (2011, 419–20).

95. Fukuyama (2011, 23–25, 110–19). Fukuyama (2000) embraced the concept of social capital. I have argued elsewhere that this misapplies the c-word to vague phenomena that are neither financial nor monetary (Hodgson 2014).

circumstances, making a distinction between 'capital-intensive' and 'coercion-intensive' extractive mechanisms and regions:[96]

> In the *coercion-intensive* mode, rulers squeezed the means of war from their own populations and others they conquered, building massive structures of extraction in the process. . . . In the *capital-intensive* mode, rulers relied on compacts with capitalists . . . to rent or purchase military force, and thereby warred without building vast permanent state structures. . . . In the intermediate *capitalized coercion mode*, rulers did some of each, but spent more of their effort than did their capital-intensive neighbours on incorporating capitalists and sources of capital directly into the structures of their states. . . . France and England eventually followed the capitalized coercion mode, which produced full-fledged national states earlier than the coercion-intensive and capital-intensive modes did. Driven by the pressures of international competition (especially by war and preparation for war) all three paths eventually converged on [unprecedented] concentrations of capital and coercion. . . . From the seventeenth century onward the capitalized coercion form proved more effective in war, and therefore provided a compelling model for states that had originated in other combinations of coercion and capital.[97]

This is a powerful argument, helping to explain the emergence and building of nation states. Capital and capitalism are central concepts. But Tilly—like so many others—treated capital as capital goods, and he confused the latter with finance capital. His definition of *capital* is as follows: 'Let us think of *capital* generously, including any tangible mobile resources, and enforceable claims on those resources.' In short, for Tilly, capital is mobile material stuff, or enforceable claims upon mobile material stuff. But what about land and buildings? Tilly's insertion of the word 'mobile' excludes them. Yet when more land became alienable and mortgageable, land and buildings became crucial security for raising loans. Tilly's definition also excludes intangible assets, such as patents and bonds. These grew in importance in the eighteenth and nineteenth centuries. They too were sometimes used as collateral to raise loans. His definition of capital is not generous enough. Finance does not appear in the index of his major work on *Coercion, Capital and European States*. It is not about capital in the everyday sense employed by businesspeople and accountants,

96. Tilly (1992, 15–16, 21).
97. Tilly (1992, 30–31).

which would include both immobile and intangible assets. There is much discussion of taxation, but little on other financial institutions. The roles of mortgaging and markets for debt are unmentioned.[98]

Tilly wrote: 'Rulers relied heavily on formally independent capitalists for
loans.' But there is nothing in Tilly's definition of a *capitalist* that implies that
he or she has money to lend. For Tilly, capitalists are merely 'people who spe-
cialize in the accumulation, purchase, and sale of capital'. There is no mention
of money here. *Capitalism* is defined in terms redolent of Marx, as a 'system in
which wage-workers produce goods by means of materials owned by capitalists'. There is no mention of financial institutions.[99]

My account puts the growth of finance at the centre in the explanation of
the rise of capitalism. A set of financial institutions based on collateralizable
property and credit creation were developed during the eighteenth century.
These institutions were required in part to finance war, and the state played a
crucial role in their evolution. Much legislation was required to make them
work effectively. The expansion of financial and other markets helped to enhance the conditions for the Industrial Revolution.

98. Tilly (1992, 17). Contra Tilly, Veblen (1904, 1908a, 1908b) and Commons (1924, 1934)
stressed the importance of intangible as well as tangible assets.

99. Tilly (1992, 17, 29).

5

Finance and Industrialization

We have the spirit of feudalism rife and rampant in the midst of the antagonistic development of the age of Watt, Arkwright and Stephenson. . . . So great is its power and prestige that it draws to it the support and homage of even those who are the natural leaders of the newer and better civilization. Manufacturers and merchants as a rule seem only to desire riches that they may be enabled to prostrate themselves at the feet of feudalism.

—RICHARD COBDEN (1863)

The apparent paradox of slow growth in times of rapid technological change disappears when we examine the role of private finance.

—PETER TEMIN AND JOACHIM VOTH (2013)

THIS CHAPTER EXPLORES the role of finance and financial institutions in the Industrial Revolution.[1] How did industrial entrepreneurs finance their ventures? What were their sources of finance? To what degree was finance scarce or constrained? Did that matter? Conventional wisdom has it that entrepreneurs could draw on their savings or borrow from family and friends if needed. The esteemed economic historian Michael Postan wrote in 1935:

> At the beginning of the Industrial Revolution . . . on the whole the insufficiency of capital was local rather than general. . . . There were enough rich people in the country to finance an economic effort far in excess of the modest activities of the leaders of the Industrial Revolution. . . . The reservoirs of savings were full enough, but conduits to connect them to the

---

1. This chapter uses material from Hodgson (2021b).

wheels of industry were few and meagre. . . . The pioneers of the factory system had to draw almost entirely on their private savings, or on the assistance of friends.[2]

According to Postan, there was adequate finance, but banks and financial markets were underdeveloped. Consequently, entrepreneurs relied on savings or borrowed money from friends. Similarly, Herbert Heaton wrote: 'External supplies of capital were, however, less important than the personal or family funds which the industrialists scraped together and ventured in the new productive equipment.' Heaton mentioned one case of raising a mortgage, by the famous Matthew Boulton. Otherwise, his account suggests that the entrepreneurs drew on their savings or borrowed largely from family or friends. In slightly different versions, this became the conventional wisdom. As Alex Trew put it: 'The general argument runs that an individual entrepreneur, especially a good one, could find the start-up capital required or use reinvested profits to expand as and when conditions allowed.'[3]

The purpose of this chapter is not to overturn this conventional wisdom. Using savings or borrowing from family and friends may have been the norm. But we need more evidence, and there are some grounds to be sceptical. Even if borrowing from family and friends was widespread, it may have been insufficient in some cases. There are two issues here: the extent of borrowing from family and friends, and the question of whether that borrowing was sufficient.

Both issues have been brought into question. Thomas S. Ashton wrote: 'It is true that self-financing was a marked feature of the period, but it would be an error to consider it as universal. . . . The country dealer or manufacturer often needed more capital than could be obtained from his own resources or those of his partners and friends.' Rondo Cameron and his colleagues also questioned the ubiquity of self-financing: they pointed out that short-term credit was sometimes used to finance fixed investment in buildings and machinery. Peter Mathias noted wryly: 'As more case histories reveal the number of instances in which this generalization about banks not financing industrial investment was broken, the generalization may itself come under some suspicion.' But as yet we do not have enough evidence to refute the conventional wisdom.[4]

2. Postan (1935, 2–3).

3. Heaton (1937, 4), Trew (2010, 988).

4. Ashton (1955, 26, 180), Cameron et al. (1967, 11, 55), Mathias (1969, 177). See also Heaton (1937), Mathias (1983, 130–36), Crouzet (1990, chap. 5), King and Timmins (2001, 114–20),

Some prominent enterprises borrowed mainly from family and friends. But in these cases, we often find additional borrowing from elsewhere. In 1784 Samuel Greg built a water-driven cotton mill at Quarry Bank in Styal, near Manchester. It was financed by family money, including from a sugar plantation using slave labour in the Caribbean. In her study of this family business, Mary B. Rose wrote that 'the firm made little use of external sources of long-term capital'. She noted that access to these sources of finance was inhibited because of a necessary reliance on a legal partnership arrangement. Businesses could not then be incorporated as legal persons. Each partner was legally liable if there was a default on the loan. Nevertheless, in 1803 the Greg partnership raised a mortgage on a farm property valued at £2,000 (about £190,000 in 2021 purchasing power). In 1821 they raised a loan of £1,500 (about £140,000 in 2021 purchasing power) using another mill property in Lancashire as security. In 1828 a large loan from the Bank of Manchester was in existence. Rose explained that the adverse economic conditions in the 1820s, plus the purchase of a large mill in Bury in Lancashire, 'made imperative the use of external sources of finance to supplement retained profits'. She noted that 'the owning of land, available as security for loans, could prove a positive advantage to the mill-owner'. Even with this exemplary case dominated by family financing, other sources of money were exploited. Finance as well as savings was important.[5]

Beyond the trusted circle of family and friends, larger loans would typically require collateral, as with a mortgage. Legal and other institutional arrangements for mortgaging evolved only slowly, yet there is some evidence of loans obtained via mortgages. Records by attorneys show substantial mortgaging activity in the eighteenth century. In her study of the financing of the West Riding Woollen Industry in Yorkshire, Pat Hudson demonstrated that the mortgage market 'developed rapidly in the eighteenth century through the activities of intermediaries such as attorneys, and much mortgaging and land transfer was occurring by the end of the century'. But Robert C. Allen noted the lack of estimates of the overall volume of mortgaging. We know relatively little about the extent and nature of borrowing before the nineteenth century, or for what it was used. An adequate picture of the role of finance is lacking.[6]

The seventeenth and eighteenth centuries saw expanding British trade and colonization. There were many expensive and risky overseas ventures that

5. Rose (1977, 37, 47–48, 51–52; 1986), Beckert (2015, 56–63).
6. Anderson (1969a), Miles (1981), Hudson (1986, 85), Allen (1992, 104).

required long-term finance. If financial institutions were sufficiently developed to provide some of this, then it may be presumed that they were also deployed in aid of entrepreneurial activity in the homeland.

Empirical research has underlined the importance of finance in the modern era. In a macroeconomic study, Peter L. Rousseau amassed evidence for the Dutch Republic (1640–1794), England (1720–1850), the United States (1790–1850) and Japan (1880–1913). His econometric analysis indicated that, in all cases, the emergence of financial institutions including financial markets was crucial in enabling growth and industrialization.[7]

Pointing to experiences in many countries, Trew noted that the conventional wisdom concerning finance in the British Industrial Revolution 'runs against the large body of empirical evidence . . . that suggests that financial development is strongly correlated with, and perhaps leads, the level of economic growth'.[8] Ross Levine surveyed multinational evidence, and concluded: 'While subject to ample qualifications and countervailing views, the preponderance of evidence suggests that both financial intermediaries and markets matter for growth and that reverse causality alone is not driving this relationship. Furthermore, theory and evidence imply that better developed financial systems ease external financing constraints facing firms, which illuminates one mechanism through which financial development influences economic growth'.[9] The role of finance is crucial because it no longer limits the funding of innovation and economic growth to the flows of savings and profits. With finance, enterprises can expand more rapidly. Was Britain an exception? Did it manage to take off industrially without the extensive help of financial institutions?

Britain pioneered industrialization. Because they faced British competition, the countries that followed were under greater pressure to restructure. Their states were impelled to intervene more extensively in their economies, and to promote the development of banking and financial markets.[10] But this still leaves open the question of whether underdeveloped financial institutions restrained British growth.

7. Rousseau (2003).

8. Trew (2010, 988).

9. Levine (2005, 865). See also King and Levine (1993), Rajan and Zingales (1998), Beck et al. (2003), Carlin and Mayer (2003), Sarma and Pais (2011), Kendal (2012) and Raghutla and Chittedi (2021).

10. Gerschenkron (1962).

One possibility is that borrowing from family and others might have been prevalent partly because of the underdevelopment of financial institutions and their inability to supply adequate loans. Postan hinted at this in the earlier quote. Philip Cottrell and Joel Mokyr speculated that if the imperfections in Britain's capital markets had been reduced earlier, then the Industrial Revolution might have been boosted. Larry Neal stressed the interconnection of finance and industry and pointed to the slow development of banking and stock markets. Despite the Financial Revolution of 1660–1760, the relatively immature and precarious state of financial institutions and financial markets may have limited economic development during the eighteenth and early nineteenth centuries.[11]

The notion that the development of capitalism is both empowered and constrained by finance may be described as the Schumpeterian hypothesis, because of Schumpeter's emphasis on the role of finance in supporting innovation. He stressed that an innovating entrepreneur 'must resort to credit . . . which cannot like an established business be financed by returns from previous production'. This source of finance is not 'purchasing power which already exists in someone's possession' but may be 'supported by securities which are not themselves circulating media'. With appropriate financial institutions, credit based on collateral can create new purchasing power.[12]

As yet, we have insufficient data to confirm or refute this hypothesis in the English case. This chapter provides only a little new empirical evidence, and it does not resolve the foremost issues of dispute. Instead it frames the argument and points to some key areas where research needs to be done to begin to answer some pressing questions. The Schumpeterian hypothesis would be falsified if capitalist innovation and growth were uncorrelated with the availability and development of finance. The limited evidence that we have so far suggests otherwise.

The Schumpeterian Hypothesis in English Perspective

In line with the Schumpeterian hypothesis, limited finance might help to explain that, despite growing innovation and industrialization, Britain's overall

---

11. Postan (1935, 2–3), Cottrell (1980, 33), Mokyr (1993, 104–5), Neal (1994), Dickson (1967), Roseveare (1991), Carruthers (1996), Wennerlind (2011), Hodgson (2017b), Hoppit (1987), Williamson (1987).

12. Schumpeter (1934, 69, 73).

rate of growth from 1760 to 1820 was very slow—in the region of 0.2 per cent per annum in GDP per capita. In the same period, industrial output per capita increased by an average of 0.7 per cent per annum. Many innovations took place from 1760 to 1820, but they did not lead to growth above 1 per cent. In part this was due to the relatively small size of the innovating sectors in the early years. But it is likely that their growth was constrained. In the following fifty years growth picked up significantly. From 1820 to 1870 GDP per capita growth averaged 1.1 per cent, and the growth of industrial output per capita roughly trebled to 2.0 per cent.[13]

Growth was held back before 1820 for several reasons. The Bubble Act of 1720 put severe restriction on the formation of joint stock companies. It was not repealed until 1825. Many firms were partnerships, and these were vulnerable if any partner got into financial difficulties. Loans were limited for additional reasons. In 1714 the highest legal rate that could be charged for a loan was lowered to 5 per cent, and this ceiling lasted until the 1820s, when the most restrictive usury regulations were repealed. The usury laws created disincentives to lend money. Unable to charge high-risk premiums on loans, lenders rationed credit and were inclined to ask for greater security. As will be elaborated further in this chapter, progress with land registration was highly limited, thus inhibiting the use of landed wealth as collateral.[14]

Patenting inventions was cumbersome and costly. Patents evolved from seventeenth-century instruments of royal patronage into the intellectual property of inventors and manufacturers. The British patent system was systematized and became more accessible during the reign of Queen Anne (1702–14). But it was expensive and fallible. In 1733 John Kay took out a patent on his flying shuttle. Kay filed lawsuits against alleged infringements, but the costs of litigation often exceeded the expected compensation. His legal expenses nearly made him bankrupt. The annual number of patents awarded remained low until a marked rise after about 1760, with an acceleration thereafter. But numerous important innovations were not patented.[15]

13. Data from Broadberry et al. (2015, 241–44). Some earlier studies report higher per capita growth rates (Mokyr, 1993, 9).

14. Temin and Voth (2013).

15. There were moves to provide open access to technological knowledge. The Society for the Encouragement of Arts, Manufactures and Commerce, founded in 1754, offered grants to inventors who were willing to allow others to copy their ideas. Dutton (1984), Sullivan (1989), Griffiths et al. (1992), MacLeod (2002), Ashton (1968, 10).

War had positive and negative economic effects. Military procurement stimulated innovation, industrial production and employment. For example, John Wilkinson patented a more accurate method of boring an iron cannon in 1774. Watt's long search for a method of producing a cylinder to the required accuracy for his steam engine was at last resolved. While a Newcomen engine could work without a close-fitting piston, it was vital for Watt's machine. This did not mean that all innovation was driven by war. Ashton pointed out that patent applications were more numerous in times of peace. Also on the negative side, war exacerbates political and economic uncertainty. Some economic historians have argued that state spending and borrowing for war crowded out industrial and other private investment.[16]

Financial markets are constrained by communications technology. Partly for reasons of national defence and state administration, the English state began to develop a postal network in the sixteenth century, under Henry VIII and Elizabeth I. This facilitated the conveyance of documents and valuables. It was opened up for use by the public in 1635 under Charles I. Until the nineteenth century brought the railways and the telegraph, nationwide communication of detailed information was no faster than the speed of a horse. Some government policies hindered financial development, including restrictions on banks and joint stock companies.[17]

What do we know about the size and growth of the financial sector in the eighteenth century? Cameron and his colleagues estimated that the capital invested in English banking (excluding the Bank of England) increased by a factor of 2.2 from 1775 to 1800, and again by a factor of 1.5 from 1800 to 1825. Total banking assets, as a proportion of English national income, increased from 15.2 per cent in 1775, to 27.9 per cent in 1800 and to 29.6 per cent in 1825. These figures show a large rise in the size of the financial sector in the final quarter of the eighteenth century, followed by another increase in the first quarter of the nineteenth.[18]

Broadberry and his colleagues provided estimates at fifty-year intervals of the overall size of the British financial services sector. The volume of financial

16. Roll (1930, 25), Ashton (1968, 73), Rosenberg (1969, 5). Williamson (1984) and Temin and Voth (2013) claimed that government war expenditures 'crowded out' private borrowing. Heim and Mirowski (1987), Clark (2001) and Ventura and Voth (2015) qualified or contested such arguments.

17. Heblich and Trew (2019), Temin and Voth (2013, 185).

18. Cameron et al. (1967, 32–35).

services was about the same in 1700 as it was in 1650. But from 1700 to 1750 this sector increased by a factor of 2.6. This suggests some growth in financial services *before* the beginning of the Industrial Revolution. From 1750 to 1800 it increased by a factor of 3.1. From 1800 to 1850 the increase was by a factor of 2.6. This is consistent with later evidence from other countries that the growth of financial services and markets enables industrial growth.[19]

There is corroborative evidence from the nineteenth century. A microeconomic analysis of geographically distributed data from 1817 to 1881, by Stephan Heblich and Alex Trew, found evidence of causal mechanisms through which banks enabled industrial growth. Their work suggests that industrial employment was positively related to the activity of the country banks.[20]

At present we are unable to test the Schumpeterian hypothesis definitively because too little empirical work has been done for the eighteenth century. Note that the Schumpeterian emphasis on financial institutions largely concerns the conditions and enablers of innovation and investment, not their drivers. The hypothesis is compatible, for example, with Mokyr's stress on the energizing role and innovative potential of Enlightenment science and culture. It can also be dovetailed with the emphasis on the roles of ideas and innovations in the work of McCloskey, as long as her hasty dismissal of institutions is annulled.[21]

The Industrial Revolution has been a foremost topic in economic history for well over a century, but our knowledge of seventeenth- and eighteenth-century financial institutions and activities is still patchy. Temin and Voth noted that, with some exceptions, 'banks and other forms of intermediation are hardly ever mentioned in modern treatments of the Industrial Revolution'. Perhaps the explanation of the lacuna is this simple: material technology is visible, but institutions are mainly beyond sight.[22]

The possibility of a 'shortage of capital' is considered in the following section. The chapter then moves on to discuss the evolution of key institutional underpinnings of finance before 1820. There is a particular focus on the growing alienability of land and on the legislation that made mortgaging more practicable.

19. Broadberry et al. (2015, 164), Rajan and Zingales (1998), Beck et al. (2003), Levine (2005).

20. Heblich and Trew (2019).

21. Mokyr (2009), McCloskey (2010, 2016a, 2016b).

22. Temin and Voth (2013).

Was There 'No Shortage of Capital'?

Did eighteenth-century industrial entrepreneurs face a shortage of funds? As noted, some economists look to interest rates for indications of excess supply or excess demand for loans. But many economic historians have argued that interest rates are poor guide on this score. Financial markets were relatively underdeveloped, and usury laws restricted lending. In these circumstances interest rates are a highly imperfect guide.[23]

It is vital to distinguish between a *need* for finance and an economic *demand* for finance. Generally, demand is not the same as need. As Adam Smith put it in his *Wealth of Nations*: 'A very poor man may be said in some sense to have a demand for a coach and six; he might like to have it; but his demand is not an effectual demand.'[24] If the want is not backed by money, then it is not an economic demand. Many demands for finance must be backed by security or means of future payment. An entrepreneur may be in dire *need* of additional finance but unable to express an economic *demand* for it because of a lack of secure collateral or of perceived repayment capacity. Collateral was often crucial in creating this demand. Any unbacked *need* for money would have no discernible signal or effect on the supply of finance.

Nevertheless, several prominent economic historians have insisted that capital was available. François Crouzet argued that 'the eighteenth century capital market seems, to twentieth century eyes, badly organized, but the creators of modern industry do not seem to have suffered too much from its imperfection. . . . English industry . . . seems to have overflowed with capital.' It is unclear whether Crouzet was referring to finance capital or capital goods. Likewise, in his account of the Industrial Revolution, the Marxist historian Eric Hobsbawm wrote: 'There was neither a relative nor an absolute shortage of capital.' This is also ambiguous, as Hobsbawm also failed to distinguish between finance capital and capital goods. Joan Robinson was clear that she meant finance, but she gave it a trailing role: 'There is a general tendency for the supply of finance to move with the demand for it . . . where enterprise leads finance follows.'[25] Similarly, H. John Habakkuk argued further that if there

23. Pressnell (1960), Pollard (1958, 221–22), Clark (1996), Quinn (2001), Temin and Voth (2013).

24. Smith ([1776] 1976, 73).

25. Crouzet, (1965, 187–88), Hobsbawm (1969, 39), Robinson made her statement in 1952 and republished it without amendment in 1979 (Robinson, 1952, 86; 1979b, 20). The Cambridge

had been a greater need for finance, then financial institutions would have grown up to satisfy it: 'Financial institutions adapt themselves to meet the principal economic needs of their period and that English banks concentrated on the provision of working-capital because that was what industry needed; if there had been a large unsatisfied demand from industry to finance fixed capital, financial institutions would, with relative ease, have adapted themselves to meet this need, or new institutions would have arisen for the purpose.'[26] Habakkuk confused the need for finance with demand. His claim that financial institutions automatically grow up to meet needs is countered by more recent evidence from several countries, which suggests that limited financial capacity is a crucial constraint.[27] Furthermore, an economic demand for substantial finance cannot be expressed without the legal and institutional machinery of alienable property, collateral, pricing and contract. These institutional arrangements were dependent on a series of legislative acts, which were neither easy nor automatic.

Another approach is to look at the comparative usage of fixed and variable capital goods in the early phases of the Industrial Revolution. For Pollard, in his seminal study, fixed capital is 'buildings, machinery, etc.' and circulating capital is 'stocks, stores, etc.' So in both cases here, by *capital* he meant *capital goods*. The argument is that greater deployments of fixed capital goods would require greater tranches of long-term finance. Perhaps the fixed capital goods could act as collateral for the loan. But that is not made clear. Pollard concluded: 'The need for fresh capital, especially for fixed assets, has been less than is often supposed, since much capital could be generated from within the existing domestic manufacturing and associated credit systems.' Fixed capital goods of lower value were taken to imply a lesser need for long-term finance.[28]

Pollard concluded that 'the banks provided little long-term capital because little long-term capital was demanded.' Again this neglects the point that any economic demand for finance requires particular institutions to be expressed.

---

capital controversies of the 1960s and 1970s did not seem to have altered her overall opinion on this point. Her main dissent from the orthodox position was to point out that there is no aggregate measure of heterogenous capital goods that is independent of an assumed vector of weights, such as of prices (Robinson, 1953). Sraffa (1960) confirmed this point.

26. Habakkuk (1962, 175).

27. Beck et al. (2003), Rousseau (2003), Levine (2005), Emenalo et al. (2018).

28. Pollard (1964, 304, 313).

Pollard endorsed Postan's supposition that internal savings or loans from family and friends were the prevalent sources of finance. Neal called this the 'Postan-Pollard story'. But Pollard went further than Postan by suggesting that savings or loans from family and friends were adequate, as well as the normal means of finance. In yet another ambiguous statement, Ronald M. Hartwell claimed that 'the capital needs of early industrialization were modest'. Similarly, starting with capital goods and then shifting to finance, Sushil Khanna asserted that 'the requirements of fixed investment were very modest and the threshold of entry into factory production quite low . . . there was no "capital scarcity" in 18th century England'. Noting 'how low the capital-labour ratio was during the industrial revolution', Khanna then claimed that 'capital equivalent to about four months' wages was enough to start a firm.' Then, in parenthesis: 'Boulton and Watt, who had the monopoly of steam engines for 25 years, launched their firm in 1775 with a capital of only £3370.'[29]

The celebrated Matthew Boulton and James Watt partnership has been studied in detail. Does the launch of their steam engine business with 'only £3370' (which was equivalent to about £460,000 in 2021 purchasing power) confirm that finance was adequate for their industrial ambitions? No. Watt's early development of his steam engine relied on the finance of John Roebuck, who held a share of the patent that Watt took out in 1769. Five years later Roebuck was in financial difficulties, and he transferred his share in the patent to Boulton. When they started in 1775, Boulton and Watt did not themselves manufacture many steam engines. Instead, they generally patented their designs and allowed others to manufacture the engines on licence. They drew up and sold plans and acted as consulting engineers. According to Eric Roll, the 'most important' reason for this delegated arrangement 'was undoubtedly the lack of sufficient capital' to finance and set up a works themselves. It was not until 1795 that they focused on manufacturing steam engines for sale.[30]

Hence, apart from their Soho premises near Birmingham, Boulton and Watt owned limited fixed capital goods in the early years. But that did not mean that their financial needs were small and satisfied. The early decades of their business were fraught with financial difficulties. Roll noted their 'serious

---

29. Pollard (1964, 308), Postan (1935), Neal (1994, 152), Hartwell (1965, 173), Khanna (1978, 1889–92, 1897).

30. Roll (1930, 24–26), Cule (1935), Ashton (1968, 56).

lack of capital which . . . hampered the growth of the business and more than once presented the partners with the prospect of immediate collapse'.[31] Postan also wrote on the precarious state of the Boulton-Watt partnership in its early years:

> Boulton had to sink into the venture nearly the whole of his fortune, including £25,000 [about £3.4 million in 2021 purchasing power] brought him by his wife and sums raised by the sale of his estate and the mortgage on his father's property. In the most critical period in the history of the firm, the bankers who financed him by short-term loans failed him, and more than once he had to depend, even for short-term accommodation, on the assistance of clients and friends, including Wilkinson and Wedgwood.[32]

J. E. Cule noted several mortgages by Boulton. One was raised in 1769 in Amsterdam with the premises near Birmingham as partial security, another in 1778, and yet another in 1787 or 1788, using, respectively, London and country banks. Addressing all entrepreneurs, Heaton indicated that 'fixed capital requirements' were not necessarily large: 'Yet they were frequently large enough to harass and perplex those who needed funds for building or equipping a plant of their own; for they were often the last straw on a back that already bore a heavy load.' Heaton added in a footnote: 'We know of . . . the strain on Boulton's resources when he was erecting his Soho factory.' Heaton summed up Boulton's desperate need for finance. The firm survived 'after many years of grim abstinence, of pared family budgets, and of frantic efforts to find supplementary funds outside'.[33]

The assumed relationship between fixed capital goods and the need for finance capital seems partly driven by the ambiguity of the word *capital*. Fixed capital and circulating capital goods are seen to relate to long-term and short-term finance, respectively. In reality, the connection is much looser. The example of Boulton and Watt shows clearly that the ratio of fixed to circulating capital is at best a weak indicator of the need for finance. It also demonstrates that, contrary to Robinson and Habakkuk, financial institutions did not readily spring up to rescue entrepreneurs in dire need.[34]

---

31. Roll (1930, 38).
32. Postan (1935, 4).
33. Cule (1935, 28, 83), Heaton (1937, 4–5), Ashton (1968, 84–85).
34. Habakkuk (1962, 175).

From Factor Prices to Collateral

Allen showed that England (compared with France and elsewhere) had a relatively high-wage economy for some time before the Industrial Revolution. He also noted that Britain had abundant cheap sources of energy, particularly coal. He too argued that interest rates provide little indication of a need for finance. Instead, Allen turned to the substitution of capital goods for labour, prompted largely by the lower price of the former relative to the latter.[35]

In his criticism of Allen's argument, Mokyr pointed to evidence suggesting that relatively few inventions were designed to save labour. Firms will try to save on all costs, not simply those from the relatively expensive inputs. Above all, innovative effort is always constrained by the extent of useful knowledge.[36]

Thomas Newcomen produced an early steam engine in about 1710. Its main use was to pump water out of mines. Hundreds of these engines were installed. Watt greatly improved the Newcomen engine by adding a separate condenser, more than doubling its fuel efficiency. But Boulton and Watt 'had little prospect of supplying many of their engines to collieries where coals were cheap and where the saving of fuel was of little importance', as Roll put it. The cheapness of coal was here an impediment, not a spur, to technological progress. Boulton and Watt got around this problem by offering their engines to the Cornish tin and copper mines. Unlike the Midlands and North of England, there was no coal in remote Cornwall: it was shipped there from South Wales. The local expensiveness of coal gave the Watt engine an advantage. But also in that county, there was a severe shortage of the skilled labour required to assemble and maintain the engines. Parts for their steam engines had to be transported by road or canal to Bristol, from where coastal vessels conveyed them to their Cornish destinations. There, the superior Watt engines quickly replaced the Newcomen machines. This strategy established the Boulton and Watt business before they developed and manufactured rotative steam engines after 1795.[37]

Relative prices of factor inputs clearly mattered. But this story is not about substituting relatively cheap capital for relatively expensive labour. A Cornish tin mining enterprise circa 1780 had the choice of a Newcomen engine or a slightly smaller, equally powerful, more expensive and hugely coal-saving engine

35. Allen (2009).
36. Mokyr (2009, 268–72), who follows Rosenberg (1969, 2).
37. Roll (1930, 60–67).

by Boulton and Watt.[38] There are several kinds of capital goods involved in these options, including coal and two types of steam engine. Both skilled and unskilled labour are relevant. Neither capital goods nor labour are homogenous. The oversimplified rhetoric of *capital* obscures this heterogeneity.

We have no way of ascertaining the value of aggregated capital goods without knowing their individual prices. As the Cambridge economist Piero Sraffa showed, the value of aggregate capital goods is not independent of relative prices, wage levels and profits. Yet it is relative prices that are said to drive the choice of combination of *capital* and *labour*. As both capital goods and labour are heterogeneous, there may be no simple relationship between prices and aggregate outcomes. The Cambridge capital theory debates showed the severe limitations of $Q = f(K, L)$ and of the idea of marginal substitutions between these aggregated factors of production. Aggregated prices of 'capital' relative to 'labour', as displayed by Allen, are highly problematic for this reason.[39] As Mokyr pointed out: 'Factor-saving biases can only be identified in models in which labour and capital are comparatively homogeneous. If technological change replaces skilled artisans with proletarians, or replaces one form of capital with another, the measurement problems can become insuperable.'[40]

Capital goods are needed for production through time. They can also be used as collateral for borrowing money to invest in more capital goods. Yet much of the focus of economic historians has been on savings, which come out of profits, as the main options for raising finance. The relative neglect of possible collateralization of fixed assets is unfortunate. Collateralization requires developed financial and legal institutions to deal with property and debt. In a capitalist economy, the insufficient development of these institutions will constrain growth.[41]

The Precarious Evolution of the Banking System

In the eighteenth century the number of banks increased significantly. There were about 24 London banks in the 1725, 52 in 1785 and 70 in 1800. In the UK provinces there were about a dozen country banks in 1750, 119 in 1784, 280 in

---

38. Brunt (2006, 89–90) quoted the cost of an early Watt engine as £2,000 (equivalent to about £200,000 in 2022 prices). But the savings in coal costs for Cornish clients, compared to the Newcomen engine, were estimated at £2,000 per annum.

39. Sraffa (1960), Harcourt (1972), Allen (2009, 138–39).

40. Mokyr (1994, 15).

41. De Soto (2000), Steiger (2006, 2008), Besley and Ghatak (2008), Arruñada (2012, 2017), Heinsohn and Steiger (2013), Hodgson (2015a, 2015b).

1793, reaching to a peak of 707 in 1812. Country banks played an important and growing role during the Industrial Revolution. Liam Brunt argued that some of them resembled modern venture capitalists who invested in high-risk industries on the basis of inside information. But country banks were often insecure. Their numbers fluctuated, due to failures and amalgamations. They issued notes payable on demand. An Act of Parliament of 1708 prevented private banks with more than six partners from issuing bank notes. They had neither corporate status nor limited liability. One partner in financial difficulties could break the bank.[42]

As noted in the previous chapter, the eighteenth-century financial system enlarged the possibilities for credit creation. Once legal institutions supporting collateralizable property, credit money and the sale of debt were in place, a new dynamic was unleashed. But this new system was and is vulnerable to waves of speculation, causing unsustainable booms and damaging slumps.[43]

It is here that the stabilizing capacities of central banks are important. In his history of central banks in several countries, Charles Goodhart examined their evolution from being bankers for the government to taking responsibility for the whole financial system. Then the central bank would not treat other banks as rivals and take some responsibility for their welfare. But this did not begin to happen in Britain until the nineteenth century. Before 1820 the Bank of England had a limited stabilizing role.[44]

Before the rise of larger private banks in the nineteenth century, the country banks, with their size limited by legislation, were too small to serve many financial needs. They also lacked adequate financial and infrastructural support from the central bank. Crucially, the Bank of England was formed to fight wars rather than to support industry. As Charles W. Calomiris and Stephen H. Haber noted: 'The politicized nature of the Bank of England meant that in spite of its immense size, it did little to knit the hundreds of small goldsmith and country banks together into anything that resembled a network.'[45]

42. See Dawes and Ward-Perkins (2000, 1:6), Kindleberger (1984, 77–79), Mathias (1969, 169), Pressnell (1958), Brunt (2006), Mokyr (2009, 222–25), Desan (2014, 378), Heblich and Trew (2019). Dawes and Ward-Perkins (2000, 1:6) pointed out that the rise in numbers in the 1790s may in part be due to the publication in that decade of the *Universal British Directory*, which for the first time listed banks that may have existed earlier.

43. Beutel (1938), Shientag (1941), Baker (1979), Lawrence (2002).

44. Goodhart (1988).

45. See Dawes and Ward-Perkins (2000, 1:6), Kindleberger (1984, 77–79), Mathias (1969, 169), Pressnell (1958), Heblich and Trew (2019). The quote is from Calomiris and Haber (2014, 97).

The role of the Bank of England as a financial guarantor of banking stability was severely compromised by its corrupt political entanglement with both Parliament and the Crown. Financial favours were regularly exchanged between politicians and bankers. Ministers were lobbied, cajoled and given stipends for their compliance. Many investors shunned the Bank of England in the eighteenth century because of its politicized administration, its exposure to sovereign debt and its rampant cronyism. The Bank of England was a tarnished centrepiece of an inadequate banking system. Calomiris and Haber wrote:

> This situation kept the supply of bank credit for private purposes quite low throughout the eighteenth and early nineteenth centuries, precisely when it could have fostered the economic growth that industrialization made possible. The scarcity of credit helps to explain the puzzling disparity between the remarkable technological progress witnessed in England from 1750 to 1840 and the tepid overall economic growth of that period. . . . The bottom line was that England's industrialists, as well as other risky private borrowers, were starved for funds.[46]

Until 1797 the Bank of England paid bonuses to Treasury officials. Then, as part of wider efforts to reduce state corruption in the face of ballooning national debt, Prime Minister William Pitt put an end to these payments. But the Bank of England and business interests maintained their separation. This divorce of London finance and British industry continued well into the twentieth century. By then, other developed countries had established much closer relationships between industry and finance. The separation of City finance from British industry has taken some blame for lower rates of investment and productivity growth.[47]

To help gauge the extent to which the slow development of the English financial system restrained industrial growth until sometime in the nineteenth century, we need evidence on the extent of creation of credit through the use of financial institutions in the eighteenth and nineteenth centuries. Security or collateral are the foundations of credit. The main store of wealth was land. Among other things, we need evidence on potential and actual mortgaging by entrepreneurs and shareholders.

---

46. Calomiris and Haber (2014, 98).
47. Ingham (1984). For a later analysis, see Carlin and Mayer (2003).

The Development of Mortgage Activity

As Benito Arruñada explained, there need to be safeguards to ensure that the mortgagor has genuine title to the land, and its boundaries are not under dispute. A partial solution is the formation of land registries, as Hernando de Soto has pursued in contemporary Peru. But as Arruñada further elaborated, an operable system of land registration requires trustworthy financial intermediaries plus legal and administrative institutions that are relatively efficient and mostly free of corruption. Even today, only a minority of countries fulfil these conditions.[48]

The Low Countries had an extensive and well-organised system of land registration as early as the seventeenth century. England was far behind. The previous chapter noted the land register around the Isle of Ely in 1663. By 1700 there was some clamour for further land registries, to facilitate land mortgaging and the raising of capital. Registries with records of conveyances and mortgages were established in the West Riding of Yorkshire in 1704, the East Riding of Yorkshire in 1707, Middlesex in 1708 and the North Riding of Yorkshire in 1735. These early land registries seem rarely explored by economic historians, although they helped the use of land as collateral.[49]

Powerful landowners resisted the extension of land registries to other counties in the eighteenth and nineteenth centuries because of fears that they would lead to greater systematic taxation of their landed property. Once again, the aristocracy and the landed gentry held back institutional changes that could have helped to promote innovation and economic development. But lenders and borrowers adapted to the limitation. From the end of the seventeenth century there is some evidence of mortgaging in parts of England that lacked land registries. But more finance, at cheaper rates, could have been made available if effective land registries had been widely established.

Despite these problems, some private banks developed a growing mortgage business. In their study of Hoare's Bank in London, Temin and Voth reported: 'Mortgages were the single most important security offered in the years before 1710.' Joslin also noted several cases of lending via mortgages by the London private banks in 1739–84. But again the evidence is limited. What is certain is that all UK private banks remained small until after the Joint-Stock Bank Act

48. Arruñada (2012, 2017), De Soto (2000), Dam (2006a, 2006b).
49. Van Bochove et al. (2015). Tate (1944), Sheppard et al. (1979) and Sheppard and Belcher (1980) explored the early land registries in England.

of 1826, which replaced the 1708 Act, allowed private joint stock banks in addition to the Bank of England and heralded a more effective banking system. Even then, it was not until 1858 that banks and other businesses could register as corporations and benefit from limited liability.[50]

In his study of country banking, Leslie Pressnell noted the growing need for long-term finance, including for major agricultural improvements: 'Loans by way of mortgage were procurable in London, from banks and insurance companies and through the multitudinous lawyers of the capital.' Pressnell concluded: 'Much the most important means of raising money privately in the eighteenth century was the property mortgage.' Mathias cited several enterprises that obtain loans from banks, but without much further detail. His list includes Francis Egerton, the Duke of Bridgewater, who borrowed £25,000 (about £4.0 million in 2021 purchasing power) from a London bank to help finance the Lancashire canal that opened with his name in 1761, plus Richard Arkwright and other industrial entrepreneurs. The evidence we have so far is patchy, but it reveals important cases where mortgages were raised on land, buildings or other assets to finance industry or infrastructure.[51]

Infrastructural development was crucial to prepare the ground for industrialization. In her study of the English turnpike trusts, Brenda Buchanan noted the early development 'of the concept of the "mortgage" beyond its landed origins. . . . Before 1793 the tolls formed the only security, and these were assigned to three landed trustees. Each mortgagee had "all the Right Title and Interest in and to the said Tolls".' J. R. Ward found a similar innovation in mortgaging arrangements in the early canals and river improvements, where the rights to barge tolls where sometimes mortgaged. He noted a mortgage on a landed estate for river improvements as early as 1698. His data, which are summarized in table 5.1, also show that the Sun Insurance Company provided some mortgages. Ward's data are gleaned from archives in Bedfordshire, Oxfordshire and Sheffield. The sample is not intended to be comprehensive, but it relates to a central area of commercial activity in England. Even this geographically highly limited sample shows substantial mortgaging activity for canal construction, growing and then peaking in the second half of the eighteenth century.[52]

By using the records of attorneys, B. L. Anderson established that mortgaging occurred in Lancashire throughout the eighteenth century, and M. Miles

---

50. Temin and Voth (2013, 50), Joslin (1960), Grossman (2010, 28–29).

51. Pressnell (1958, 344; 1960, 187), Ashton (1968, 84), Mathias (1969, 175–76).

52. Buchanan (1986, 230), Ward (1974).

TABLE 5.1. Number of mortgages raised for canal building in an area of central England including Bedford, Oxford and Sheffield

1660–79	1670–99	1700–19	1720–39	1740–59	1760–79	1780–99
38	71	86	109	133	151	105

Source: Ward (1974, 166).

and Pat Hudson found significant post-1750 evidence of borrowing and mortgaging in the West Riding of Yorkshire, where there was a land registry. Anderson noted examples of mortgages on urban dwellings in Lancashire: 'It is clear that the practice of borrowing and lending on mortgage had taken root among all classes right from the beginning of the [eighteenth] century.' Mortgaging became no longer the exclusive device of the rich.[53]

The impressive study by Philip T. Hoffman and his co-workers of peer-to-peer lending from 1740 to 1899 in France warns us of the amount of financial 'dark matter' that may be out of sight in Britain and elsewhere. Hoffman and his colleagues showed that peer-to-peer lending in France was huge, in rural as well as urban areas, almost a century before French industrialization and the rise of its banks. In 1740 nearly a third of French families borrowed money. Much of this lending involved mortgages and was facilitated by the use of *notaires*. This borrowing was not generally from family and friends. It could not rely on trust alone. As well as acting in their capacity as state officials to authorize and record contracts, the *notaires* often served as financial intermediaries, by matching lenders with borrowers and arranging loans. Before 1850 lenders and borrowers were rarely more than a day on horse apart because the lender might have to visit the borrower to retrieve the debt. Nevertheless, lending flourished.[54]

Hoffman and his colleagues were able to access data on the extent of this lending because of surviving central records. The closest equivalent positions in Britain to the French *notaires* were the attorneys or scriveners. But these have never been state officials, and no central British records of such lending exist. Finding comparable data of peer-to-peer lending in Britain will be a much harder task. But the French case suggests that much British financial activity may be hidden and dispersed in the archives.

53. Anderson (1969a, 1969b), Miles (1981), Hudson (1986). Quote is from Anderson (1969b, 18).

54. Hoffman et al. (2019).

This raises the question that if finance was available in 1740, why did France not industrialize until well into the nineteenth century? France had an inferior system of credit creation that inhibited its military and industrial efforts. Bruce Carruthers noted several factors, including pre-1789 state despotism alongside a fragmented legal system, revolutionary turbulence from 1789, and the slow development of larger private companies. In addition, unlike England and the Netherlands in the eighteenth century, there 'was no developed capital market upon which the state could market its debt. Rather, France raised money through a complex and cumbersome system of tax farms, private bankers and venal offices.' Financial institutions in France in the eighteenth century were well behind their Dutch and British rivals.[55]

In Britain, when peer-to-peer and bank lending were inadequate, borrowers approached other financial institutions. A. H. John highlighted the role of insurance companies in providing mortgages: 'In the first half of the [eighteenth] century the only office to make great use of mortgages was the Sun Fire, to be followed later by the Equitable.' The mortgaging function of insurance companies expanded after 1750. G. E. Mingay noted: 'By the end of the eighteenth century the Equitable and Sun Fire Offices alone had some £776,000 [about £81 million in 2021 purchasing power] invested in mortgages.'[56]

Further archival research might help to resolve some important questions. For instance, it is clear that as the Industrial Revolution progressed, shareholders financed many joint stock enterprises. But where did the shareholders obtain the money to buy their shares? How many shareholders mortgaged land or buildings to fund their investments?

But the banking system was far from secure. Ellis Powell blamed the 'lending of money on farm mortgages' as the 'principal cause' of the failure of 240 country banks between 1814 and 1816. In the 1825–26 economic crisis, 60 country banks failed. The emergencies of war and successive banking failures prompted reforms and restructuring of the banking system, including the Country Bankers Act of 1826. Such observations are consistent with the hypothesis that the rickety and constrained state of British financial institutions held back growth during much of the Industrial Revolution.[57]

55. Berkeley (1750, 25–26). Carruthers (1996, 23). O'Brien (1996) emphasised differences in landownership and agricultural productivity.

56. John (1953, 155), Mingay (1963, 37).

57. Powell (1915, 118, 124), Cameron et al. (1967, 27).

TABLE 5.2. Mortgaging and financial development in Britain, 1688–1830

Year	Financial assets as a percentage of tangible assets (financial interrelations ratio)	Mortgages as a percentage of tangible assets	Mortgages as a percentage of financial assets
1688	17%	6.7%	39%
1760	40%	9.4%	23%
1800	57%	8.6%	15%
1830	76%	10.0%	13%

Source: Goldsmith (1985, 232–33).

Table 5.2 reports Raymond Goldsmith's estimates of the extent of mortgaging of assets and an index of the development of the financial sector in Britain. His figures on the extent of mortgages are 'rough conjectures'. His more reliable 'financial interrelations ratio' is the ratio of financial to tangible assets—the relative size of the financial superstructure to the tangible economy. He regarded this as the most useful macro-indicator of financial development.[58]

Table 5.2 shows the steady rise of the financial interrelations ratio from 1688 to 1830. This tracks the rising relative importance of the financial sector in this period. These years were crucial for the development of British capitalism. Goldsmith's conjectural figures on mortgages show their rise in relation to the tangible collateral during the period. But the ratio of mortgages to all financial assets declined, indicating that other financial assets—such as bonds and promissory notes—became more important, as financial institutions developed and financial services diversified.

Goldsmith's data for years after 1830 (they are not reported here—they extend into the twentieth century) show a further rising trend in the financial interrelations ratio, but one less dramatic than 1688–1830. His figures for the ratios of mortgages to tangible and financial assets show slowly declining trends into the twentieth century. The previous chapter noted that about half of English land might have been still entailed under strict settlement at the end of the nineteenth century. The scope for mortgaging land remained constrained.

There is evidence that the country banks, despite their limitations and vulnerability, were crucial in financing industrial growth. Figures 5.1 and 5.2 use data from a large survey of country banks, here covering the years from 1688

58. Goldsmith (1985, 229, 232–33).

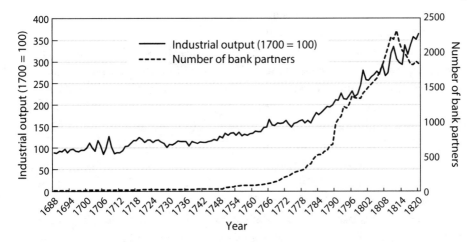

FIGURE 5.1. Total size of country banks and industrial output, 1688–1820
Country bank data (*right scale*) are for England and Wales. Industrial outputs
(*left scale*) are for Britain as a whole. Data from Dawes and Ward-Perkins (2000,
vol. 2), Broadberry et al. (2015, 239–43).

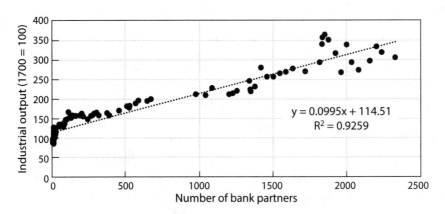

FIGURE 5.2. Correlation between total size of country banks and industrial
output in England and Wales, 1688–1820
Country bank data are for England and Wales. Industrial output is for Britain as
a whole. Data from Dawes and Ward-Perkins (2000, vol. 2), Broadberry et al.
(2015, 239–43).

to 1820. For each country bank in any given year, its number of partners is used as a rough proxy for the size of its capital.[59]

The regression in figure 5.2 suggests that these banking institutions were crucial for industrial development. The level of industrial output is closely correlated with the size of the country banking sector. We may hypothesize that this correlation resulted from the capacity of the country banks to lend money for industrial investment. Of course, correlation does imply causation. Much deeper statistical analysis is required. (Also some adjustment must be made to deal with the fact that the country banking data are for England and Wales, while the industrial output data are from Britain as a whole.) But the results give strong prime facie evidence to support the claim that the size of the country bank sector was a major empowering factor for industrial growth.

Financial institutions were essential for economic development, but their limitations and weaknesses kept growth on a leash. While the growing banking sector enabled growth, it also set its limits. Restricted to no more than six partners, country bank expansion was severely constrained. This held back industrial development. Yet finance was a crucial enabler of innovation, investment and growth. Constraining as well as enabling factors were important.[60]

Conclusion: Challenging the Conventional Wisdom

The conventional wisdom, laid down by Postan, simplified by Pollard and endorsed by many others, is that finance for industrial development was provided by savings or by borrowing from family and friends, and that financial institutions otherwise played a secondary role. This jars against widespread international evidence of the importance of financial institutions in economic development. Some economic historians, such as Mathias, have paid more attention to mortgaging activity, but they found insufficient evidence to challenge the conventional wisdom. While the 'Postan-Pollard story' may have some empirical foundation, at least in the early years of the

---

59. Dawes and Ward-Perkins (2000). The author is very grateful to Alex Trew for access to this data. Heblich and Trew (2019) analysed the same dataset—in much more depth than here—from 1817 to 1881. They did not analyse the pre-1817 period.

60. Grajzl and Murrell (2022c) provided data to show that between 1765 and 1865 that developments in case law on debt and finance were very important drivers of England's real per-capita GDP.

Industrial Revolution, it may also be that the nascent state of British financial institutions restricted borrowing, hindered entrepreneurship and helped to account for the remarkably slow rate of growth of industrial output from 1760 to 1820. The constraining role of limited finance is in line with the Schumpeterian hypothesis.[61]

This hypothesis raises a number of questions, for many of which we do not yet have adequate answers. An alternative source of finance to borrowing from family and friends, once the legal and other institutional conditions were in place, was the mortgaging of property, including land and buildings. This chapter has established that there was a significant amount of mortgaging activity after 1670, but its overall extent cannot yet be gauged, other than by rough estimates. Too little research has been done. The land registries of Middlesex and Yorkshire, existing from the early eighteenth century, have not yet been explored systematically with the issue of mortgaging in mind. The surviving records of the seventeenth-century insurance companies, country banks, attorneys or scriveners—with a few notable exceptions—seem likewise little disturbed by such queries. We need more evidence to assess the Schumpeterian hypothesis in the English case.

Future empirical research on financial activity in eighteenth-century Britain should attempt to estimate the following:

1. The extent to which finance for entrepreneurship was provided out of savings or by borrowing from family or friends.
2. The extent to which finance for entrepreneurship was otherwise provided through peer-to-peer lending intermediaries, banks or other financial institutions.
3. Concerning (2), the extent to which landed and other property could or was used as collateral to obtain loans.
4. The different uses to which familial, collateralized or other loans were put, including agricultural improvements, infrastructural or industrial investments, or conspicuous consumption.
5. The overall degree to which the underdeveloped state of financial institutions acted as a constraint on industrial growth.

Answers to questions (1) and (2) would determine the relative importance of borrowing from family and friends versus financial institutions. Note that

61. Postan (1935), Pollard (1964), Mathias (1969).

(1) is logically independent of (3), (4) and (5). If the conventional wisdom concerning (1) were confirmed (or disconfirmed), then this would not determine the answer to (3), (4) or (5). All five issues are in want of systematic empirical assessment.

Why have research efforts in this direction been insufficient? Mokyr noted an obsession with industry and manufacturing rather than finance.[62] This fixation may emanate from a view of the economy as a physical machine. Much of economics is framed by a vision of physical inputs, forces and outputs. This pervasive notion goes back to the physiocrats and Adam Smith. It has sustained a physical definition of capital, and a frequent failure to distinguish finance capital from capital goods. The mental models and metaphors that dominate the work of many economic historians have diverted attention away from the crucial issue of finance.

As Carol Heim and Philip Mirowski argued in the *Journal of Economic History*: 'The idea that "the economy" consists of a unified pool of potentially mobile resources—rather than distinct and possibly nonintersecting sets of economic relationships—is so standard in neoclassical theory that many economists take it for granted.' Even the Cambridge critics of the aggregate production function used a disaggregated formulation based on physical inputs and outputs. The outcome is that the focus has been on tangibles, including technological change. The role of financial institutions has been given insufficient attention.[63]

The physicalist perspective in economics has also meant that historically specific features—particularly institutions—are sometimes downplayed. The Industrial Revolution was a turning point in human history. Any explanation of its origins must point not only to eternities—like land, labour and capital goods—but also to novel institutions, social structures, circumstances and ideas that prompted or enabled the transformation.

Important legal developments were required to establish a modern financial system. Legal changes were neither automatic nor always responsive to business demands. Some legislation—such as that limiting interest rates, bank size and corporate formation—inhibited economic development. But other legal changes made more land saleable, enabled mortgaging, buttressed credit markets and reinforced other financial institutions.

---

62. Mokyr (2009, 266).

63. Heim and Mirowski (1987, 129), Sraffa (1960).

The stress on institutions in this analysis does not rule out other factors, such as the influence of Enlightenment ideas. But ideas always need institutions to be noticed, filtered, selected, adopted, laid down in habits, promoted and empowered. As well as ideas, we need to look more closely at key institutional developments in the eighteenth and nineteenth centuries. There is much empirical research still to be done to gauge the role of financial institutions in the British Industrial Revolution.

PART III

Legal Institutionalism and the Lessons of History

6

Agency, Institutions and Their Evolution

The readjustment of institutions and habitual views to an altered environment is made in response to pressure from without; it is of the nature of a response to stimulus. Freedom and facility of readjustment, that is to say capacity for growth in social structure, therefore depends in great measure on . . . the degree of exposure of the individual members to the constraining forces of the environment.

—THORSTEIN VEBLEN, *THE THEORY OF THE LEISURE CLASS* (1899)

The human instinct to follow rules is often based in the emotions rather than in reason. . . . It is important to resist the temptation to reduce human motivation to an economic desire for resources. Violence in human history has often been perpetrated by people seeking not material wealth but recognition.

—FRANCIS FUKUYAMA, *THE ORIGINS OF POLITICAL ORDER* (2011)

THIS CHAPTER ADDRESSES the cultural and psychological springs of motivation and the forces that bring about institutional and socio-economic change. From some general remarks about the role of habit and its primacy over reason and belief, this chapter re-examines some of the key historical changes from the fourteenth to the eighteenth century, noting how various disturbances and pressures impinged on individuals and groups and led to changed behaviours, new habits and shifting ideological alignments and developments. Legal changes are shown to be important in this particular historic context. This bolsters a perspective known as legal institutionalism. Finally, it is asked whether the processes of change outlined in this chapter are consistent with Darwinian principles. Was this historical institutional evolution Darwinian? And if so, how can this help to guide further theoretical and empirical investigation?

Darwinism means more than natural selection. It led to a sea change in philosophy and psychology, in attempts to make them consistent with the fact of human evolution from earlier life forms. The stark dualism of mind and matter had to be jettisoned. Mind somehow evolved out of matter. The proposition that mind and matter exist in different realms is inconsistent with biological evolution. Mind is an emergent property of matter itself.[1]

These intellectual developments are relevant for the analysis in this book. A key question is how and why men and women were motivated to make changes to their behaviours and to social institutions. The approach proposed here emphasises the interaction of ideas, motivations and mental states with circumstances and problems, all played out in the social and material world. This requires a psychology where beliefs and deliberations are not the prime instigators of action, but part of a process of evolving dispositions, from instincts and habits to reasons and ideas.

Beyond Folk Psychology: The Role of Habit

Towards the end of the nineteenth century, Darwinian thinking prompted a reconceptualization of the relationship between mind and matter. This was expressed in the pragmatist philosophy of Charles Sanders Peirce, William James, John Dewey and others. These ideas strongly influenced the institutional economist Thorstein Veblen. But pragmatism was eclipsed by the rise of logical positivism in the 1930s and was marginalized until the 1980s.[2] Pragmatist philosophy has since enjoyed a revival. One of its leading exponents, Hans Joas, summarized a key aspect of the pragmatist contribution in this area:

> The alternative to a teleological interpretation of action, with its inherent dependence on Cartesian dualisms, is to conceive of perception and cognition not as preceding action but rather as a phase of action by which action

1. See, for example, Bunge (1980), Dennett (1995), Joas (1996), Plotkin (1994), Richards (1987).
2. Richards (1987), Hodgson (2004).

is directed and redirected in its situational contexts. According to this alternative view, goal-setting does not take place by an act of intellect *prior to* the actual action, but is instead the result of a reflection on aspirations and tendencies that are pre-reflexive and have *already always* been operative. In this act of reflection, we thematize aspirations which are normally at work without our being actively aware of them. But where exactly are these aspirations located? They are located in our bodies. It is the body's capabilities, habits and ways of relating to its environment which form the background to all conscious goal-setting, in other words, to our intentionality. Intentionality itself, then, consists in a self-reflective control which we exercise over our current behavior.[3]

Accordingly, pragmatism overcomes the Cartesian dualism of body and mind. Pragmatists do not see intellect as an independent and ungrounded causal power, but as an emergent and active property of engaged dispositions and unfolding actions.

But a 'folk psychology' still dominates social science, where ideas or beliefs are seen as the sources of intentions, choices and actions. As critics elaborate, this ubiquitous folk psychology obscures a much more complex neurophysiological reality. These 'mind-first' explanations of human behaviour are unable to explain adequately such phenomena as sleep, memory, learning, mental illness or the effects of chemicals or drugs on our perceptions or actions. Mind-first or ideas-first conceptions sustain an unwarranted dualism or discontinuity between the mental and physical worlds, which is inconsistent with the reality of human evolution. Our mental capacities to use and process ideas evolved over millions of years, from beings who lacked ideas and were driven by instincts or habits. Among humans, ideas and intentions are emergent properties of the physical neural system. Instincts and habits came first.[4]

Much social science takes it for granted that action is motivated largely by reasons based on beliefs or preferences. This proposition is undermined by modern psychology and by the Darwinian evolutionary perspective. Reason and decision follow, both in the timespan of evolution and in an individual's thought. Experiments have shown that conscious sensations are reported about half a second after neural events, and unconscious brain processes are

---

3. Joas (1996, 158).

4. Bunge (1980); Stich (1983, 1996); P. M. Churchland (1984, 1989); P. S. Churchland (1986); Damasio (1994); Rosenberg (1995, 1998).

discernible before any conscious decision to act. This evidence suggests that our dispositions are triggered before our actions are rationalized: we often contrive reasons for actions already under way.[5]

Also found wanting is the idea prevalent in much of economics that we can explain human behaviour adequately with models involving fixed preference functions. It stretches credibility to propose that we are born with a preference function that is already able to deal with novel problems, before they appear. Capabilities, dispositions and preference must all evolve as we interact with the world and each other, and as we face new difficulties.

Furthermore, we do not simply think with the mind: thinking works through interactions with material and social contexts. 'Situated cognition' means that knowing is inseparable from doing and from its social and material settings. Ideas develop and play out in the world of social relations and material things. Human cognitive capacities are irreducible to individuals alone: they also depend upon social structures and material cues. Ideas matter. But so do institutions. Each helps to constitute the other.[6]

Humans do act for reasons. But reasons and beliefs themselves are caused and have to be explained. Reasoning itself is based on habits and instincts, and it cannot be sustained without them. It is often driven by emotions. Furthermore, consistent with the Darwinian doctrine of evolutionary continuity, where more sophisticated capacities must have evolved from relatively primitive organisms that lacked them, instincts and the capacities to form habits developed through a process of natural selection that extends way back into our pre-human past. Reason is not a first cause.

The adoption of a habit-based perspective implies neither stasis nor the absence of choice. As John Dewey argued, through our engagement with diverse and changing contexts, we develop different habits of thought and action that sometimes come into conflict with one another when triggered. Such conflicts are opportunities for choice and change. Exogenous or endogenous disruptions pose challenges that can lead to adaptations and changed habits.

5. Libet (1985, 2004), Libet et al. (1983), Wegner (2002, 2003), Wegner and Wheatley (1999), Haynes and Rees (2005a, 2005b), Haynes et al. (2007), Hodgson (2010). Libet (2004) argued that his experimental evidence is consistent with free will, which can intervene to block actions already foreshadowed in brain processes. To a large degree it depends on what precisely is meant by 'free will'.

6. Lave and Wenger (1991), Cohen and Bacdayan (1994), Hutchins (1995), Lane et al. (1996), Clark (1997).

Habit does not deny choice. On the contrary, the conflicting powers of different habits in evolving circumstances make choice inevitable.[7]

Habits are in some ways like computer programs in the brain. A habit is a disposition to engage in previously adopted or acquired behaviour (including patterns of thought) that is triggered by an appropriate stimulus or context. Habits are influenced by prior activity and have durable, self-sustaining qualities. Although formed through repetition of action or thought, habits themselves are not behaviours. If we acquire a habit, we do not necessarily use it all the time. Habit is a capacity for action, not action itself.

Habits express specific, conditional goals and are triggered by circumstances. This is in contrast to the idea that human agency can be explained essentially in terms of rational deliberation. The assumption that human behaviour is determined by appraisals of interests or by given preference functions lacks an explanation of the origin or operation of these rational capacities or preferences. These are assumed rather than explained.

The habit-based or program-based approach relies on evolutionary theory to explain the origin of systems of rule-like dispositions, which are either inherited as instincts or acquired as habits in historically specific cultural settings. Our capacities to reason and to appraise alternatives are outcomes of human evolution. Human problem-solving capacity is knowledge that is incorporated in habitual rules or programs that guide behaviour. This knowledge has been accumulated through trial and error in varied processes of human evolution and individual learning. Knowledge, in short, consists of adaptations that have emerged in evolutionary processes of selection and adaptation.[8]

Institutions and Their Evolution

Institutions are systems of established and prevalent social rules that structure social interactions. The term *rule* is broadly understood as an injunction or disposition, that in circumstances X, actors tend to, or are obliged to, do Y. A rule can be procedural (governing thought or other actions) or constitutive (allocating a function, position or status). Rules include norms of behaviour and social conventions, as well as legal or formal rules.[9]

7. Dewey (1922).

8. Holland et al. (1986), Mayr (1988, 1991), Plotkin (1994), Vanberg (2002, 2004), Hodgson (2004).

9. On rules, see Holland et al. (1986, 14–22) and Crawford and Ostrom (1995).

Institutions must involve some shared conceptions, to make rules operative. Languages, money, law, weights, measures, traffic conventions, table manners, firms and all other organizations are institutions. All institutions are social structures, but not all social structures are institutions. For example, a demographic structure of a society is not necessarily an institution. Organizations are an important subclass of institutions, with the added features of boundaries, structure, membership criteria and principles of sovereignty.[10]

We are all born into a world where institutions are handed to us from the past. As we engage with our circumstances we may reinforce existing institutions, or modify them, or help to contrive new institutional arrangements. We reinforce existing institutions by acting in compliance with them. Our conformism is perceived by others, including by those that may want change. Compliance also affects our thoughts and preferences. We may acquire habits of thought that legitimate existing institutions. Compliance can strengthen and spread normative support for existing institutional arrangements.

As Veblen wrote: 'All change in habits of life and of thought is irksome.'[11] The impacts of governments, powerful individuals or social conflicts can disrupt normal daily practice and create personal stress and heightened emotions. There can be threats to material sustenance or social status. Problems are created that people must solve. Some are more urgent than others. Solutions are found by serendipity, experiment or cooperation. Disturbances create opportunities for institutional change. These arguments are redolent of the work on *classifier systems* by John H. Holland and his co-writers:

> The [cognitive] system is continually engaged in pursuing its goals, in the course of which problem elements are constantly being recategorized and predictions are constantly being generated. As part of this process, various triggering conditions initiate inductive changes in the system's rules. Unexpected outcomes provide problems that the system solves by creating new rules as hypotheses. Concepts with shared properties are activated, thus providing analogies for use in problem solving and rule generation. . . . At

---

10. For arguments in favour of these definitions of institution and organization, with criticisms of some contrasting views, see Hodgson (2006, 2019a). Several leading scholars (Kornai, 1971; Parsons, 1983; Giddens, 1984; Scott, 1995; Dam, 2006b; Miller, 2010; Guala, 2016) saw organizations as a special form of institution.

11. Veblen (1899, 199). For an overview of theories of institutional change, see Kingston and Caballero (2009).

one level the major task of the system may be described as reducing uncertainty about the environment.[12]

Once a new institutional rule emerges, it may diffuse in a number of ways, including via long-evolved conformist, authority-compliant or prestige-oriented propensities that have been enhanced in our culture. Some rules are followed to avoid punishment, or for personal advantage. When new institutions begin to become established, the new rules and constraints not only affect behaviour but also may cause shifts in preferences and values. These are reconstitutive downward effects, where institutions change some individuals and increase overall compliance with their rules.[13]

How do new rules or institutional adaptations emerge? Mokyr considered random mutations of existing rules. He placed much weight on influential 'cultural entrepreneurs'—such as Bacon and Newton—who established and propagated major changes to our way of thinking.[14] But despite the importance of these remarkable people, many of the institutional changes we have considered in this book are more incremental and modest than the major changes in worldview promoted by Bacon or Newton. In many cases there is no record of the institutional innovators involved. Many changes are in response to pressing problems, answered by experimental attempts at solutions. They are responses to stress, and to threats to prosperity, status or survival. If they work, then ideas and rationalizations often follow. Others may imitate, and the ideas and practices spread.

In some cases a multitude of possible solutions or adaptations will appear, and the trials of experience and the powers of convention will dictate which ones survive, and which fall into disuse. In other cases the possibilities for innovation may be limited. Sometimes a new but suboptimal institution may persist, simply because it is difficult to find and establish alternatives.[15]

Some customary rules made be encoded in law. Existing laws may come under strain or be challenged by powerful interests. Legislators and judges may

12. Holland et al. (1986, 69). See also Kornai (1971) and Vanberg (2004).

13. Milgram (1974), Boyd and Richerson (1985, 1992), Henrich and Boyd (1998, 2001), Ben-Ner and Putterman (2000), Gintis (2000), Henrich and Gil-White (2001), Boyd et al. (2003), Haidt and Joseph (2004, 2008), Henrich (2004), Richerson and Boyd (2004), Gintis et al. (2005), Henrich et al. (2006, 2010), Bowles and Gintis (2011), Haidt (2012). On reconstitutive downward effects, see Hodgson and Knudsen (2004, 2010).

14. Mokyr (2016).

15. Commons (1924, 1934).

create new laws or make novel interpretations of existing ones. Through these processes, legal rules can evolve.[16]

The capacity of an economic system to create and promulgate possible solutions to pressing problems depends on a number of factors. Levels of skill and the means of communication are crucial. Consider literacy. Before 1500 the overwhelming majority of the English population were illiterate. Most problem-solving conversation had to be verbal and face-to-face. W. B. Stephens estimated that in England in around 1500 only about 10 per cent of men were literate. By about 1650 it was roughly 30 per cent, reaching 45 percent in 1714 and rising steadily. Women had lower literacy rates, reaching about 25 percent in 1714. But by the end of the nineteenth century almost all grooms and brides could sign the marriage register. Through written media, the growth of literacy made greater technological and institutional innovation and diffusion possible. Literacy vastly increases access to knowledge.[17]

Agricultural societies are typically encumbered by low skills and education, and restricted access to expertise through social networks. By contrast, industrialization creates larger clusters of specialized expertise, often in urban areas. Problem solving is aided by these concentrations of skill, with groups focusing on similar technological, economic and institutional difficulties. Improved communications and urbanization enhance the processes of learning and development. Problem-solving capacities are greatly expanded. These changes became pronounced in England in the nineteenth century.

Patterns of Institutional Change

We may describe different institutional changes in terms of their sources, sites and patterns. As a preliminary classification, the following broad categories are used:

Sources of Institutional Change

Major exogenous disruption—such as invasions or major pandemics
Exogenous pressure—including threats of war or invasion, involvement in wars abroad or politico-economic competition between states

16. On legal rules, see Ehrenberg (2016).
17. Stephens (1990, 555).

Major endogenous disruption—such as civil wars or other major internal disruptions within states

Endogenous pressure—intended or unintended pressures on actors from within states

Expressions or Sites of Institutional Change

Ideological framing—ideological rationalizations of actions or objectives

Social change—changes in social structures at the micro, meso or macro level

Economic change—changes in arrangements governing the production or distribution of wealth

Political change–changes in political institutions, forces or alignments

Legal change—legislative changes, including changes in penalties or enforcement

Adaptive and Evolutionary Processes

Practical adaptation—behavioural adaptations by individuals or groups

Institutional diffusion—the copying of institutional adaptations from elsewhere

Variation and selection—eliminative competition between institutions, habits and adaptations

In the period covered in this book (1300–1820) there were at least three major disturbances, each involving some exogenous impact or pressure: the Black Death, the Reformation and the Glorious Revolution. The English Civil War was another major disruption, but its most important institutional rupture—the creation of a republic—was reversed by the Restoration of 1660. There was no major redistribution of wealth or class power.

We look at each major disturbance and consider the multiple outcomes it triggered.

First Major Disturbance—the Black Death

The Black Death (*major exogenous disruption*) brought massive fatalities and huge socio-economic disruption. The severe shortage of agricultural labour (*endogenous pressure*) created opportunities for serfs to bargain for higher wages and better conditions (*practical adaptation*) (*variation and selection*). Changing circumstances prompted new habits of thought and enhanced expectations. In response, King Edward III attempted to fix wages (*practical adaptation*). He also levied a poll tax to help fund the English military effort in the Hundred Years' War (*legal change*) (*economic change*). These measures (*endogenous pressure*) triggered the Peasants' Revolt (*practical adaptation*). Its leader, John Ball, used biblical authority to challenge serfdom (*ideological framing*). The revolt failed.

Instead, serfdom was fatally undermined by either local renegotiation (*practical adaptation*) or fleeing to other locations to work as free labourers under a different lord (*practical adaptation*) (*variation and selection*). By the early fifteenth century, serfdom had all but disappeared. The Black Death fractured feudalism and created widespread wage labour and other changes in legal status (*endogenous pressure*) (*economic change*) (*social change*) (*legal change*) (*institutional diffusion*).

Many small farmers gained control of their land through the institutional innovation of copyhold tenure (*legal change*). This granted autonomy to the peasant in terms of use and other rights. In some cases the copyhold could be sold, leased or used as security for a mortgage. The lord of the manor retained ultimate ownership and received a small rent. But this arrangement was put under pressure by the externally induced price inflation that began in the late fifteenth century and persisted during the Tudor period (*exogenous pressure*) (*endogenous pressure*). Many landlords tried to solve this problem by enclosing the lands, evicting the copyholders and tenants, and then raising sheep for the expanding and lucrative wool trade (*practical adaptation*) (*variation and selection*) (*social change*) (*economic change*).

But enclosures and rural depopulation created a problem for government (*endogenous pressure*). Under Henry VII and Henry VIII there were concerns that the reductions in the numbers of yeoman farmers would limit the availability of men for the county levies for the armed forces. It might also reduce revenues from land taxes. Lack of men and revenue would weaken England in war (*exogenous pressure*). A patriotic ideology, involving loyalty to the Crown, played a part here (*ideological framing*). That came into conflict with the notion of economic freedom expressed by many landowners (*ideological framing*). Repeated legislation was enacted in attempts to protect small farmers and to slow down enclosures and depopulation (*legal change*) (*variation and selection*).

Second Major Disturbance—the Reformation

In the Reformation, Henry VIII's break from Rome and his conversion to Protestantism enhanced his wealth and power (*exogenous pressure*) (*practical adaptation*) (*legal change*) (*ideological framing*). It created an increased military threat from foreign powers (*exogenous pressure*). The Dissolution of the Monasteries (*major endogenous disruption*) led to significant ruptures in social structure and patterns of landownership (*variation and selection*) (*social change*) (*legal change*). Much of the newly available land was sold to the rising gentry (*practical adaptation*).

In return, the King Henry revived some feudal laws and obligations to provide him with other sources of revenue, particularly for military purposes (*exogenous pressure*). These onerous renewals included knight service (in return for land tenure) and wardship (to help ensure that the land remained in the same family). Knight service could be commuted into a tax payment. Wardship meant major state interference in family affairs when the heir to the estate had not yet reached to age of majority. These laws affected many landowners (*practical adaptation*) (*legal change*).

Although these new laws were widely resented, many of the existing aristocracy and rising gentry wanted to preserve aspects of social hierarchy inherited from feudalism (*ideological framing*) (*endogenous pressure*). These ancient measures included entails that ensured that land was retained in the same family through the generations. Land was a source of status and privilege (*ideological framing*). But entails were attacked by economic liberals (*ideological framing*) such as Bacon and Coke, who argued for the removal of these restrictions on the sale of land (*endogenous pressure*) (*legal change*). Exogenous (*exogenous pressure*) and endogenous (*endogenous pressure*) disruptions led to strife over the tenure and use of the land, and over taxation and other legal interferences (*variation and selection*) (*legal change*).

There was an ideological struggle between doctrines of commercial liberty, of family influence and status, and of allegiance to king and country (*ideological framing*) (*endogenous pressure*). This ideological conflict grew through the Tudor and early Stuart dynasties and led in 1642 to the outbreak of Civil War (*major endogenous disruption*). In this disruptive context the Levellers developed radical, democratic, liberal ideas, and the Diggers practiced a small-scale, religious, agrarian communism (*ideological framing*) (*practical adaptation*). Both groups tried to address the concerns of the small farmers (*variation and selection*). These ideologies developed out of deep feelings and grievances in a period of major political upheaval (*political change*).

The Cromwellian Protectorate rejected the Leveller demand to convert copyhold into freehold tenure, which would have protected the yeoman farmers. It looked instead to the rising gentry, favouring them by abolishing knight service and the wardship laws and by tolerating enclosures (*legal change*) (*endogenous pressure*). Under King Charles II the abolition of knight service and wardship laws was quickly confirmed. But pleas to reform copyhold fell on deaf ears (*endogenous pressure*). Rights to enclose lands were sustained. The rising legal pressure to abolish entails was met by the institutional innovation of the strict settlement, which had the same conservative effect of keeping much land within the family (*practical adaptation*) (*legal change*). Some land was alienable, and under pressure from big landowners (*endogenous pressure*), the law was reformed to make mortgaging more attractive as a means of raising finance (*variation and selection*) (*legal change*) (*economic change*).

The reigns of Charles II and James II saw increasing conflict between the monarch and Parliament (*endogenous pressure*). On one side there was a growth and systematization of liberal ideas (*ideological framing*). On the other side there were vested interests in retaining landed property within families, and in making profits from colonial slavery and the slave trade, both of which were expressed in legal changes to serve rich lobbyists (*legal change*). The Catholic sympathies of King James II heightened the conflict with the Protestant majority (*ideological framing*). There was also pressure on James to align with France in a war against the Protestant United Provinces (*exogenous pressure*).

Third Major Disturbance—the Dutch Invasion and the Glorious Revolution

Partly to forestall a possible alliance of Britain and France against the United Provinces, William of Orange invaded England in 1688 (*major exogenous disruption*). He had previously contrived the support of six nobles and a bishop, creating the myth that it was not an invasion but a 'Glorious Revolution' (*ideological framing*). After years in recess, Parliament was recalled in 1689, leading to the *Declaration of Right* (*ideological framing*), and to some legislation to limit royal power and to ensure the continuity of Parliament (*legal change*) (*political change*). Parliament approved William and his wife Mary as joint sovereigns (*legal change*) (*political change*).

The shift in the balance of power from Crown to Parliament was of great significance. But an equally important effect of the Glorious Revolution was to switch Britain's foreign alliances. The Dutch became allies. The French and Spanish became enemies. From 1688 to 1815 Britain was plunged into over a century of intense war, punctuated by relatively brief periods of peace (*exogenous pressure*). For much of this time, Crown and Parliament were bound together in common cause (*practical adaptation*).

To finance the war machine (*exogenous pressure*), a land tax was inaugurated in 1692, but its heavy rates and its unmonitored administration by the local gentry put extreme burdens on the yeoman farmers (*legal change*) (*economic change*) (*social change*). Inspired by some institutional ideas borrowed from the Dutch, the Bank of England was formed in 1694 (*institutional diffusion*) (*legal change*) as the core of a new system of public finance and state administration, involving private capital (*practical adaptation*) (*economic change*) (*political change*) (*variation and selection*). The modernization of public finance led to standardized debt contracts and the development of new taxes and state bonds. A major effect of the Glorious Revolution was an enhanced state administration and a modernized financial system.

The bursting of the South Sea Bubble in 1720 was a major setback. But the needs of renewed war (*exogenous pressure*) promoted further financial reforms (*legal change*). Among these were the legal reforms required to establish workable and extensive markets for debt (*legal change*) (*practical adaptation*) (*variation and selection*) (*economic change*). The consolidation of these legal provisions for promissory notes or negotiable instruments occurred in the 1750s. This decade also saw the launch of Consols by the state, in an effort to finance the rapidly growing national debt (*endogenous pressure*) (*practical adaptation*) (*legal change*) (*economic change*). Consols were popular among those rich enough to invest in them (*practical adaptation*). Interest from and sales of Consols helped to finance more enclosures (*practical adaptation*) (*legal change*) (*economic change*).

These were the circumstances in which the Industrial Revolution occurred. Several of the early innovations were in hosiery and other high-end textiles, reflecting economic demand from the rich (*endogenous pressure*) (*practical adaptation*) (*economic change*) (*variation and selection*). The pace of the Industrial Revolution was held back by economic inequality and by the reluctance of many of the rich to invest in anything beyond land and Consols. Also the banking system was relatively weak and vulnerable (*legal change*) (*variation and selection*). But the military needs of war (*exogenous pressure*) were spurs for technological and institutional innovation (*endogenous pressure*) (*economic change*) (*social change*) (*legal change*). War also prompted efforts to reduce state corruption and increase administrative efficiency, especially after defeat in 1783 in the American War of Independence (*exogenous pressure*) (*practical adaptation*) (*variation and selection*). In this period British trade abroad—including the slave trade—expanded massively (*practical adaptation*) (*economic change*).

The preceding is a preliminary attempt at classifying the nature, sources, sites and outcomes of prominent institutional changes in the period. The historical material is varied and complex. The taxonomy of change will need refinement and extension to enable a deeper analysis of the different processes involved. Many of the major changes considered here have a legal character. It may be possible to root the categorizations in richer empirical soil, as evidenced, for example, in Ostrom's work. But that is a task for the future.[18]

Legal Institutionalism

In modern socio-economic systems, much economic and institutional evolution involved legal changes. These were practical adaptations. Ideas and ideology surfed these waves of change and sometimes helped to consolidate movements for reform or resistance. Ideas interacted and enabled further developments. Some ideas proved more powerful than others. The tag annotations in the preceding section reveal a number of legal changes and ideas, associating them with various pressures and disruptions. Non-legal changes are included too. Both are important.

As noted previously, legal institutionalism is based on some ontological claims. One concerns the ubiquity of legal and other rules in modern society. Another concerns the nature of law, it being an essential hybrid of state and private or customary arrangements. Also law accounts for many of the powerful rules and structures of modern capitalist society. Consequently, law is a constitutive part of the institutionalized power structure and a major means through which control is exercised. Law is not simply epiphenomenal. It helps to constitute key economic institutions, including property and money. Finally, law is an important motivational force, especially when it has perceived legitimacy.[19]

18. Crawford and Ostrom (1995), Ostrom (1990, 2005), Ostrom and Basurto (2011).
19. See Hodgson (2015a, chap. 4; 2015b; 2015c) and Deakin et al. (2017).

Legal institutionalism applies to large-scale societies under the rule of law. By contrast, in smaller-scale societies where interaction is typically on a personal level, customs and norms may suffice to maintain order and cooperation. Greater complexity and stratification came with the transition from tribal to larger-scale societies, with finer divisions of labour and permanent judicial institutions. Larger, more complex and stratified societies made much interaction more impersonal. Written legal records became necessary.[20]

The existence and functioning of complex state machines depend on the creation of habits of obeisance. In specific institutional and cultural circumstances, often involving the symbols and uniforms of state or legal power, we are disposed to accept and obey legal authority. Habits of obeisance buttress respect for authority and conformity to law. Previously, religious beliefs and institutions played a major part in the legitimation of law. Mixtures of nationalism and democratic involvement also help legitimate modern legal systems.[21]

Other rules matter, but legal rules are of particular force and importance in modern societies. The power of the law is not maintained solely by coercion and threat of punishment. Tom Tyler showed that most people feel obliged to obey laws when they perceive them as legitimate, and often for moral rather than instrumental reasons. People often obey laws out of respect for authority and justice, and not because they calculate advantages and disadvantages of compliance. Dispositions to respect authority have evolved over millions of years because they aided cohesion and survival of primate and human groups.[22]

English economic history reveals that some major legal changes have impinged directly on the practice of economic agents. Some laws led to adaptations in behaviour, and some to further institutional innovations. A peasant family required to pay a new land tax faced an immediate problem that required a practical solution. They could have increased the agricultural profitability of the farm, lowered their family consumption or sold their rights to the land to a member of the local gentry. Likewise, a rich landowner who faced legislation against entails, while wanting to keep the land in the family as a source of advancement and prestige, might have favoured the legal solution of a strict settlement. Legislation can provoke local adaptations and further

20. See Hodgson (2015a, chap. 3). Greif and Tabellini (2010, 2017) argued persuasively that the formation of state legal systems with associated moral norms was crucial in Europe's economic development.

21. Milgram (1974), Tyler (1990), Hodgson (2015a, chap. 3).

22. Darwin (1871), Milgram (1974), Tyler (1990), Haidt (2012).

change. These legal changes were not superstructural reactions to an 'economic base' that had already—in some unclear manner—been altered. They were fundamental changes that required a practical solution.

Legal institutionalism does not imply that informal institutions, non-legal institutions, customs or culture are unimportant. On the contrary, they are vital. Many laws were built historically upon preceding customs. Feudal manorial law was largely customary, and some customs—such as rules concerning entails—date from the Anglo-Saxon period. As the legislative system developed, customary rules played a part in the formulation of general legal rules. Furthermore, legal institutions always depend on customs and culture to work effectively. When a supportive culture is lacking, the law may prove moribund. For example, the caste system still survives in India today, despite it having been declared illegal for many years.

But also, legislation can change custom. For example, there is some evidence, cited in the following chapter, that the customary Japanese aversions to commercial haggling and litigation may result more from draconian legislation to prevent such disputes among merchants in the eighteenth century than from earlier traditional practices or beliefs. Other cultural changes, like legal changes, can result from exogenous shocks. An example is the (possibly brief) rise of the European Marriage Pattern, as a result of the Black Death, as discussed in chapter 3. Both legal (formal) institutions and non-legal (informal) institutions can change quickly, particularly as a result of perceived exogenous pressures or disruptions.[23]

23. Williamson (2000) and Roland (2004) suggested that culture changes more slowly than legislation. This may often be true, but we lack systematic evidence, and there may be exceptions. While there is a near-consensus on the definition of an institution as a system of rules (Hodgson, 2019a), there is much less agreement on the meaning of the distinction between formal and informal institutions. Among other contrasting usages, they are used to refer to rule systems that are written/unwritten, designed/undesigned or legal/non-legal. This confusion has inhibited research. My suggestion is to adopt the legal/non-legal understanding of formal/ informal institutions. Another problem is to distinguish the concept of culture from that of an institution, where they both often refer to rules, norms, values and beliefs. One proposal is to use the word *culture* to describe a set of traits that may be found in several institutions in a specific community (Hodgson, 2001, 298–300). These cultural elements might include traits such as individualism, hierarchy and masculinity, as defined by Hofstede (1984) and others. Alesina and Giuliano (2015, 902) proposed another option, where the term *institution* is confined to 'formal institutions (formal legal systems, formal regulation)' and *culture* is applied to 'values and beliefs' and 'informal rules'. With this option, the distinction between formal and

Generalizing Darwinism

This section outlines the conceptual framework that is commonly described as generalized Darwinism. It is not a theory of everything, but a metatheoretical framework that helps guide investigation into evolving populations, with the use of auxiliary theories. We have to start by considering the general features that populations of biological, socio-economic and other entities may share. Although the details are hugely different, these general features provide the point of entry for Darwinian evolutionary ideas.

Darwinism is a system of analysis that applies to populations of entities that have important similarities but also variations. These entities retain crucial information that guides their development and behaviour, including in response to external stimuli. Variation exists among these entities and the information they retain. Entities have some capacity to pass on information to others, including to their own offspring. They must consume resources to survive, and their capacities to survive or pass on information also vary. Darwinism addresses populations with these features and provides an analytical framework for identifying key factors that require further explanation. In short, Darwinism applies to what are defined as *complex population systems*.[24]

The informational programs that the entities retain, which guide their development and behaviour and may be passed on to others, are described as *replicators*. Replication is the process of copying such retained information from one entity to another. Darwin was unaware of genetics, and he speculated about the mechanisms of replication or inheritance. In biology, the genome is an important replicator. In human social evolution there are other replicators, as noted in the following. The entities in a population that host replicators are described as *interactors*.[25]

As Robert Brandon pointed out, replicators and interactors are generalizations of the biological concepts of genotype and phenotype, respectively. Actions are phenotypical expressions, but they are insufficient to constitute an interactor. The whole phenotype must be considered.[26]

---

informal institutions is dropped, and the latter term is replaced by culture. Unfortunately, researchers are still some distance from agreement on these basic terminological issues.

24. See Hodgson and Knudsen (2010) for a much fuller account.
25. Darwin (1859). The replicator-interactor terminology originates from Hull (1988).
26. Mokyr (2016, 9), Brandon (1996, 125).

Selection refers to the variations and processes that lead to some interactors living longer or replicating information more successfully than other interactors. The simplest form of selection is *subset selection*, where some members of an anterior set are eliminated, leaving survivors in a posterior set. For example, some firms in an industry go bankrupt. The more general form of selection is *successor selection*, where new entities are formed as offspring of members of the anterior set. For example, teams leave firms to create spin-off enterprises. Some members of the anterior set may also go bankrupt. The posterior set is related to the anterior set, but it is not a subset of the anterior set. Note that *successor selection* relies on the concept of replication, as well as on entities or interactors.[27]

Although the replicator-interactor distinction is sometimes overlooked, it is also necessary to distinguish between two aspects of any selection process. The *objects* of selection are the interactors that struggle for resources to survive. They may cooperate with others in that struggle. That struggle leads to differential survival and differential replication of specific replicators. That means an altered profile of replicator information in the surviving population. That is an *outcome* of selection. The distinction between *objects* and *outcomes* of selection is important and relies on the interactor-replicator distinction.

The development of individual interactors, responding to triggers from their environment and guided by the programs in their replicators, is one major type of evolutionary change. In biology this is known as *ontogeny*—it concerns the development of an individual organism. Another important source of evolutionary change in a population is selection, as mentioned in the previous paragraph. In biology this type of evolutionary change is known as *phylogeny*—it concerns changes in a whole population.

Evolution itself is a rather loose and ambiguous word, applying to many different kinds of change. Many people equate evolution solely with ontogeny, ignoring the dynamics of selection and population change. Similarly, some scholars describe the idea that history goes through pre-ordained stages as evolutionary. Again, this concentrates on the development of one system, as if unfolding 'from within'. This neglects the evolution of populations, which are emphasized in the Darwinian framework.

This account highlights what is now widely referred to as the variation-selection-replication (V-S-R) framework. This was developed by Darwin, although he used the term *inheritance* rather than replication. The V-S-R

27. Price (1995). On spin-offs, see Bünstorf (2009).

framework is at the core of Darwinism. It describes key features of Darwinian evolutionary processes. It gives us three crucial explanatory requirements: The sources of *variation* and its replenishment must be explained. The differential survival of interactors and the differential transmission of their replicators also require explanation. The manner in which information is retained and the mechanisms of its replication are also explanatory requirements. Note that specific explanations will vary from one kind of entity to another. As Darwin elucidated, the selection mechanisms affecting the beaks of Galapagos finches are very different from the selection mechanisms that lead to the peacock's tail or to human cooperation in tribal societies. Consequently, Darwinism is not a general theory that explains everything that happens in complex population systems. It is not like the laws of physics. Instead, Darwinism is a metatheoretical framework that guides further specific, auxiliary explanations, which typically apply in some cases but not in others.[28]

It is a widespread misconception that Darwinism excludes intentionality or forethought. On the contrary, Darwin tried to explain how self-reflection, reason, foresight, purposefulness and planning evolved in humans. They are foreshadowed in the non-human animal world. As Darwin wrote: 'A little dose . . . of judgment or reason often comes into play, even in animals very low in the scale of nature.' As he repeated elsewhere: 'Animals possess some power of reasoning. Animals may constantly be seen to pause, deliberate and resolve.' He believed that animals had limited powers of reasoning and prefiguration, and he neither belittled nor denied them for humans. On the contrary, he stressed their greater importance in the human domain.[29]

Darwinism does not take intentionality as given. It upholds that intentionality and other human mental capacities must have evolved from similar but less developed attributes among our pre-human ancestors. Intentionality among humans is an evolved capacity. Darwinism insists that intentionality must be explained and not simply assumed.

We should also note that Darwinian evolution does not necessarily lead to greater efficiency or progress. While the peacock's tail makes him more attractive to the peahen, and thus more likely to produce offspring, the tail also makes the peacock more vulnerable to predators. This dynamic of sexual selection is

---

28. Darwin (1859, 1871). Some authors use the words variation-selection-retention (Campbell, 1965). Retention is vital for replication to occur. Hence the replication concept embraces the retention of information as well.

29. Darwin (1859, 208; 1871, 1:46).

not necessarily optimal. Darwin denied that natural selection necessarily led to improvement. As he wrote in a letter to Charles Lyell in 1859: 'The theory of Natural Selection . . . implies no necessary tendency to progression.' In regard to human society, Darwin also wrote: 'We are apt to look at progress as the normal rule in human society; but history refutes this. . . . We must remember that progress is no invariable rule.' Evolutionary progress in human society is not inevitable.[30]

Applying Darwinism to Economic and Scientific Evolution

In human societies there are several different types of population. There are populations of states. Within states, there are different organizations, some of which together form populations. For example, there are populations of families and of business firms. The human individuals in a society also form a population. Information plays a crucial role throughout the system: it can be retained and replicated. Some members of these populations are more successful than others. Human societies are complex population systems.

Several authors, including Thorstein Veblen and Donald Campbell, have argued that Darwinian principles apply to the evolution of human society.[31] But clearly, the populations and processes involved in human society are very different from those found elsewhere, such as in the biological world. Does the V-S-R framework still apply?

Consider nation states. They are different from one another—variety exists for historical and geographical reasons. There is rivalry between them. In the long run, over thousands of years, some states get eliminated and new ones are born. The creation or elimination of states implies selection. But in shorter periods of time, in the order of a hundred years, selection is infrequent at the level of nation states. States are born or eliminated infrequently. In shorter time spans, selection is less important as a mechanism of change. Changes in states are then mostly matters of institutional development, prompted by external or internal pressures. Ontogeny becomes more important than phylogeny. Internal developmental processes are paramount, including those prompted by exogenous shocks.

30. F. Darwin (1887, 2:210), Darwin (1871, 1:166, 177).
31. Veblen (1898a, 1899), Campbell (1965). Hodgson and Knudsen (2010, 6–13, 18–21) cited additional precursors.

When secession occurs, such as when the United States gained independence from Britain in 1783, institutional characteristics from the mother country are often passed onto the new offspring state. These include important features of the legal system. In addition, some states copy the institutions of others. Japan voluntarily copied some European institutions after the Meiji Restoration. These are all processes of replication.

Selection becomes more important when we look within nations. The selection of organizations, families and individuals is frequent, even with shorter time scales, say decades. For example, growing industrialization led to competition among manufacturing firms. New enterprises appeared and others went under. At this level and timescale there is strong selection pressure and a clear process of selection. Selection upon organizations changed the distribution of habits (including skills) in the participating population. Some individuals were more successful than others, affecting their chances of survival and procreation. Patterns of habit and skill were altered, partly by selection processes and partly by adaptive developments in response to new challenges. There was also the replication of ideas from one organization (including families as well as firms) to another.

There were strong, two-way interactions between state institutions and the V-S-R processes at the organizational and individual levels. Legislation and taxation are examples. They had strong downward effects on farmers and landowners. It seems, for example, that many yeoman farmers were forced to sell their farms as a result of the 1692 land tax. There were upward effects too, for example after the Restoration, when the big landowners put pressure on Chancery to reform mortgage law.

Consider the importance of exogenous disruptions. Following Charles Tilly and others, this book has emphasized the ways in which rivalries and conflicts between nations force their states to adapt. Raising taxes for war puts downward pressures on organizations and individuals. War can also create business opportunities and spur technological innovation. At the level of the state, exogenous disruption is often more important than selection. But these disruptions can intensify selection at the organizational and individual levels.

Exogenous disruptions are important in biology too, and their importance is not confined to catastrophic extinctions that wipe out most species and provide opportunities for survivors. As the biologist and ecologist Wayne P. Sousa argued:

> Disturbance is both a major source of temporal and spatial heterogeneity in the structure and dynamics of natural communities and an agent of

natural selection in the evolution of life histories. . . . A disturbance is a discrete, punctuated killing, displacement, or damaging of one or more individuals (or colonies) that directly or indirectly creates an opportunity for new individuals (or colonies) to become established. Both physical and biological processes act as agents of disturbance. . . . Regimes of disturbance vary considerably along a number of spatial and temporal scales.[32]

The mechanisms and details are different in the human social world, but exogenous disturbances are an important feature in biological contexts as well.

Consider the evolution of science. At the most basic level, ideas are transmitted from individuals to individuals. Individuals are a type of interactor. Their habits of thought (ideas) are a type of replicator. But science would not be able to progress very far, or at much speed, if that were the whole story. Organizations are important too. Mokyr stressed the importance of the European 'Republic of Letters' as a crucible for exchanging, criticizing and developing ideas. But it lacked sufficient organized authority to establish modern science. Organized authority in science depends on closer, more organized and more intensive interactions. These can help to refine the selection process and, under the right conditions, promote experts who are more knowledgeable and ideas that are more useful. In the evolution of science, an efficacious selection environment is vital.

Hence, crucial for the evolution of science in Britain was the creation of learned societies and networks. The Royal Society of London for Improving Natural Knowledge was founded in 1660. The Society for the Encouragement of Arts, Manufactures and Commerce was founded in 1754. The Lunar Society of Birmingham (it held its meetings when the moon was full) met regularly from the 1760s, and its attendees included Matthew Boulton, Erasmus Darwin, Richard Lovell Edgeworth, Samuel Galton, Joseph Priestley, James Watt and Josiah Wedgwood.[33]

Some other early scientific groups met in the London coffee houses. These institutions and meetings created networks of scientists and inventors and

32. Sousa (1984, 354–57). See also Vermeij (1995).

33. Erasmus Darwin was a physician and scientist, and a grandfather of Charles Darwin and Francis Galton. Richard Lovell Edgeworth was a politician and inventor, and a grandfather of the economist Francis Y. Edgeworth. Samuel Galton was an arms manufacturer and the other grandfather of Francis Galton. Joseph Priestley is one of those credited with the isolation and discovery of oxygen. Josiah Wedgwood was a pottery entrepreneur and the other grandfather of Charles Darwin. Clearly, family connections were important too.

established interactive communities of researchers. They established routines for the scrutiny of new candidates to ensure that their deliberations were well-informed. Darwin was not a lone scientific entrepreneur. He built up a network of collaborators and critics to help test and refine his ideas. These organizations and networks foreshadowed the modern institutions of science, as located in universities and other research institutes.[34]

The organized authority of experts, involving sufficient mutual trust, helps to obtain assent to scientific claims. Trust and authority are necessary because no one can be an expert on more than a tiny fraction of the relevant knowledge. These considerations bring in institutions, as well as culture. These scientific organizations are the *interactors* of modern scientific research and technological development. They evolve in response to external pressures, through internal selection of people and ideas.[35]

Darwinism as a Unifying Theoretical Framework

In sum, Darwinian ideas including the V-S-R framework can be usefully applied to the socio-economic changes that occurred in England from 1300 to 1820 and thereafter. But Darwinian ideas, as in biology and elsewhere, are insufficient on their own. They provide a metatheoretical framework to guide further empirical and theoretical investigation. Auxiliary hypotheses, immersed in empirical data, are also required.

How do the over-arching Darwinian principles generate relevant questions and guide research? Consider an example. Human socio-economic evolution has accelerated in the past few millennia, with even more spectacular developments in the past few hundred years. What has caused this remarkable acceleration of economic output and socio-economic complexity? Generalized Darwinism helps us look for answers. Theorists working in this area have asked about the conditions under which replication can lead to increased complexity. Part of the answer involves improvements in replicative or copying fidelity of key information in socio-economic systems, including institutional rules and technology. This insight directs our attention to dramatic improvements in the accuracy, speed and reliability of information storage and transmission in the last few hundred years, from the spread of moveable type printing in the

34. See Edgeworth and Edgeworth (1844, 118–19), as quoted in Hodgson (2019d, 6), Kitcher (1993, 11–31), Polanyi (1962).

35. Polanyi (1958, 1962), Hull (1988), Kitcher (1993).

fifteenth century to computers and the internet today. Modern socio-economic evolution has seen the development of new social modes of storing and replicating information. Previously, there have been major informational transitions, from the evolution of language and writing to modern institutions that process laws and sustain progress in science and technology. We must investigate further, but the framework of generalized Darwinism points us in these directions.[36]

As another example, we have noted that the role of selection, in shorter timeframes than millennia, is less at the level of states. At the state level, instead of selection, there is an important dynamic of military and political rivalry and exogenous disruptions, leading to more significant selection pressures at lower levels. The absence of strong eliminative selection on nation states in shorter time periods has focused our attention on the importance of internal mechanisms and exogenous pressures that lead to institutional or policy changes within states. The Darwinian idea of multi-level selection, operating at different speeds and intensities, has led to more specific questions about evolutionary change, with a focus on selection, variety-creation and replication at levels below and within states themselves. This is another example of how new questions are guided and generated by the Darwinian framework. The framework itself does not provide the answers, but it guides the lines of enquiry. Empirical work is vital to answer those questions. Darwinism is not the answer to everything.

The use of a Darwinian framework to guide and inspire research in economic history dovetails with the psychological perspective outlined earlier in this chapter, where 'ideas first' or 'mind first' perspectives were demoted in favour of evolutionary-grounded approaches based on instincts and habits. Instinctive capacities evolved first. Then some species acquired the capacity to form habits. Then humans evolved and became capable of rational deliberation and the communication of ideas. The temporal and ontological primacy of instinct and habit, over reason and ideas, applies over millions of years. That primacy is also present in the development (ontogeny) and daily functioning of each human being: reason and ideas are built upon and empowered by habits, passions and emotions.

Shifts in circumstances can create new problems requiring a solution. Humans adapt by deploying a repertoire of feelings and reasons. They often

36. Hodgson and Knudsen (2010, chaps. 6–9).

cooperate with others to try to find a way forward. Ideologies are often too ambiguous to serve as primary movers. The power of religion, for example, typically depends on contestable scriptural interpretations of selected texts. Typically, ideas come in to rationalize the chosen solutions. Changes in human society stir up long-evolved instincts, channelled into habits of thought and behaviour, leading to action legitimated by systems of ideas.

7

A Comparison with Japan and Concluding Remarks on Economic Development

[The] British ... are paying the penalty for having been thrown into the lead and so having shown the way. ... The shortcomings of this British industrial situation are visible chiefly by contrast with what the British might be doing if it were not for the restraining dead hand of their past achievement.

—THORSTEIN VEBLEN, *IMPERIAL GERMANY* (1915)

THIS BOOK FOCUSES on England. The emphasis has been on the institutions that helped or hindered its economic development. These include the legal forms of landownership, and the financial institutions necessary for industrial investment, innovation and growth. Other studies of economic development in multiple countries have also underlined the importance of finance, of land tenure, of effective legal systems and of capable state administrations. Some development scholars have stressed the importance of alienable landed property, with appropriate institutions including land registries and viable mortgage facilities. These may help to form a pump-priming system for the financing of industrial entrepreneurship and innovation. Accordingly, can other countries learn lessons from the English experience?[1]

1. On financial development, see King and Levine (1993), Rajan and Zingales (1998), Beck et al. (2003), Rousseau (2003), Levine (2005), Sarma and Pais (2011), Kendal (2012), Emenalo et al. (2018), Heblich and Trew (2019), Raghutla and Chittedi (2021). On land alienability and

As a step toward a fuller answer, this chapter begins with a comparison of Britain and Japan, notwithstanding the huge differences in their histories and culture. The choice of Japan is not random. By reasonable criteria, very few countries that could be classified as underdeveloped in 1950 have become developed by the year 2000. Japan is one. It is one of only a few economies that have moved from low to high levels of development since 1950.

Of course, it all depends on what we mean by underdevelopment and development. What could 'underdeveloped' in 1950 mean? Consider Angus Maddison's GDP per capita figures for selected countries. A 1950 maximum of $2,000 (expressed in 1990 dollars) GDP per capita per year is a reasonable threshold to capture underdevelopment. To identify development, we need a second threshold. A 1998 level of $12,000 minimum GDP per capita per year (expressed in 1990 dollars) is chosen. The development threshold is six times greater than the one for underdevelopment. Examining Maddison's data, very few countries have moved from below the 1950 threshold of $2,000 per capita to above the 1998 threshold of $12,000 per capita. They are, namely, Japan, South Korea and Taiwan.[2]

Some other countries came close, including Greece, Hong Kong, Portugal, Singapore and Spain. But Greece was below the $12,000 threshold in 1998, and Hong Kong, Portugal, Singapore and Spain were above the $2,000 threshold in 1950. Hong Kong and Singapore could reasonably be excluded because of their lower populations and smaller land areas. Funding from the European Union significantly boosted the development of Greece, Portugal and Spain in the 1980s and 1990s. These special circumstances provide another reason for excluding them. We are left with Japan, South Korea and Taiwan.

Notably, Korea was a Japanese colony from 1910 to 1945 and Taiwan was a Japanese colony from 1895 to 1945. These countries adopted some Japanese institutions. Korea was divided into two in 1945. Hence the choice of Japan has significance for Taiwan and South Korea as well. Despite a major growth slowdown since 1990, Japan is a key exemplar of successful economic development.

Table 7.1 compares Japan, South Korea and Taiwan with the United States. Japanese economic growth has been spectacular. The figures for South Korea

---

mortgaging, see De Soto (2000), Dam (2006a, 2006b), Steiger (2006, 2008), Arruñada (2012, 2017), Heinsohn and Steiger (2013), Hodgson (2015a, 2015b).

2. Maddison (2003, 276–327).

TABLE 7.1. GDP per capita in Japan, South Korea and the United States, 1870–2020

Year	Japan	South Korea	Taiwan	United States
In 1990 US\$ per year				
1870	737	663	554	
1950	1,926	770	936	9,561
1998	20,410	12,152	15,012	26,453
As a percentage of US GDP per capita in the same year				
1950	20.1%	8.1%	9.8%	100.0%
1998	77.2%	45.9%	56.7%	100.0%
2020	66.4%	67.9%	86.7%	100.0%

Sources: For 1870, 1950 and 1998: Maddison (2003, 212, 277–79, 304; 2007, 385) in 1990 US\$. For 2020: World Bank (2021).

and Taiwan are even more impressive. Instead of the \$2,000 and \$12,000 thresholds discussed earlier, an alternative way of looking at comparative development would be to examine each country's GDP per capita as a percentage of the US level, in the same year. These calculations appear in the bottom three rows of the table. (These percentages are less meaningful for 1870, as the United States was not the world leader in GDP per capita at that time. In 1870 that leader was the United Kingdom, by some margin.) Japan, South Korea and Taiwan all moved from below 21 per cent of US GDP per capita in 1950 to above 66 per cent in 2020. No other country has achieved such rapid and complete transitions from underdevelopment to development.[3]

Japan was heavily bombed during the Second World War, and some of the economic growth for a decade or so after 1945 may be due to aided reconstruction of buildings and infrastructure. But this would be insufficient to explain its spectacular growth from 1955 to 1990.

3. China is now the largest economy in the world in terms of purchasing power parity (PPP) GDP. But its nominal GDP (which reflects its weight on world markets) was estimated in 2022 at about 78 per cent of that of the US (International Monetary Fund, 2022). In GDP per capita terms, China is still well behind the leading developed countries. In 2020 Chinese GDP per capita (by one PPP measure) was estimated at 27 per cent of the level in the US (Central Intelligence Agency, 2022). Chinese growth has slowed, and further growth will require major institutional reforms (Rodrik, 2003; Hodgson and Huang, 2013; Hodgson 2015a, 335–43). It is very unlikely that China will soon overtake the leading developed countries in GDP per capita terms.

Some Institutional Aspects of Japanese Development

Until the end of the sixteenth century, Japan was divided into a number of warring states. Moves towards national unification were made under the *daimyo* (lord) Oda Nobunaga in the 1560s, and they gathered momentum from 1585 under the leadership of Toyotomi Hideyoshi, who eventually became the emperor's chief minister and advisor. But local states retained some autonomy until after the Meiji Restoration.

Remarkably, Nobunaga established a register of land in areas under his political control. Hideyoshi followed Nobunaga's example to establish a basic land survey of the whole of Japan in the 1590s, and he reorganized the system of landownership. Land was allotted to about 270 local *daimyo*, who acquired duties of administration and were granted rights of taxation. They taxed about 40 per cent of peasant produce. *Daimyo* rights and duties were inherited by succeeding members of their families. The countryside became a system of villages, with small farmers under territorial, hereditary lords. The *daimyo* themselves were under the control of the *shogun* (military ruler), who was nominally appointed by the emperor.[4]

Land registration happened much earlier in feudal Japan than in capitalist England. But the Japanese land registry of the 1590s was not updated regularly. There was local resistance to new surveys, partly out of fear of increased taxation being a consequence of more accurate registries of ownership. This landowner resistance to registration is redolent of England in the eighteenth century. Land in Japan could not be sold or mortgaged until the eighteenth century, when wealthy merchants began to circumvent the national laws governing landownership.[5]

The Tokugawa Shogunate ruled Japan from 1603 to 1868. Japanese society was consolidated as a rigid class system, and trade with the outside world was severely restricted. Central control by the *shogun* was combined with a degree of autonomy by the *daimyo* at a local level. The *shogun* kept the families of the *daimyo* in Edo (the old name of Tokyo and home of the Shogunate) as hostages, to keep the *daimyo* under control. The Shogunate imposed drastic restrictions on the power of the emperor, who remained largely a ceremonial figurehead. The legal system relied extensively upon customary precedents.

4. Lockwood (1954, 3–4), Oda (1992, 19).
5. Oda (1992, 23).

But national legislation increased during this period, leading to a more system-atized and comprehensive body of law.[6]

In 1742 a systematic legal code was enacted. But its provisions for legal rights were limited. The law was used more as an instrument of political con-trol than as a means to establish individual or group rights. It was not designed primarily to deal with disputes over property or contracts. Instead, informal settlements or compromises in such disputes were encouraged, sometimes by the threat of state punishment of both parties. The modern Japanese reputa-tion for the extra-legal resolution of disputes in part may have an historic ori-gin in institutional changes and state directives in the eighteenth century. The supposed Japanese aversion to litigation seems to have more to do with its evolving legal institutions than being something inherent and longstanding in the Japanese culture. From 1742 to 1868 markets for goods, and some financial markets, developed in Japan, along with the increasing wealth of the low-status merchant class.[7]

For Japan to modernize, the conservative resistance of the Shogunate had to be broken. In 1853, and then in 1854, American gunships arrived in Tokyo Bay. They forced insular feudal Japan to trade much more widely with the outside world and to open up more of its ports. An internal movement for reform gathered momentum. It turned to the young Emperor Meiji as a fig-urehead. To get the farmers on their side, the reformers promised large reduc-tions in burdensome land taxes. The reformers marched on Kyoto and took the Imperial Palace. In the Meiji Restoration of 1868, Imperial rule was re-stored. The Shogunate was defeated in a subsequent civil war. In contrast to England, institutional change was facilitated by shifting power upwards towards the hereditary ruler, rather than by a Parliament countervailing the powers of the monarch. Also in contrast to England, the Meiji forces relied on the support of the peasant farmers and the military, rather than the lords and large landowners.

Under the Meiji Emperor and his ministers, Japan began to copy Western political, legal and military institutions and to adopt Western technological know-how. It developed a modern state administration. The fear that Western powers could colonise Japan, as they had already done in many places in East Asia, was a spur to rapid modernization and militarization. The legal system

---

6. Anderson (1974, 441–58).

7. Smith (1988), Oda (1992, 20–24), Sorenson (2010). Ginsburg and Hoetker (2006) sum-marised the scholarly debate over the causes of lower litigation rates in Japan.

was modernised, partly to encourage foreign governments to accept Japanese jurisdiction over trade and residence within Japanese territory. In an effort to stimulate indigenous Japanese entrepreneurship, foreign direct investment was generally disallowed. Modernisation was in part a defensive reaction to perceived external threats, and in part to grasp opportunities provided by expanded involvement in international trade.[8]

One of the first acts of the Meiji regime in 1868 was to declare that the farmers with customary possession of the land would own it outright. This often meant that the richer village farmers became owners of the land, leaving other farmers still working as tenants. Restrictions on what crops could be grown were abolished in 1871. In another major reform in that year, the previous feudal arrangements based on landed domains was replaced by a system of prefectures under the control of the Imperial government. The *daimyo* were replaced by the centrally appointed governors.[9]

Extensive changes were made to the law and governance of landed property. In 1872 the previous prohibition on buying and selling land was annulled. Title deeds were issued to the landowning farmers. A major land reform began in 1873, leading to the replacement of the feudal land tax by a modernized system, based on a new and comprehensive survey of landed property, with a nationally uniform rate of tax replacing wide local variations. By about 1875 Japan had an effective modern land registry. The amount of taxable land was increased by about 48 per cent, by updating the records of land usage and finding land that had been hidden from the records. But variations in previous concealment meant that the effects of the new land surveys were uneven, with some peasants facing a heavier tax burden than before. The Japanese land reforms had a number of objectives, including to enhance private property rights and to facilitate Japanese economic expansion and military capability. Another aim was to remove the hereditary sources of income and power from the *daimyo*, thus quashing a possible threat to Imperial rule. The *daimyo* received compensation for their lost privileges. They were bought off to achieve land reform.[10]

Subsequently, there was a steady rise in agricultural productivity. Land mortgaging became more frequent. Sometimes mortgages were raised to fund

8. Oda (1992, 24–26).

9. Waswo (1977).

10. Lockwood (1954, 26, 513–14, 521), Dore (1959), Nakamura (1966), Oda (1992, 25–26), Sorenson (2010).

agricultural improvements. In other cases they were raised to pay taxes. Mort-gage default bankrupted some farmers, and richer landowners sometimes took over their land. The Meiji land reforms crushed feudalism, but they were fol-lowed by growing inequality in landownership among farmers.[11]

Not without some resistance, the *samurai* were compensated by pensions and government bonds. Many of them took positions in the public administra-tion or education. Others became industrial entrepreneurs. Unlike England, the aristocracy (below the emperor and consisting of the *daimyo* and the *samurai*) lost much of its influence. The Japanese state machine was dominated by the military and the ministerial bureaucracies. Japan implemented a strategy of 'elite redeployment' that removed vested interest groups that blocked progress.[12]

After Japan took some institutional inspiration from France, German (par-ticularly Prussian) legal and political ideas became more influential. The first constitution, drafted with German advice, was adopted in 1889. Property rights were declared inviolate, except by just legal process to remove them. The em-peror was sanctified and freed from parliamentary or other control. The role of the Diet (parliament) was to assist and support the emperor. Civil, com-mercial and criminal laws were drafted with the help of German advisors in the 1890s. Unlike England, Japan did not develop a system of common law. It adopted a German-style civil code. The Bank of Japan was founded in 1882 using the Belgian central bank as a model. The banking system was reorga-nized, with a leading role for the central bank. As William W. Lockwood noted, there was 'a persistent bias in favor of monetary expansion'. In the 1890s Japan began a process of rapid industrialization under the slogan: 'Enrich the coun-try and strengthen the army.'[13]

Among the major drivers of financial development were defence and military expansion. After victories in wars against China (1894–95) and Russia (1904–5), Japan gained control of Korea and Taiwan. Japanese legal rules on land tenure and other matters spread to Korea and Taiwan and several other colonies.[14] A few years with representative democracy (1912–26) were overshadowed by increasing expansionism and the growing power of the military. Universal adult male suffrage was introduced in 1925. But the army and authoritarian nationalists became more influential. Civil liberties

11. Bird (1977), Waswo (1977).

12. Lockwood (1954, 10), Yamada (2022).

13. Lockwood (1954, 11, 514–17, 520), Oda (1992, 27–32), Sorenson (2010).

14. Smitka (1998), Yoo and Steckel (2016).

were eroded. Japan invaded Manchuria in 1931 and other parts of China in 1937. The Diet became a rubber stamp for the military, and full military rule began in 1936. The attack on Pearl Harbor in 1941 brought Japan fully into the Second World War. Japan surrendered after atomic bombs were dropped on Hiroshima and Nagasaki in 1945. It was then an impoverished nation, much destroyed by war.

The Allied occupation from 1945 led to major economic restructuring and the re-instigation of representative democracy. American political and legal institutions became an important influence for post-war Japan. Women were given the vote for the first time. As well as the adoption of a new constitution, major land reforms were enforced under Allied pressure. One-third of the farmland was purchased by the government and sold to its tenants at a reduced price. These reforms amounted to a radical redistribution of landed wealth. But restrictions were imposed on the sale of land, to prevent the agglomeration of large estates by the rich.[15]

Japanese GDP per capita grew at an average annual rate of 1.48 per cent from 1870 to 1913, 0.88 per cent from 1913 to 1950, and a massive 8.06 per cent per annum from 1950 to 1973. A new industrial model emerged in the 1930s, combining corporate networks and state strategic guidance. After the Second World War, the developmental state was a key driver of economic expansion. The country was transformed from an isolated agricultural backwater into a major industrial power.[16]

Just before to the Meiji Restoration, literacy rates in Japan were about 35 per cent for men and 8 per cent for women. It is estimated that by 1910 about 70–80 per cent of males and 60–75 per cent of females were literate. For the population as a whole, literacy rates more than trebled in fifty years.[17]

Japanese economic development was powered by a growing financial sector. Despite relatively high interest rates, finance was instrumental in promoting new agricultural and industrial technologies. The strategic influence of the state was also crucial. Data gathered by David J. Ott show that in the 1878–85 business cycle the net issue of primary securities, including the national government debt, local government bonds, corporate bonds and corporate stock,

15. Dore (1959), Sorenson (2010).

16. Maddison (2007, 176), Johnson (1982, 1995), Dore (1986), Smith (1988), Vestal (1993), Wolferen (1993), Morris-Suzuki (1996), Okazaki and Okuno-Fujiwara (1999), Steinmo (2010, chap. 3).

17. Dore (1965, 321), Taira (1971).

amounted to only 4.1 per cent of national income. The national government debt was then zero. By the 1902–8 business cycle, the net issue of primary securities amounted to 16.3 per cent of national income, almost two-thirds of which was national government debt. During the 1938–46 period, the net issue of primary securities amounted to 31.2 per cent of national income, almost two-thirds of which was again national government debt. These data show that Japan built up substantial financial capacity prior to its defeat in the Second World War. For several years after the war, these figures were much lower, as Japan was rebuilding its financial, corporate and administrative institutions. But financial institutions remained central to Japanese development.[18]

Raymond W. Goldsmith's financial data provide a complementary picture. The financial intermediation ratio (the ratio of claims against financial institutions to all financial assets) rose from 25.5 per cent in 1875 to 41.2 per cent in 1929. This 1929 ratio was higher than that in all other countries mentioned by Goldsmith, including France, Germany, Great Britain and the United States. This confirms the strength of Japan's financial institutions in the interwar period.[19]

In Japan the financial interrelations ratio (the ratio of financial to tangible assets) was 30.4 per cent in 1885. This compares with financial interrelations ratios in Britain of 74.7 per cent and the United States of 62.9 per cent in the same year. In 1912–13 the financial interrelations ratios were 63.7 per cent in Japan, 143.2 per cent in Britain and 80.0 per cent in the United States. In 1955 the financial interrelations ratio in Japan was 53.9 per cent, compared with 177.0 in Britain in 1948 and 112.0 per cent in the United States in 1950. While Japan was then much poorer than the leading Western economies, its financial system developed rapidly.[20]

A crucial difference between Japan and England is that the Meiji Restoration successfully disempowered key elites, including those that had control over the land. By contrast, rich English landed families retained and enlarged their power and influence, and the yeoman farmers became extinct. In Japan, way ahead of England, land registration was completed in the 1870s. This enabled a more efficient system of land taxation that was less punitive for most small farmers. Land reforms after the Second World War enhanced the influence and economic viability of small farmers. Consequently, Japan

18. Lockwood (1954, 288–91, 513), Ott (1961).
19. Goldsmith (1985, 136).
20. Goldsmith (1985, 109–14).

today is one of the more equal of developed economies in terms of the distribution of wealth.[21]

Contrary to the literature on 'legal origins', Japan's adoption of a system of civil law (in contrast to England's common law system) does not seem to have inhibited growth.[22] The Japanese financial system grew rapidly, reaching a high level of development as early as 1929. Initially under a strong military aegis, Japan established a powerful developmental state, which was radically adapted under a democratic regime in the post-war period.

Possible Explanations of Japanese Development

The Japanese success story challenges some institutional theories of economic development. In particular, the claim by Douglass North and Barry Weingast that economic development is promoted by 'secure property rights', where the power of the monarch is countervailed by a relatively strong parliament, does not work in Japan.[23] On the contrary, the institutional foundations of Japanese modernization were built by revolutionary oligarchs, using the emperor as their figurehead. From 1868 to 1945 Japan was bound together by nationalist ideology and Imperial symbolism, heightened by real or proclaimed military threats from outside. Landed property rights became relatively secure, not because the Diet kept the emperor under control, but because the Meiji regime relied on the support of the small landowning farmers, the merchants and the manufacturers.

Deirdre McCloskey's emphasis on the positive role of liberal ideas does not fare well for the period before 1945 in Japan. From 1870 to 1913, under nationalist and authoritarian rule, GDP per capita grew faster in Japan than in Britain in the same period. Liberal and democratic values became pervasive in Japan only after the Allied occupation in 1945.

Marxists fare no better. There has been protracted dispute among Marxists on whether the Meiji Restoration was a bourgeois revolution. Perry Anderson

21. In terms of incomes, the most egalitarian countries, such as Denmark, Finland, Norway and Sweden, are more equal than Japan. But if we turn to inequalities in the distribution of wealth, Japan is much more equal than Norway or Sweden (Credit Suisse Research Institute, 2019; OECD, 2021).

22. Glaeser and Shleifer (2002). For a review of the evidence on the importance (or otherwise) of legal origins, see Dam (2006b, chap. 2).

23. North and Weingast (1989).

pointed out that it was one of the most abrupt transitions from feudalism to capitalism, and the Meiji insurgents had substantial support from the merchants and manufacturers. But it was not a seizure of power by the bourgeoisie. Although devoted to capitalism, the Meiji state was monarchical and militaristic.[24]

Robert Allen pointed to the contrast between England, where landownership became concentrated into the hands of the aristocracy and rich gentry, and the fast-growing economies of South Korea and Taiwan, where small farmers own much of the agricultural land. After the Meiji Restoration and the land reforms of the 1870s, Japan became a land of small, owner-occupied, family farms. The aristocracy was deprived of land and power. Similar arrangements spread from Japan to its colonies. Based on his evidence from England, Allen surmised that small-scale, owner-occupied farming is generally more conducive to economic development. By contrast, the concentrated, large-scale landownership in England hindered economic growth and created mass unemployment. These arguments may help to explain the spectacular economic transformation of Japan, South Korea and Taiwan in the second half of the twentieth century.

From the little evidence we have, it seems that a greater proportion of Japanese land was alienable in 1880 than in the same year in England. With viable registration, this alienable land could be used as collateral to raise finance. As later in South Korea and Taiwan, land registration greatly facilitates sales and mortgage transactions.[25]

Because of the radical land reforms and the relegation of the aristocracy from power, Japan was not held back by a landowning aristocracy and gentry, as in England. The demotion of big landowners was possible in Japan because the Imperial bureaucracy and the military were dominant from 1868 to 1945. After 1945, further land reforms redistributed land still further. By contrast, in Britain the aristocracy still retains enormous wealth and influence. Even where members of the lower classes have risen to take over powerful positions in the British government and state machine, they have done so within institutions that bear the hallmarks of aristocratic supremacy. These include the enduring elitist elements in the British education system.

24. Hoston (1991), Anderson (1974, 461), Marx (1973a, 69).
25. Yoo and Steckel (2016) provided quantitative evidence of the economic effectiveness of land registration in a Japanese island colony.

As with England, much more empirical work needs to be done on Japan, South Korea and Taiwan to establish relative importance of the factors highlighted in this analysis. If corroboration of some key points were forthcoming, then they would apply not only to England but also to the three most remarkable cases of economic transformation into developed countries in the second half of the twentieth century, despite their different histories, structures and cultures. It would also illuminate the kind of institutions that are needed to cross the 'middle income trap' and move into the ranks of the developed countries. Few apart from these three Asian countries have made this transition.[26]

The experiences in both Britain and Japan suggest that a major precondition of economic development is the building of a relatively efficient state administration, effective methods of gathering taxes, and public and private institutions that enable the financing of military defence and economic infrastructure. In both cases, state-building was driven by the needs of war and the expansion of empire. A stress on the 'security of property rights' is insufficient. The nature of property and its connection with finance and politics have to be better understood. On this we can learn lessons from Britain, Japan, South Korea and Taiwan, despite their very different histories and cultures.

Land registration is important, but it is only part of the story. Britain may have been held back by the absence of a universal land registry until the late twentieth century, but it still became the first industrial nation. The United States still lacks a universal land registry and relies instead on title insurance for real estate transactions. The World Bank has been promoting land registries in developing countries, but with mixed success. They are difficult to operate effectively when there is widespread corruption in the state and its legal system. Good governance is necessary to make land registration work. In addition, for poor farmers, land registration can be relatively costly, with few or any perceived benefits. Unless counter measures are in force, introducing systematic land registration can lead to speculative land acquisition, often favouring males with influential social connections, thus creating a more unequal structure of landownership, while further disadvantaging women and the poor. Effective land registration is difficult to establish. It is not a panacea.[27]

Consider Japanese economic development, using the categories and tags deployed in the English case in the preceding chapter. In the much shorter period from 1850 to 1960, Japan experienced two major exogenous shocks.

26. See, for example, Lee (2013).
27. Bromley (2009), Deininger and Feder (2009, esp. 240), Arruñada (2017, 2018).

Exogenous Shocks Led to the Meiji Restoration of 1868
(major exogenous disruption) (political change) (legal change)

The arrival of US warships in Tokyo Bay in 1853 and 1854 forced Japan to trade with the outside world. From 1868 the new Meiji regime was concerned to modernise and militarize Japan *(endogenous pressure)*, to expand its territory and to protect it from assault by foreign powers *(exogenous pressure)*. It built up support among the small farmers and made them a powerful group *(practical adaptation)* by implementing land reform and land registration *(legal change) (social change) (economic change) (variation and selection)*. To finance industrialization and militarization *(practical adaptation)* the government imposed a uniform land tax *(legal change) (economic change)*. Former landlords *(daimyo)* received compensation, along with the samurai *(practical adaptation) (social change)*. Institutional, legal and technological ideas were borrowed from abroad *(institutional diffusion) (practical adaptation) (legal change) (exogenous pressure)*. A modern financial system was developed *(practical adaptation) (legal change) (economic change) (variation and selection)*. Japan defeated China and Russia *(exogenous pressure)* and expanded its territory. Military rule began in 1936, leading to further expansionism *(endogenous pressure) (political change) (legal change) (economic change)*.

Second Major Exogenous Shock—the Occupation of Japan by
the Allies in 1945 (major exogenous disruption) (political
change) (social change) (legal change)

Allied authority *(exogenous pressure)* led to several major institutional changes *(practical adaptation) (variation and selection) (major endogenous disruption)* including the introduction of a Western-style democracy *(institutional diffusion)* and further land reform *(legal change) (political change) (economic change) (social change)*. Partly making use of Western industrial knowledge and organization *(institutional diffusion)*, Japan built a rapidly growing modern industrial economy *(economic change) (social change)*.

This short analysis shows that exogenous shocks and perceived pressures prompted important legal and social changes that led to Japan's economic development. With two major exogenous shocks in the space of less than a hundred years, the outcome in Japan was much more spectacular than in Britain.

The commonalities and the differences are both important. The shared lessons include the importance of an effective state administration and the empowering role of finance based on a banking system with substantial state and private involvement, markets for debt and the use of well-defined alienable property as collateral. Some differences lie to a degree in the different kinds of exogenous shocks and internal adaptations that were involved in provoking and enabling development. Britain and Japan are very different, but they carry lessons in common.

Concluding Question: Is Economic Development Achievable without War?

State-driven development can lift countries out of widespread poverty and build the foundations of industrial growth, as exhibited in Japan after 1868, in South Korea after 1953, in Taiwan after 1950 and (most spectacularly in growth terms) in China after 1978.[28] But no economy has moved into the ranks of the developed economies, at least in terms of GDP per capita, without having substantial private enterprise, extensive markets and a mixed economy. All such economies require a strong financial sector. No country in the world has reached high levels of development without an effective array of financial institutions.

But we should avoid the conclusion that 'better financial institutions' is a simple recipe for economic development, just as 'secure property rights' or 'free markets' or 'privatization' or 'land registration' have promoted previously. North wrote: 'Privatization is not a panacea for solving poor economic performance.' As Peter Evans put it, we should avoid 'institutional monocropping'. There is no single institutional key to development. As the present study has demonstrated, institutions always depend on and are moulded by complex structures involving other institutions. Concentrating on one imagined institutional solution to the neglect of this surrounding institutional environment can lead to major distortions, including concentrated vested interests and a failure to generate sufficient institutional variety for further experimentation.[29]

Nevertheless, with due caution about the historical, institutional and cultural differences, the British and Japanese cases bring some major lessons for countries moving from low to higher levels of per capita income. Financial

28. But, as noted earlier, China is still far behind the most developed countries in terms of GDP per capita.

29. North (1994, 366), Evans (2004, 31–32), Ostrom and Basurto (2011, 336–37).

institutions are crucial, along with the development of a reliable state admin-istration and a relatively autonomous and effective legal system.

Calomiris and Haber argued convincingly that the development of finan-cial systems depends crucially on political institutions. While democracy is not essential for economic progress, stable parliamentary systems provide ad-ditional checks and balances, which can reduce corruption. Electorates in representative democracies can put pressure on governments to regulate banks and make more credit available. Calomiris and Haber's case studies in-dicate that the differences between democratic and autocratic regimes in this respect are dramatic. But they also found evidence that democracies can some-times exacerbate instability.[30]

It is possible that different types of institutional arrangements and policies are necessary at different levels of development. Japan developed substantially from 1868 to 1945, without being a secure democracy. South Korea and Taiwan developed rapidly from the 1960s, but they did not become democracies until the late 1980s. In the United Kingdom, democracy was limited and corrupt for a long while. The Great Reform Bill of 1832 began a long process of gradually extending the franchise. Evidence on the economic effects of democracy is mixed, but the positive economic effects of democracy seem to be stronger at from middle- to high-income levels.[31]

The development of effective financial institutions is not easy. Consider mortgaging to obtain loans. Many countries have mortgages in name, but often there is little reduction in the interest rate compared with that for unsecured loans. This means that the institutional arrangements behind the mortgage are inadequate. Benito Arruñada asked: 'Why, then, are so many countries in the world unable to provide institutional support for mortgages? The answer is, simply, that providing such institutional support is not easy.' With or without land registries, the institutional foundations of finance have to be adequate and secure. Courts dealing with property disputes have to function effectively without corruption or long delays. Financial development remains a major condition for

30. Calomiris and Haber (2014).

31. Rodrik and Wacziarg (2005), Acemoglu et al. (2014). But Pozuelo et al. (2016) argued that the apparent empirical correlation between democracy and economic growth does not mean that the former causes the latter. Instead, they suggested that economic turmoil is respon-sible for causing or facilitating many democratic transitions. Knutsen (2015) provided evidence that democracy can help promote technological innovation, and autocracies have slower tech-nological change than democracies.

economic development. And in turn, financial development depends on a relatively impartial legal system and an effective state administration.[32]

The capacity to adapt and change is a major condition for sustained economic development. Particularly important from the perspective of this book is the need for ongoing reform of the state administration and legal institutions. Hence a major challenge for the developing world today is to build up a relatively efficient and well-governed state administration and legal system, without depending on the external threat of war. Historically, war has been the greatest builder and reformer of many states, as well as being a massive destroyer of lives and resources. But things are different today. Robert Neild argued that, partly because of the relative cheapness of highly destructive weapons, military competition no longer works to reform state administration or reduce corruption. Furthermore, the human costs of military conflict are enormous, and we have somehow to find a better path.[33]

But the fact remains that major institutional changes in the fundamental areas that matter for economic development typically depend on exogenous shocks. Often, politico-economic systems need jolting into major reform. Apart from war, likely shocks in the future include further pandemics and the dislocating effects of climate change. But such shocks will not bring beneficial institutional changes without effective governance and the adaptive capacity of all major institutions. Institutional researchers need to focus on the crucial questions of adaptability and sound governance. Adaptability and sound governance enhance the chances of effective and constructive responses to internal pressures and to exogenous shocks.

In nature, evolution and selection can lead to the emergence of fitter and more complex organisms. But as a number of biologists have pointed out, evolution operates on a second-order level as well. It is increasingly acknowledged that evolution is not simply about variety or adaptation, but also, at the highest level, about the ongoing capacity to evolve further in changing circumstances. Evolution can lead to greater abilities to adapt in response to changing pressures—the evolution of evolvability. This should become a maxim for politico-economic evolution too. Politico-economic systems need to develop

---

32. Arruñada (2012, 43). Dam (2006b, 201–3) gave examples of developing countries where the courts take five or more years to deal with disputes over mortgage default, or they are even unable to process such claims. On the influence of the rule of law on economic development, see Dam (2006b), Haggard at al. (2008) and Haggard and Tiede (2009).

33. Neild (2002, 131).

the capacity to adapt more effectively to multiple and unforeseen pressures and shocks. Future work in this area may be able to make use of the literature on complex adaptive systems. The concern is not simply with individual or institutional changes to such systems, but also with overall enhancements of its adaptability.[34]

What kinds of political, economic and legal institutions are most effective in responding to disruptions, foreseen or unforeseen? What kinds of adaptations are likely to be most successful? History can provide a useful source of insight on these questions, as well as institutional analysis, broadly conceived and drawing from multiple disciplines.

34. Holland et al. (1986), Campbell (1987), Wimsatt and Schank (1988), Holland (1992, 2006), Wills (1989), Houle (1992), Depew and Weber (1995), Wagner and Altenberg (1996), Harper (2014).

REFERENCES

Acemoglu, Daron, and James A. Robinson. 2012. *Why Nations Fail: The Origins of Power, Prosperity, and Poverty*. New York: Random House and London: Profile.

Acemoglu, Daron, Simon Johnson and James A. Robinson. 2005a. 'Institutions as a Fundamental Cause of Long-Run Growth', in *Handbook of Economic Growth, Volume 1A*, ed. Philippe Aghion and Steven N. Durlauf. North Holland: Elsevier, 385–472.

———. 2005b. 'The Rise of Europe: Atlantic Trade, Institutional Change and Economic Growth', *American Economic Review* 95 (3), June, 546–79.

Acemoglu, Daron, Suresh Naidu, Pascual Restrepo and James A. Robinson. 2014. 'Democracy Does Cause Growth', National Bureau of Economic Research, Working Paper 20004, Cambridge, MA.

Aghion, Philippe, and Peter Howitt. 1998. *Endogenous Growth Theory*. Cambridge, MA: MIT Press.

Alchian, Armen A. 1965. 'Some Economics of Property Rights', *Il Politico* 30, 816–29. Reprinted in Armen A. Alchian, *Economic Forces at Work*. Indianapolis, Ind.: Liberty Press, 1977, 127–49.

Aldrich, Howard E., Geoffrey M. Hodgson, David L. Hull, Thorbjørn Knudsen, Joel Mokyr and Viktor J. Vanberg. 2008. 'In Defence of Generalized Darwinism', *Journal of Evolutionary Economics* 18 (5), October, 577–96.

Alesina, Alberto, and Paola Giuliano. 2015. 'Culture and Institutions', *Journal of Economic Literature* 53 (4), December, 898–944.

Allen, Douglas W. 2012. *The Institutional Revolution: Measurement and the Economic Emergence of the Modern World*. Chicago: University of Chicago Press.

Allen, Robert C. 1992. *Enclosure and the Yeoman: The Agricultural Development of the South Midlands 1450–1850*. Oxford: Clarendon Press.

———. 1999. 'Tracking the Agricultural Revolution in England', *Economic History Review* 52 (2), May, 209–35.

———. 2009. *The British Industrial Revolution in Global Perspective*. Cambridge: Cambridge University Press.

———. 2015. 'The High Wage Economy and the Industrial Revolution: A Restatement', *Economic History Review* 68 (1), 1–22.

Allen, Robert C., and J. L. Weisdorf. 2011. 'Was There an "Industrious Revolution" before the Industrial Revolution? An Empirical Exercise for England, c. 1300–1830', *Economic History Review* 64 (3), 715–29.

Anderson, B. L. 1969a. 'The Attorneys and the Early Capital Market in Lancashire', reprinted in *Capital Formation in the Industrial Revolution*, ed. François Crouzet. London: Methuen, 1972, 223–55.

———. 1969b. 'Provincial Aspects of the Financial Revolution in the Eighteenth Century', *Business History* 11 (1), 11–22.

Anderson, Perry. 1964. 'Origins of the Present Crisis', *New Left Review*, no. 23, January/February, 26–53.

———. 1974. *Lineages of the Absolutist State*. London: NLB.

Angeles, Luis. 2011. 'Institutions, Property Rights, and Economic Development in Historical Perspective', *Kyklos* 64 (2), May, 157–77.

Aoki, Masahiko. 2001. *Toward a Comparative Institutional Analysis*. Cambridge, MA: MIT Press.

Arruñada, Benito. 2012. *Institutional Foundations of Impersonal Exchange: Theory and Policy of Contractual Registries*. Chicago: University of Chicago Press.

———. 2016. 'Coase and the Departure from Property', in *The Elgar Companion to Ronald H. Coase*, ed. Claude Ménard and Elodie Bertrand. Cheltenham, UK: Edward Elgar, 305–19.

———. 2017. 'Property as Sequential Exchange: The Forgotten Limits of Private Contract', *Journal of Institutional Economics* 13 (4), December, 753–83.

———. 2018. 'How to Make Land Titling More Rational', Universitat Pompeu Fabra, Department of Economics and Business, Working Paper No. 1575.

Arthur, W. Brian (1990) 'Positive Feedbacks in the Economy', *Scientific American* 262 (2), February, 80–85.

———. 1994. *Increasing Returns and Path Dependence in the Economy*. Ann Arbor: University of Michigan Press.

———. 2006. 'Out-of-Equilibrium Economics and Agent-Based Modeling', in *Handbook of Computational Economics, Vol. 2: Agent-Based Computational Economics*, ed. Leigh Tesfatsion and Kenneth L. Judd. Amsterdam: North-Holland, 1551–64.

Ashley, Maurice. 1966. *The Glorious Revolution of 1688*. London: Hodder and Stoughton.

Ashton, Thomas S. 1955. *An Economic History of England: The 18th Century*. London: Methuen.

———. 1968. *The Industrial Revolution*. Oxford: Oxford University Press.

Ayres, Clarence E. 1943. 'The Twilight of the Price System', *Antioch Review* 3, Summer, 162–81.

———. 1944. *The Theory of Economic Progress*. Chapel Hill: University of North Carolina Press.

Bagehot, Walter. 1919. *Lombard Street: A Description of the Money Market* (1st ed. 1873). London: John Murray.

Bailey, Mark. 2016. *The Decline of Serfdom in Late Medieval England: From Bondage to Freedom*. Rochester, NY: Boydell Press.

Baker, J. H. 1979. 'The Law Merchant and the Common Law before 1700,' *Cambridge Law Journal* 38 (2), November, 295–322.

———. 2019. *An Introduction to English Legal History*, 5th ed. Oxford: Oxford University Press.

Bank of England. 1970. *The Bank of England: History and Functions*. Debden, UK: Gordon Chalmers Fortin.

———. 2021. 'Public Sector Debt Outstanding in the United Kingdom', Federal Reserve Bank of St. Louis, FRED Economic Data. https://fred.stlouisfed.org/series/PSDOTUKA.

Bar, Michael, and Oksana Leukhina. 2010. 'Demographic Transition and Industrial Revolution: A Macroeconomic Investigation', *Review of Economic Dynamics* 13, 424–51.

Baring-Gould, Sabine. 1906. *A Book of Cornwall*. London: Methuen.

Barzel, Yoram. 1989. *Economic Analysis of Property Rights*. Cambridge: Cambridge University Press.

———. 2002. *A Theory of the State: Economic Rights, Legal Rights, and the Scope of the State*. Cambridge: Cambridge University Press.

Baumgartner, Frank, and Bryan D. Jones. 1993. *Agendas and Instability in American Politics*. Chicago: University of Chicago Press.

Beck, Thorsten, Asli Demirgüç-Kunt and Ross Levine. 2003. 'Law, Endowments, and Finance', *Journal of Financial Economics* 70, 137–81.

Becker, Sascha O., Steven Pfaff and Jared Rubin. 2016. 'Causes and Consequences of the Protestant Reformation', *Explorations in Economic History* 62, October, 1–25.

Becker, Sascha O., and Ludger Woessmann. 2009. 'Was Weber Wrong? A Human Capital Theory of Protestant Economic History', *Quarterly Journal of Economics* 124 (2), May, 531–96.

Beckert, Sven. 2015. *Empire of Cotton: A New History of Global Capitalism*. London: Penguin.

Beckett, J. V. 1984. 'The Pattern of Landownership in England and Wales, 1660–1880', *Economic History Review* 37 (1), February, 1–22.

Beinhocker, Eric D. 2006. *The Origins of Wealth: Evolution, Complexity, and the Radical Remaking of Economics*. New York: Random House.

Benedictow, Ole J. 2004. *The Black Death 1346–1353: The Complete History*. Woodbridge, UK: Boydell Press.

Bell, Duncan. 2014. 'What Is Liberalism?' *Political Theory* 42 (6), 682–715.

Bell, Stephanie A. 2001. 'The Role of the State and the Hierarchy of Money', *Cambridge Journal of Economics* 25 (2), March, 149–63.

Ben-Ner, Avner, and Louis Putterman. 2000. 'Some Implications of Evolutionary Psychology for the Study of Preferences and Institutions', *Journal of Economic Behavior and Organization* 43 (1), September, 91–99.

Berg, Maxine, and Pat Hudson. 1992. 'Rehabilitating the Industrial Revolution', *Economic History Review*, New Series, 45 (1), February, 24–50.

Berkeley, George. 1750. *The Querist, Containing Several Queries, Proposed to the Consideration of the Public*. London: Innys, Davis, Hitch, Bower and Cooper.

Berman, Harold J. 1983. *Law and Revolution: The Formation of the Western Legal Tradition*. Cambridge, MA: Harvard University Press.

———. 2003. *Law and Revolution II: The Impact of the Protestant Reformations on the Western Legal Tradition*. Cambridge, MA: Harvard University Press.

Besley, Timothy, and Maitreesh Ghatak. 2008. 'Creating Collateral: The de Soto Effect and the Political Economy of Legal Reform', Working Paper, London School of Economics.

Beutel, Frederick K. 1938. 'The Development of Negotiable Instruments in Early English Law', *Harvard Law Review* 51 (5), 813–45.

Biancalana, Joseph. 2001. *The Fee Tail and the Common Recovery in Medieval England 1176–1502*. Cambridge: Cambridge University Press.

Bird, Richard M. 1997. 'Land Taxation and Economic Development: The Model of Meiji Japan', *Journal of Development Studies* 13 (2), 162–74.

Blackledge, Paul. 2019. 'Historical Materialism', in *The Oxford Handbook of Karl Marx*, ed. Matt Vidal, Tony Smith, Tomás Rotta and Paul Prew. Oxford: Oxford University Press, 37–56.

Blackstone, Sir William. 1765–1769. *Commentaries on the Laws of England*, 4 vols. Oxford: Clarendon Press.

Bloch, Marc. 1962. *Feudal Society,* trans. from French edition of 1939–1940 by L. A. Manyon, foreword by M. M. Postan. London: Routledge and Kegan Paul.

Blomstrom, Magnus, Richard E. Lipsey and Mario Zejan. 1996. 'Is Fixed Investment the Key to Economic Growth?' *Quarterly Journal of Economics* 111 (1), February, 269–76.

Blum, Jerome. 1957. 'The Rise of Serfdom in Eastern Europe', *American Historical Review* 62 (4), July, 807–36.

———. 1981. 'English Parliamentary Enclosures', *Journal of Modern History,* 53 (3), September, 477–504.

Bogart, Dan. 2005. 'Did Turnpike Trusts Increase Transportation Investment in Eighteenth Century England?' *Journal of Economic History* 65 (2), June, 439–68.

———. 2011. 'Did the Glorious Revolution Contribute to the Transport Revolution? Evidence from Investment in Roads and Rivers', *Economic History Review* 64 (4), November, 1073–1112.

Bogart, Dan, and Gary Richardson. 2011. 'Property Rights and Parliament in Industrializing Britain', *Journal of Law and Economics* 54 (2), May, 241–74.

Botticini, Maristella, and Zvi Eckstein. 2012. *The Chosen Few: How Education Shaped Jewish History, 70–1492.* Princeton, NJ: Princeton University Press.

Boulding, Kenneth E. 1966. 'The Economics of Knowledge and the Knowledge of Economics', *American Economic Review (Papers and Proceedings)* 56 (1), March, 1–13.

Bourdieu, Pierre. 1986. 'The Forms of Capital,' in *Handbook of Theory and Research for the Sociology of Education,* ed. John G. Richardson. New York: Greenwood, 241–58.

Bouscasse, Paul, Emi Nakamura and Jón Steinsson. 2021. 'When Did Growth Begin? New Estimates of Productivity Growth in England from 1250 to 1870', NBER Working Paper 28623. https://www.nber.org/system/files/working_papers/w28623/w28623.pdf.

Bowen, Huw V. 1995. 'The Bank of England during the Long Eighteenth Century: 1694–1815', in *The Bank of England,* ed. Richard Roberts and David Kynaston. Oxford: Oxford University Press, 1–18.

Bowles, Samuel and Gintis, Herbert. 2011. *A Cooperative Species: Human Reciprocity and its Evolution* (Princeton, NJ: Princeton University Press).

Boyd, Robert, Herbert Gintis, Samuel Bowles and Peter J. Richerson. 2003. 'Evolution of Altruistic Punishment', *Proceedings of the National Academy of Sciences* 100 (6), March, 3531–35.

Boyd, Robert, and Peter J. Richerson. 1985. *Culture and the Evolutionary Process.* Chicago: University of Chicago Press.

———. 1992. 'Punishment Allows the Evolution of Cooperation (or Anything Else) in Sizable Groups', *Ethology and Sociobiology* 13, 171–95.

Braddick, Michael. 1996. *The Nerves of State: Taxation and the Financing of the English State, 1558–1714.* Manchester, UK: Manchester University Press.

Brailsford, H. N. 1961. *The Levellers and the English Revolution.* London: Cresset Press.

Brandon, Robert N. 1996. *Concepts and Methods in Evolutionary Biology.* Cambridge: Cambridge University Press.

Braudel, Fernand. 1979. *Afterthoughts on Material Civilization and Capitalism.* Baltimore, MD: Johns Hopkins University Press.

———. 1984. *Civilization and Capitalism, 15th–18th Century, Vol. 3: The Perspective of the World.* London: Collins.

Braun, Eduard. 2015. 'Carl Menger's Contribution to Capital Theory', *History of Economic Ideas* 23 (1), 77–99.

———. 2020. 'Carl Menger: *Contribution to the Theory of Capital* (1888), Section V', *Journal of Institutional Economics* 16 (4), August, 557–68.

Brenner, Robert. 1976. 'Agrarian Class Structure and Economic Development in Pre-Industrial Europe', *Past and Present*, no. 70, February, 30–75.

Brewer, Holly. 1997. 'Entailing Aristocracy in Colonial Virginia: "Ancient Feudal Restraints" and Revolutionary Reform', *William and Mary Quarterly*, third series, 54 (2), April, 307–46.

———. 2021. 'Creating a Common Law of Slavery for England and Its New World Empire'. *Law and History Review* 39 (4), November, 765–834.

Brewer, John. 1989. *The Sinews of Power: War, Money and the English State, 1688–1783*. New York: Knopf.

Briggs, Chris, and Jaco Zuijderduijn, eds. 2018. *Land and Credit: Mortgages in the Medieval and Early Modern European Countryside*. London: Palgrave Macmillan.

Broadberry, Stephen N., Bruce M. S. Campbell, Alexander Klein, Mark Overton and Bas van Leeuwen. 2015. *British Economic Growth 1270–1870: An Output-Based Approach*. Cambridge: Cambridge University Press.

Bromley, Daniel W. 2009. 'Formalising Property Relations in the Developing World: The Wrong Prescription for the Wrong Malady', *Land Use Policy* 26 (1), 20–27.

Brunt, Liam. 2006. 'Rediscovering Risk: English Country Banks as Proto-Venture Capital Firms in the Industrial Revolution', *Journal of Economic History* 66 (1), March, 74–102.

Buchanan, Brenda J. 1986. 'The Evolution of the English Turnpike Trusts: Lessons from a Case Study', *Economic History Review* 39 (2), May, 223–23.

Bunge, Mario A. 1980. *The Mind-Body Problem: A Psychobiological Approach*. Oxford: Pergamon.

Bünstorf, Guido. 2009. 'Opportunity Spin-Offs and Necessity Spin-Offs', *International Journal of Entrepreneurial Venturing* 1 (1), 22–40.

Button, Graham, ed. 1993. *Technology in Working Order: Studies of Work, Interaction and Technology*. London: Routledge.

Callinicos, Alex. 2009. *Making History: Agency, Structure, and Change in Social Theory*. Chicago: Haymarket.

Calomiris, Charles W., and Stephen H. Haber. 2014. *Fragile by Design: The Political Origins of Banking Crises and Scarce Credit*. Princeton, NJ: Princeton University Press.

Calvin, William H. 2002. *A Brain for All Seasons: Human Evolution and Abrupt Climate Change*. Chicago: University of Chicago Press.

Cameron, Rondo, Olga Crisp, Hugh T. Patrick and Richard Tilly. 1967. *Banking in the Early Stages of Industrialization*. Oxford: Oxford University Press.

Campbell, Bruce M. S. 2010. 'Nature as Historical Protagonist', *Economic History Review* 63 (2), May, 281–314.

Campbell, Donald T. 1969. 'Ethnocentrism of Disciplines and the Fish-Scale Model of Omniscience', in *Interdisciplinary Relationships in the Social Sciences*, ed. Muzafer Sherif and Carolyn Wood Sherif. Chicago: Aldine, 328–48. Excerpted in Hodgson (2022b).

Cannadine, David. 1977. 'Aristocratic Indebtedness in the Nineteenth Century: The Case Re-opened', *Economic History Review, New Series* 30 (4), November, 624–50.

———. 1980. 'Aristocratic Indebtedness in the Nineteenth Century: A Restatement', *Economic History Review, New Series* 33 (4), November, 569–73.

Cannan, Edwin. 1921. 'Early History of the Term Capital', *Quarterly Journal of Economics* 35 (3), May, 469–81.

Campbell, Donald T. 1965. 'Variation, Selection and Retention in Sociocultural Evolution', in *Social Change in Developing Areas: A Reinterpretation of Evolutionary Theory*, ed. H. R. Barringer, G. I., Blanksten, and R. W. Mack. Cambridge, MA: Schenkman, 19–49. Reprinted in *General Systems* 14, 1969, 69–85.

Campbell, John H. 1987. 'The New Gene and Its Evolution', in *Rates of Evolution*, ed. K. Campbell and M. F. Day. London: Allen and Unwin, 283–309.

Cantoni, Davide. 2015. 'The Economic Effects of the Protestant Reformation: Testing the Weber Hypothesis in the German Lands', *Journal of the European Economic Association* 13 (4), August, 561–98.

Carlin, Wendy, and Colin Mayer. 2003. 'Finance, Investment, and Growth', *Journal of Financial Economics* 69 (2), July, 191–226.

Carlton, Charles. 1995. *Going to the Wars: The Experience of the British Civil Wars 1638–1651*. London: Routledge.

Carruthers, Bruce G. 1996. *City of Capital: Politics and Markets in the English Financial Revolution*. Princeton, NJ: Princeton University Press.

Castor, Helen. 2006. *Blood and Roses: One Family's Struggle and Triumph during the Tumultuous Wars of the Roses*. New York: Harper Collins.

Centre for Global Economic History, University of Utrecht, Netherlands. "Data." http://www .cgeh.nl/data#conflict. Accessed 27 July 2021.

Central Intelligence Agency. 2022. 'Real GDP Per Capita', in *CIA World Factbook*. https://www .cia.gov/the-world-factbook/field/real-gdp-per-capita/country-comparison.

Chamberlain, Hugh. 1695. *A Proposal for Erecting a General Bank: Which May Be Justly Called the Land Bank of England*. London: Whitlock.

Chandler, Alfred D., Jr. 1977. *The Visible Hand: The Managerial Revolution in American Business*. Cambridge, MA: Harvard University Press.

Chapman, S. D. 1972. *The Cotton Industry in the Industrial Revolution*. London: Macmillan.

Cheshire, Edward. 1854. 'The Results of the Census of Great Britain in 1851, with a Description of the Machinery and Processes Employed to Obtain the Returns; Also an Appendix of Tables of Reference', *Journal of the Statistical Society of London* 17 (1), March, 45–72.

Churchland, Patricia S. 1986. *Neurophilosophy: Toward a Unified Science of the Mind-Brain*. Cambridge, MA: MIT Press.

Churchland, Paul M. 1984. *Matter and Consciousness*. Cambridge, MA: MIT Press.

———. 1989. *A Neurocomputational Perspective: The Nature of Mind and the Structure of Science*. Cambridge, MA: MIT Press.

Cipolla, Carlo M. 1965. *Guns, Sails and Empires: Technological Innovation and the Early Phases of European Expansion, 1400–1700*. New York: Pantheon.

Clapham, John H. 1966. *The Bank of England: A History. Volume One, 1694–1797*. Cambridge: Cambridge University Press.

Clark, Andy. 1997. *Being There: Putting the Brain, Body and World Together Again*. Cambridge, MA: MIT Press.

Clark, Gregory. 1996. 'The Political Foundations of Modern Economic Growth: England, 1540–1800', *Journal of Interdisciplinary History* 26 (4), Spring, 563–88.

———. 1998a. 'Land Hunger: Land as a Commodity and as a Status Good, England, 1500–1910', *Explorations in Economic History* 35, 59–82.

———. 1998b. 'The Charity Commission as a Source in English Economic History', *Research in Economic History* 18, 1–52.

———. 1998c. 'Commons Sense: Common Property Rights, Efficiency, and Institutional Change', *Journal of Economic History* 58 (1), 73–102.

———. 2001. 'Debt, Deficits, and Crowding Out: England, 1727–1840', *European Review of Economic History* 5 (3), December, 403–36.

———. 2007. *A Farewell to Alms: A Brief Economic History of the World*. Princeton, NJ: Princeton University Press.

Coase, Ronald H. 1937. 'The Nature of the Firm', *Economica*, New Series, 4, November, 386–405.

Cobban, Alfred. 1964. *The Social Interpretation of the French Revolution*. Cambridge: Cambridge University Press.

Cohen, Avi J., and Geoffrey C. Harcourt. 2003. 'Whatever Happened to the Cambridge Capital Theory Controversies?', *Journal of Economic Perspectives* 17 (1), Winter, 199–214.

Cohen, Gerald A. 1978. *Karl Marx's Theory of History: A Defence*. Oxford: Oxford University Press.

Cohen, Michael D., and Paul Bacdayan. 1994. 'Organizational Routines Are Stored as Procedural Memory—Evidence from a Laboratory Study', *Organization Science* 5 (4), November, 554–68.

Cole, Daniel H. 2015. '"Economic Property Rights" as "Nonsense upon Stilts": A Comment on Hodgson's Article', *Journal of Institutional Economics* 11 (4), September, 725–30.

Cole, Daniel H., and Peter Z. Grossman. 2002. 'The Meaning of Property Rights: Law versus Economics?' *Land Economics* 78 (3), August, 317–30.

Coleman, D. C. 1966. 'The "Gentry" Controversy and the Aristocracy in Crisis, 1558–1641', *History* 51 (172), 165–78.

Coleman, James S. 1988. 'Social Capital in the Creation of Human Capital', *American Journal of Sociology* 94 (supplement), S95–S120.

Collins, Harry. 2010. *Tacit and Explicit Knowledge*. Chicago: University of Chicago Press.

Collins, Harry, and Martin Kusch, eds. 1998. *The Shape of Actions—What Humans and Machines Can Do*. Cambridge, MA: MIT Press.

Collins, Randall. 1988. *Theoretical Sociology*. San Diego, CA: Harcourt, Brace, Jovanovich.

Commons, John R. 1893. *The Distribution of Wealth*. London: Macmillan.

———. 1924. *Legal Foundations of Capitalism*. New York: Macmillan.

———. 1934. *Institutional Economics—Its Place in Political Economy*. New York: Macmillan.

Comninel, George C. 1987. *Rethinking the French Revolution: Marxism and the Revisionist Challenge*. London: Verso.

Corning, Peter A. 2003. *Nature's Magic: Synergy in Evolution and the Fate of Humankind*. Cambridge: Cambridge University Press.

———. 2005. *Holistic Darwinism: Synergy, Cybernetics and the Bioeconomics of Evolution*. Chicago: University of Chicago Press.

Corns, Thomas N., Ann Hughes and David Loewenstein, eds. 2009. *The Complete Works of Gerrard Winstanley, Vol. 2.* Oxford: Oxford University Press.

Cottrell, Philip L. 1980. *Industrial Finance, 1830–1914: The Finance and Organization of English Manufacturing Industry.* London: Methuen.

Cox, Gary W. 2012. 'Was the Glorious Revolution a Constitutional Watershed?' *Journal of Economic History* 72 (3), September, 567–600.

———. 2016. *Marketing Sovereign Promises: Monopoly Brokerage and the Growth of the English State.* Cambridge: Cambridge University Press.

Crafts, Nicholas. F. R., and C. Knick Harley. 1992. 'Output Growth and the British Industrial Revolution: A Restatement of the Crafts-Harley View', *Economic History Review* 45 (4), November, 703–30.

Crawford, Sue E. S., and Elinor Ostrom. 1995. 'A Grammar of Institutions', *American Political Science Review* 89 (3), September, 582–600.

Credit Suisse Research Institute. 2019. *Global Wealth Databook 2019.* Zurich: Credit Suisse Research Institute.

Crouzet, François. 1965. 'Capital Formation in Great Britain During the Industrial Revolution', *Proceedings of the Second Conference of Economic History.* The Hague. Reprinted in *Capital Formation in the Industrial Revolution*, ed. François Crouzet. London: Methuen, 1972, 162–222.

———. 1990. *Britain Ascendant: Comparative Studies in Franco-British Economic History.* Cambridge: Cambridge University Press.

Cule, J. E. 1935. 'The Financial History of Matthew Boulton: 1759–1800', PhD thesis, University of Birmingham.

Curott, Nicholas A. 2017. 'Adam Smith's Theory of Money and Banking', *Journal of the History of Economic Thought* 39 (3), 323–47.

Dafoe, Allan. 2015. 'On Technological Determinism: A Typology, Scope Conditions, and a Mechanism', *Science, Technology, and Human Values* 40 (6), November, 1047–76.

Dam, Kenneth W. 2006a. 'Land, Law and Economic Development', University of Chicago Law and Economics, Olin Working Paper No. 272. https://papers.ssrn.com/sol3/papers.cfm?abstract_id=876659.

———. 2006b. *The Law-Growth Nexus: The Rule of Law and Economic Development.* Washington, DC: Brookings Institution.

Damasio, Antonio R. 1994. *Descartes' Error: Emotion, Reason, and the Human Brain.* New York: Putnam.

Darby, Henry C. 1977. *Domesday England.* Cambridge: Cambridge University Press.

Darwin, Charles R. 1859. *On the Origin of Species by Means of Natural Selection, or the Preservation of Favoured Races in the Struggle for Life.* London: John Murray.

———. 1871. *The Descent of Man, and Selection in Relation to Sex*, 2 vols. London: John Murray and New York: Hill.

Darwin, Francis, ed. 1887. *Life and Letters of Charles Darwin: Including an Autobiographical Chapter*, 3 vols., 3rd ed. London: John Murray.

David, Paul A. 1994. 'Why Are Institutions the "Carriers of History"? Path Dependence and the Evolution of Conventions, Organizations and Institutions', *Structural Change and Economic Dynamics* 5 (2), 205–20.

Davidson, Paul. 1972. *Money and the Real World*. London: Macmillan.

Davies, Godfrey. 1959. *The Early Stuarts 1603–1660*, 2nd ed. Oxford: Clarendon Press.

Davis, Ralph. 1954. 'English Foreign Trade, 1660–1700', *Economic History Review*, New Series 7 (2), 150–66.

Dawes, Margaret, and C. Neville Ward-Perkins. 2000. *The Country Banks of England and Wales*, 2 vols. Canterbury: Chartered Institute of Bankers.

de Pinto, Isaac. 1774. *An Essay on Circulation and Credit: In Four Parts; and a Letter on the Jealousy of Commerce*, trans. from French edition of 1771. London: Ridley.

de Soto, Hernando. 2000. *The Mystery of Capital: Why Capitalism Triumphs in the West and Fails Everywhere Else*. New York: Basic Books.

de Tocqueville, Alexis. 1838. *Democracy in America*, trans. Henry Reeve from French edition of 1835, intro. John C. Spencer. New York: George Adlard.

Deakin, Simon, David Gindis, Geoffrey M. Hodgson, Kainan Huang andKatharina Pistor. 2017. 'Legal Institutionalism: Capitalism and the Constitutive Role of Law', *Journal of Comparative Economics* 45 (1), February, 188–200.

Deaton, Angus. 2013. *The Great Escape: Health, Wealth, and the Origins of Inequality*. Princeton, NJ: Princeton University Press.

Defoe, Daniel. 1727. *A Tour Thro' the Whole Island of Great Britain, Divided into Circuits or Journeys*. London: Strahan.

Deininger, Klaus, and Gershon Feder. 2009. 'Land Registration, Governance, and Development: Evidence and Implications for Policy', *World Bank Research Observer* 24 (2), August, 233–66.

Dennett, Daniel C. 1995. *Darwin's Dangerous Idea: Evolution and the Meanings of Life*. London: Allen Lane and New York: Simon and Schuster.

Dennison, Tracy, and Sheilagh Ogilvie. 2014. 'Does the European Marriage Pattern Explain Economic Growth?' *Journal of Economic History* 74 (3), September, 651–93.

Depew, David J., and Bruce H. Weber. 1995. *Darwinism Evolving: Systems Dynamics and the Genealogy of Natural Selection*. Cambridge, MA: MIT Press.

Desan, Christine. 2014. *Making Money: Coin, Currency and the Coming of Capitalism*. Oxford: Oxford University Press.

Dewey, John. 1922. *Human Nature and Conduct: An Introduction to Social Psychology*. New York: Holt.

Diamond, Jared. 1997. *Guns, Germs and Steel: A Short History of Everybody for the Last 13,000 Years*. London: Jonathan Cape.

Dickson, Peter G. M. 1967. *The Financial Revolution in England: A Study in the Development of Public Credit, 1688–1756*. London: Macmillan.

Dong, Guanghui, Xin Jia, Chengbang An, Fahu Chen, Yan Zhao, Shichen Tao, and Minmin Ma. 2012. 'Mid-Holocene Climate Change and Its Effect on Prehistoric Cultural Evolution in Eastern Qinghai Province, China', *Quaternary Research* 77, 23–30.

Dopfer, Kurt. 2004. 'The Economic Agent as Rule Maker and Rule User: *Homo Sapiens Oeconomicus*', *Journal of Evolutionary Economics* 14 (2), May, 177–95.

Dopfer, Kurt, John Foster and Jason Potts. 2004. 'Micro-Meso-Macro', *Journal of Evolutionary Economics* 14 (3), July, 263–79.

Dopfer, Kurt, and Jason Potts. 2008. *The General Theory of Economic Evolution*. London: Routledge.

Dore, Ronald P. 1959. *Land Reform in Japan*. London: Athlone.

———. 1965. *Education in Tokugawa Japan*. Berkeley: University of California Press.

———. 1986. *Flexible Rigidities: Industrial Policy and Structural Adjustment in the Japanese Economy 1970–1980*. Stanford, CA: Stanford University Press and London: Athlone Press.

Dosi, Giovanni, Christopher Freeman, Richard Nelson, Gerald Silverberg and Luc L. G. Soete, eds. 1988. *Technical Change and Economic Theory*. London: Pinter.

Doyle, William. 2002. *The Oxford History of the French Revolution*, 2nd ed. Oxford: Oxford University Press.

Draper, N. 2008. 'The City of London and Slavery: Evidence from the First Dock Companies, 1795–1800', *Economic History Review*, New Series, 61 (2), May, 432–66.

Duby, Georges. 1974. *The Early Growth of the European Economy*. Ithaca, NY: Cornell University Press.

Dutton, Harry I. 1984. *The Patent System and Inventive Activity during the Industrial Revolution, 1750–1852*. Manchester, UK: Manchester University Press.

Easterly, William. 2001. *The Elusive Quest for Growth: Economists' Adventures and Misadventures in the Tropics*. Cambridge, MA: MIT Press.

Easterly, William, and Ross Levine. 2001. 'It's Not Factor Accumulation: Stylized Facts and Growth Models', *World Bank Economic Review* 15 (2), 177–219.

Edgeworth, Richard Lovell, and Maria Edgeworth. 1844. *Memoirs of Richard Lovell Edgeworth Esq. Begun by Himself and Concluded by His Daughter, Maria Edgeworth*, 3rd ed. London: Richard Bentley.

Edwards, Bryan. 1806. *The History, Civil and Commercial of the British Colonies in the West Indies*, 4 vols. Philadelphia: Humphreys.

Ehrenberg, Kenneth M. 2016. *The Functions of Law* (Oxford: Oxford University Press.

Eldredge, Niles, and Stephen Jay Gould. 1977. 'Punctuated Equilibria: The Tempo and Mode of Evolution Reconsidered', *Paleobiology* 3, 115–51.

Elster, Jon. 1983. *Explaining Technical Change*. Cambridge: Cambridge University Press.

Eltis, David. 2001. 'The Volume and Structure of the Transatlantic Slave Trade: A Reassessment', *William and Mary Quarterly* 58 (1), January, 17–46.

Emenalo, Chukwunonye, Francesca Gagliardi and Geoffrey M. Hodgson. 2018. 'Historical Institutional Determinants of Financial System Development in Africa', *Journal of Institutional Economics* 14 (2), April, 345–72.

English, Barbara, and John Saville. 1983. *Strict Settlement: A Guide for Historians*. Hull: University of Hull Press.

Epstein, Stephan R. 2000. *Freedom and Growth: The Rise of States and Markets in Europe, 1300–1750*. London: Routledge.

Epstein, Steven A. 1991. *Wage Labor and Guilds in Medieval Europe*. Chapel Hill: University of North Carolina Press.

Eric, Roll. 1930. *An Early Experiment in Industrial Organisation: Being a History of the Firm of Boulton and Watt 1775–1805*. Abingdon, UK: Frank Cass.

Ertman, Thomas. 1997. *Birth of the Leviathan: Building States and Regimes in Medieval and Early Modern Europe*. Cambridge: Cambridge University Press.

Evans, Peter B. 2004. 'Development as Institutional Change: The Pitfalls of Monocropping and the Potentials of Deliberation', *Studies in Comparative International Development* 39 (4), December, 30–52.

Evans, Peter B., Dietrich Rueschemeyer and Theda Skocpol, eds. 1985. *Bringing the State Back In*. Cambridge: Cambridge University Press.

Fagan, Brian M. 2000. *The Little Ice Age: How Climate Made History, 1300–1850*. New York: Basic Books.

Faundez, Julio. 2016. 'Douglass North's Theory of Institutions: Lessons for Law and Development', *Hague Journal on the Rule of Law*, July, 1–47.

Ferguson, Niall, ed. 1998. *Virtual History: Alternatives and Counterfactuals*. London: Macmillan.

———. 2001. *The Cash Nexus: Money and Power in the Modern World, 1700–2000*. London: Penguin).

Fetter, Frank A. 1927. 'Clark's Reformulation of the Capital Concept', in *Economic Essays Contributed in Honor of John Bates Clark*, ed. Jacob H. Hollander. New York: Macmillan, 136–56.

———. 1930. 'Capital', in *Encyclopaedia of the Social Sciences*, ed. Edwin R. A. Seligman and Alvin Johnson. New York: Macmillan, 3: 187–90. Reprinted in *Journal of Institutional Economics* 4 (1), April 2008, 127–37.

Field, Alexander J. 1991. 'Do Legal Systems Matter?', *Explorations in Economic History* 28 (1), 1–35.

Fogel, Robert W. 2004. *The Escape from Hunger and Premature Death, 1700–2100: Europe, America, and the Third World*. Cambridge: Cambridge University Press.

Frank, Lawrence Kelso. 1925. 'The Significance of Industrial Integration', *Journal of Political Economy* 33 (2), April, 179–95.

Franklin, Benjamin. 1810. *The Way to Wealth; Or, "Poor Richard Improved"*, 1st ed., 1758. London: Darton. https://www.gutenberg.org/files/43855/43855-h/43855-h.htm, accessed 20 April 2021.

French, Henry R., and Richard W. Hoyle. 1999. 'The Land Market of a Pennine Manor: Slaidburn, 1650–1780', *Continuity and Change* 14 (3), 349–83.

Fukuyama, Francis. 2000. 'Social Capital and Civil Society', International Monetary Fund Working Paper WP/00/74, 1–18.

———. 2011. *The Origins of Political Order: From Prehuman Times to the French Revolution*. London: Profile Books and New York: Farrar, Straus and Giroux.

Furubotn, Eirik G., and Svetozar Pejovich. 1972. 'Property Rights and Economic Theory: A Survey of Recent Literature', *Journal of Economic Literature* 10 (4), December, 1137–62.

Gardiner, Samuel Rawson. 1906. *The Constitutional Documents of the Puritan Revolution 1625–1660*, 3rd, ed. Oxford: Oxford University Press.

Gascoigne, Neil, and Tim Thornton. 2013. *Tacit Knowledge*. Durham, UK: Acumen.

Gayton, Juliet. 2018. 'Mortgages Raised by Rural English Copyhold Tenants 1605–1735', in *Land and Credit: Mortgages in the Medieval and Early Modern European Countryside*, ed. Chris Briggs and Jaco Zuijderduijn. London: Palgrave Macmillan, 47–80.

Gendron, John H. 2021. 'Employment Preservation and Textile Regulation in Early Modern England, 1550–1640', *Journal of Institutional Economics* 17 (4), August, 549–43.

Gentles, Ian. 1997. 'The New Model Officer Corps in 1647: A Collective Portrait', *Social History* 22 (2), May, 127–44.

Georgescu-Roegen, Nicholas. 1971. *The Entropy Law and the Economic Process*. Cambridge, MA: Harvard University Press.

Gerschenkron, Alexander. 1962. *Economic Backwardness in Historical Perspective: A Book of Essays*. Cambridge, MA: Belknap Press.

Giddens, Anthony. 1979. *Central Problems in Social Theory*. Berkeley: University of California Press.

———. 1984. *The Constitution of Society: Outline of the Theory of Structuration*. Cambridge: Polity Press.

Gingerich, Daniel W., and Jan P. Vogler. 2021. 'Pandemics and Political Development: The Electoral Legacy of the Black Death in Germany', *World Politics*, 1–48. https//doi.org/10.1017/S0043887121000034.

Ginsburg, Tom, and Glenn Hoetker. 2006. 'The Unreluctant Litigant? An Empirical Analysis of Japan's Turn to Litigation', *Journal of Legal Studies* 35 (1), January, 31–59.

Gintis, Herbert, Samuel Bowles, Robert Boyd and Ernst Fehr, eds. 2005. *Moral Sentiments and Material Interests: The Foundations of Cooperation in Economic Life*. Cambridge, MA: MIT Press.

Glaeser, Edward L., and Andrei Shleifer. 2002. 'Legal Origins', *Quarterly Journal of Economics* 117 (4), November, 1193–1229.

Goldman, Alvin I. 1999) *Knowledge in a Social World*. Oxford: Oxford University Press.

———. 2009. 'Social Epistemology: Theory and Applications', *Royal Institute of Philosophy Supplement* 64, 1–18.

Goldsmith, Raymond W. 1985. *Comparative National Balance Sheets: A Study of Twenty Countries, 1688–1978*. Chicago: University of Chicago Press).

———. 1987. *Premodern Financial Systems*. Cambridge: Cambridge University Press.

Goodhart, Charles A. E. 1988. *The Evolution of Central Banks*. Cambridge, MA: MIT Press.

———. 2009. 'The Continuing Muddles of Monetary Theory: A Steadfast Refusal to Face Facts', *Economica* 76, October, 821–30.

Gordon, Robert W. 1984. 'Critical Legal Histories', *Stanford Law Review* 36 (57), 57–125.

Gould, Stephen Jay. 2002. *The Structure of Evolutionary Theory*. Cambridge, MA: Harvard University Press.

Graeber, David. 2011. *Debt: The First 5,000 Years*. New York: Melville House.

Graeber, David, and David Wengrow. 2021. *The Dawn of Everything: A New History of Humanity*. London: Allen Lane.

Grajzl, Peter, and Peter Murrell. 2016. 'A Darwinian Theory of Institutional Evolution Two Centuries Before Darwin?', *Journal of Economic Behavior and Organization* 131A, November, 346–72.

———. 2019. 'Toward Understanding 17th Century English Culture: A structural topic model of Francis Bacon's ideas', *Journal of Comparative Economics*, 47, 111–35.

———. 2021a. 'A Machine-Learning History of English Caselaw and Legal Ideas Prior to the Industrial Revolution I: Generating and Interpreting the Estimates', *Journal of Institutional Economics* 17 (1), February, 1–19.

———. 2021b. 'A Machine-Learning History of English Caselaw and Legal Ideas Prior to the Industrial Revolution II: Applications', *Journal of Institutional Economics* 17 (2), April, 201–16.

———. 2022a. 'Lasting Legal Legacies: Early English Legal Ideas and Later Caselaw Development during the Industrial Revolution', *Review of Law and Economics*, 1–57.

———. 2022b. 'Of Families and Inheritance: Law and Development in Pre-Industrial England', ms.

———. 2022c. 'Did Caselaw Foster England's Economic Development During the Industrial Revolution? Data and Evidence', unpublished.

———. 2022d. 'Using Topic-Modeling in Legal History, with an Application to Pre-Industrial English Caselaw on Finance', *Law and History Review*.

Gray, Charles Montgomery. 1963. *Copyhold, Equity and the Common Law*. Oxford: Oxford University Press.

Greif, Avner, and Guido Tabellini. 2010. 'Cultural and Institutional Bifurcation: China and Europe Compared', *American Economic Review: Papers & Proceedings* 100, May, 135–40.

———. 2017. 'The Clan and the Corporation: Sustaining Cooperation in China and Europe', *Journal of Comparative Economics* 45, 1–35.

Griffiths, Trevor, Philip A. Hunt and Patrick K. O'Brien. 1992. 'Inventive Activity in the British Textile Industry, 1700–1800', *Journal of Economic History* 52 (4), December, 881–906.

Grossman, Richard S. 2010. *Unsettled Account: The Evolution of Banking in the Industrialized World since 1800*. Princeton, NJ: Princeton University Press.

Guala, Francesco. 2016. *Understanding Institutions: The Science and Philosophy of Living Together*. Princeton, NJ: Princeton University Press.

Guinnane, Timothy W. 2011. 'The Historical Fertility Transition: A Guide for Economists', *Journal of Economic Literature* 49 (3), September, 589–614.

Habakkuk, H. John. 1940. 'English Landownership, 1680–1740', *Economic History Review*, 1st series, 10, 2–17.

———. 1950. 'Marriage Settlements in the Eighteenth Century', *Transactions of the Royal Historical Society*, 4th series, 32, 15–30.

———. 1958. 'The Market for Monastic Property, 1539–1603', *Economic History Review*, New Series, 10 (3), 362–80.

———. 1960. 'The English Land Market in the Eighteenth Century', in *Britain and the Netherlands*, ed. J. S. Bromley and E. H. Kossmann. London: Chatto and Windus, 154–73.

———. 1962. *American and British Technology in the Nineteenth Century*. Cambridge: Cambridge University Press.

———. 1979. 'The Rise and Fall of English Landed Families, 1600–1800: I', *Transactions of the Royal Historical Society*, 5th series, 29, 187–207.

———. 1980. 'The Rise and Fall of English Landed Families, 1600–1800: II', *Transactions of the Royal Historical Society*, 5th series, 30, 199–221.

———. 1981. 'The Rise and Fall of English Landed Families, 1600–1800: III. Did the Gentry Rise?', *Transactions of the Royal Historical Society*, 5th series, 31, 195–217.

———. 1994. *Marriage, Debt, and the Estates System: English Landownership, 1650–1950*. Oxford: Clarendon Press.

Haggard, Stephan, Andrew MacIntyre and Lydia Tiede. 2008. 'The Rule of Law and Economic Development', *Annual Review of Political Science*, 11, 205–34.

Haggard, Stephan, and Lydia Tiede. 2011. 'The Rule of Law and Economic Growth', *Annual World Development* 39 (5), 673–85.

Hahn, Frank H. 1991. 'The Next Hundred Years', *Economic Journal* 101 (1), January, 47–50.

Haidt, Jonathan. 2012. *The Righteous Mind: Why Good People Are Divided by Politics and Religion*. London: Penguin.

Haidt, Jonathan, and Craig Joseph. 2004. 'Intuitive Ethics: How Innately Prepared Intuitions Generate Culturally Variable Virtues', *Daedalus* 133 (4), Fall, 55–66.

———. 2008. 'The Moral Mind: How Five Sets of Innate Intuitions Guide the Development of Many Culture-Specific Virtues, and Perhaps Even Modules', in *The Innate Mind, Vol. 3*, ed. Peter Carruthers, S. Laurence and S. Stich. Oxford: Oxford University Press, 367–444.

Hale, Robert Lee. 1952. *Freedom through Law: Public Control of Private Governing Power*. New York: Columbia University Press.

Hall, Peter A., and David Soskice, eds. 2001. *Varieties of Capitalism: The Institutional Foundations of Comparative Advantage*. Oxford: Oxford University Press.

Harcourt, Geoffrey C. 1972. *Some Cambridge Controversies in the Theory of Capital*. Cambridge, Cambridge University Press.

Harley, C. Knick. 1982. 'British Industrialization before 1841: Evidence of Slower Growth during the Industrial Revolution', *Journal of Economic History* 42 (2), 267–89.

Harper, David A. 2014. 'Property Rights as a Complex Adaptive System: How Entrepreneurship Transforms Intellectual Property Structures', *Journal of Evolutionary Economics* 24, 335–55.

Harrington, James, 1747. *The Oceana and Other Works of James Harrington, with an Account of His Life*, 3rd ed. London: Millar.

Harris, Tim, 2006. *Revolution: The Great Crisis of the British Monarchy, 1685–1720*. London: Allen Lane.

Hart, Herbert L. A. 1961. *The Concept of Law*. Oxford: Oxford University Press.

Hart, Marjolein 't. 1991. '"The Devil or the Dutch": Holland's Impact on the Financial Revolution in England, 1643–1694', *Parliaments, Estates, and Representation* 11 (1), June, 39–52.

Hartwell, Ronald M. 1965. 'The Causes of the Industrial Revolution: An Essay in Methodology', *Economic History Review*, New Series, 18 (1), 164–82.

Harvey, P. D. A., ed. 1984. *The Peasant Land Market in Medieval England*. Oxford: Oxford University Press.

Haskins, George L. 1977. 'Extending the Grasp of the Dead Hand: Reflections on the Origins of the Rule against Perpetuities', *University of Pennsylvania Law Review* 126, 19–46.

Hayek, Friedrich A. 1948. *Individualism and Economic Order*. London: Routledge and Chicago: University of Chicago Press.

Haynes, John-Dylan, and Geraint Rees. 2005. 'Predicting the Orientation of Invisible Stimuli from Activity in Human Primary Visual Cortex', *Nature Neuroscience* 8 (5), May, 686–91.

———. 2005. 'Predicting the Stream of Consciousness from Activity in Human Visual Cortex', *Current Biology* 15 (14), 1301–7.

Haynes, John-Dylan, K. Sakai, G. Rees, S. Gilbert, C. Frith and R. Passingham. 2007. 'Reading Hidden Intentions in the Human Brain', *Current Biology* 17 (4), 323–28.

Heaton, Herbert. 1937. 'Financing the Industrial Revolution', *Bulletin of the Business Historical Society* 11 (1), February, 1–10.

Heblich, Stephan, and Alex Trew. 2019. 'Banking and Industrialization', *Journal of the European Economic Association* 17 (6), December, 1753–96.

Heim, Carol E., and Philip Mirowski. 1987. 'Interest Rates and Crowding-Out during Britain's Industrial Revolution', *Journal of Economic History* 47 (1), March, 117–39.

Heinsohn, Gunnar, and Otto Steiger. 2013. *Ownership Economics: On the Foundations of Interest, Money, Markets, Business Cycles and Economic Development*, trans. and ed. Frank Decker. London: Routledge.

Heldring, Leander, James A. Robinson and Sebastian Vollmer. 2020. 'The Long-Run Impact of the Dissolution of the English Monasteries', NBER Working Paper 21450, rev. version, National Bureau of Economic Research. http://www.nber.org/papers/w21450.

Heller, Michael A. 2008. *The Gridlock Economy: How Too Much Ownership Wrecks Markets, Stops Innovation, and Costs Lives*. New York: Basic Books.

Hendriks-Jansen, Horst. 1996. *Catching Ourselves in the Act: Situated Activity, Interaction, Emergence, Evolution and Human Thought*. Cambridge, MA: MIT Press.

Henrich, Joseph. 2004. 'Cultural Group Selection, Coevolutionary Processes and Large-Scale Cooperation', *Journal of Economic Behavior and Organization* 53 (1), February, 3–35.

Henrich, Joseph, and Robert Boyd. 1998. 'The Evolution of Conformist Transmission and the Emergence of Between Group Differences', *Evolution and Human Behavior* 19, 215–42.

———. 2001. 'Why People Punish Defectors: Why Conformist Transmission Can Stabilize Costly Enforcement of Norms in Cooperative Dilemmas', *Journal of Theoretical Biology* 208 (1), 79–89.

Henrich, Joseph, Jean Ensminger, Richard McElreath, Abigail Barr, Clark Barrett, Alexander Bolyanatz, Juan Camilo Cardenas, Michael Gurven, Edwins Gwako, Natalie Henrich, Carolyn Lesorogol, Frank Marlowe, David Tracer and John Ziker. 2010. 'Markets, Religion, Community Size, and the Evolution of Fairness and Punishment', *Science* 327 (5972), 1480–84.

Henrich, Joseph, and Francisco J. Gil-White. 2001) 'The Evolution of Prestige: Freely Conferred Deference as a Mechanism for Enhancing the Benefits of Cultural Transmission', *Evolution and Human Behavior* 22 (3), 165–96.

Henrich, Joseph, Richard McElreath, Abigail Barr, Jean Ensminger, Clark Barrett, Alaexander Bolyanatz, Juan Camilo Cardenas, Michael Gurven, Edwins Gwako, Natalie Henrich, Carolyn Lesorogol, Frank Marlowe, David Tracer and John Ziker. 2006. 'Costly Punishment Across Human Societies'. *Science* 312, no. 5781, 1767–70.

Hexter, Jack H. 1958. 'Storm Over the Gentry', *Encounter* 10 (5), May, 22–34.

———, ed. 1992. *Parliament and Liberty: From the Reign of Elizabeth to the English Civil War*. Stanford, CA: Stanford University Press.

Hill, Christopher. 1940. 'The Agrarian Legislation of the Interregnum', *English Historical Review*, 55 (218), April, 222–50.

———. 1948. 'The English Civil War Interpreted by Marx and Engels', *Science and Society* 12 (1), Winter, 130–56.

———. 1948/1949. 'Land in the English Revolution', *Science and Society* 13 (1), Winter, 22–49.

———. 1956. 'Recent Interpretations of the Civil War', *History*, New Series, 41 (141/143), February–October, 67–87.

———. 1961. *The Century of Revolution 1603–1714*. London: Van Nostrand Reinhold.

———. 1965. *The Intellectual Origins of the English Revolution*. Oxford: Oxford University Press.

———. 1975. *The World Turned Upside Down: Radical Ideas during the English Revolution*. Harmondsworth, UK: Penguin.

———. 1980. 'A Bourgeois Revolution?' in *Three British Revolutions: 1641, 1688, 1776*, ed. J. G. A. Pocock. Princeton, NJ: Princeton University Press, 109–39.

Hilton, Rodney H. 1969. *The Decline of Serfdom in Medieval England*. London: Macmillan.

Hobsbawm, Eric J. 1969. *Industry and Empire*. Harmondsworth, UK: Penguin.

Hobson, John A. 1926. *The Evolution of Modern Capitalism: A Study of Machine Production*, rev. ed. London: Walter Scott and New York: Charles Scribner's.

Hodgson, Geoffrey M. 1984. *The Democratic Economy: A New Look at Planning, Markets and Power*. Harmondsworth, UK: Penguin.

———. 1988. *Economics and Institutions: A Manifesto for a Modern Institutional Economics*. Cambridge: Polity Press and Philadelphia: University of Pennsylvania Press.

———. 1989. 'Institutional Rigidities and Economic Growth', *Cambridge Journal of Economics* 13 (1), March, 79–101.

———. 1996. 'An Evolutionary Theory of Long-Term Economic Growth', *International Studies Quarterly* 40, 393–412.

———. 1997. 'The Ubiquity of Habits and Rules', *Cambridge Journal of Economics* 21 (6), November, 663–84.

———. 1991. 'Economic Evolution: Intervention Contra Pangloss', *Journal of Economic Issues* 25 (2), June, 519–33.

———. 1993. *Economics and Evolution: Bringing Life Back Into Economics*. Cambridge: Polity Press and Ann Arbor: University of Michigan Press.

———. 2001. *How Economics Forgot History: The Problem of Historical Specificity in Social Science*. London: Routledge.

———. 2004. *The Evolution of Institutional Economics: Agency, Structure and Darwinism in American Institutionalism*. London: Routledge.

———. 2006. 'What Are Institutions?' *Journal of Economic Issues* 40 (1), March, 1–25.

———. 2007. 'Evolutionary and Institutional Economics as the New Mainstream?' *Evolutionary and Institutional Economics Review* 4 (1), September, 7–25.

———. 2010. 'Choice, Habit and Evolution', *Journal of Evolutionary Economics* 20 (1), January, 1–18.

———. 2013a. *From Pleasure Machines to Moral Communities: An Evolutionary Economics without Homo Economicus*. Chicago: University of Chicago Press.

———. 2013b. 'Come Back Marshall, All Is Forgiven? Complexity, Evolution, Mathematics and Marshallian Exceptionalism', *European Journal of the History of Economic Thought* 20 (6), December, 957–81.

———. 2014. 'What Is Capital? Economists and Sociologists Have Changed Its Meaning—Should It Be Changed Back?' *Cambridge Journal of Economics* 38 (5), September, 1063–86.

———. 2015a. *Conceptualizing Capitalism: Institutions, Evolution, Future*. Chicago: University of Chicago Press.

———. 2015b. 'Much of the "Economics of Property Rights" Devalues Property and Legal Rights', *Journal of Institutional Economics* 11 (4), December, 683–709.

———. 2015c. 'What Humpty Dumpty Might Have Said about Property Rights—and the Need to Put Them Back Together Again: A Response to Critics', *Journal of Institutional Economics* 11 (4), December, 731–47.

———. 2016. 'Varieties of Capitalism: Some Philosophical and Historical Considerations', *Cambridge Journal of Economics* 40 (3), May, 941–60.

———. 2017a. 'Introduction to the Douglass C. North Memorial Issue', *Journal of Institutional Economics* 13 (1), March, 1–23.

———. 2017b. '1688 and All That: Property Rights, the Glorious Revolution and the Rise of British Capitalism', *Journal of Institutional Economics* 13 (1), March, 79–107.

———. 2018. *Wrong Turnings: How the Left Got Lost*. Chicago: University of Chicago Press.

———. 2019a. 'Taxonomic Definitions in Social Science, with Firms, Markets and Institutions as Case Studies', *Journal of Institutional Economics* 15 (2), April, 207–33.

———. 2019b. *Evolutionary Economics: Its Nature and Future*, in *Cambridge Elements in Evolutionary Economics*, series ed. John Foster and Jason Potts. Cambridge: Cambridge University Press.

———. 2019c. *Is Socialism Feasible? Towards an Alternative Future*. Cheltenham, UK: Edward Elgar.

———. 2019d. *Is There a Future for Heterodox Economics? Institutions, Ideology and a Scientific Community*. Cheltenham, UK: Edward Elgar.

———. 2020. 'How Mythical Markets Mislead Analysis: An Institutionalist Critique of Market Universalism', *Socio-Economic Review* 18 (4), October, 1153–74.

———. 2021a. 'On the Limits of Markets', *Journal of Institutional Economics* 17 (1), February, 153–70.

———. 2021b. 'Financial Institutions and the British Industrial Revolution: Did Financial Underdevelopment Hold Back Growth?' *Journal of Institutional Economics* 17 (3), June, 429–48.

———. 2021c. *Liberal Solidarity: The Political Economy of Social Democratic Liberalism*. Cheltenham, UK: Edward Elgar).

———. 2022a. 'Culture and Institutions: A Review of Joel Mokyr's *A Culture of Growth*', *Journal of Institutional Economics* 18 (1), February, 159–68.

———. 2022b. 'Donald T. Campbell on the Institutions of Scientific Knowledge and the Limits to Interdisciplinarity', *Journal of Institutional Economics*, 18 (6), December, 969–80.

———. 2023. 'Thorstein Veblen and Socialism', *Journal of Economic Issues*, forthcoming.

Hodgson, Geoffrey M., and Kainan Huang. 2013. 'Brakes on Chinese Economic Development: Institutional Causes of a Growth Slowdown', *Journal of Economic Issues* 47 (3), September, 599–622.

Hodgson, Geoffrey M., and Thorbjørn Knudsen. 2004. 'The Complex Evolution of a Simple Traffic Convention: The Functions and Implications of Habit', *Journal of Economic Behavior and Organization* 54 (1), 19–47.

———. 2010. *Darwin's Conjecture: The Search for General Principles of Social and Economic Evolution*. Chicago: University of Chicago Press.

Hoffman, Philip T., David S. Jacks, Patricia A. Levin and Peter H. Lindert. 2002. 'Real Inequality in Europe since 1500', *Journal of Economic History* 62 (2), June, 322–55.

Hoffman, Philip T., Gilles Postel-Vinay and Jean-Lauren Rosenthal. 2019. *Dark Matter Credit: The Development of Peer-to-Peer Lending and Banking in France*. Princeton, NJ: Princeton University Press.

Hofstede, Geert. 1984. *Culture's Consequences: International Differences in Work-Related Values*. London: Sage.

Holland, John H. 1992. 'Complex Adaptive Systems', *Daedalus* 121 (1), Winter, 17–30.

————. 2006. 'Studying Complex Adaptive Systems', *Journal of Systems Science and Complexity* 19, 1–8.

Holland, John H., Keith J. Holyoak, Richard E. Nisbett and Paul R. Thagard. 1986. *Induction: Processes of Inference, Learning and Discovery*. Cambridge, MA: MIT Press.

Honoré, Antony M. 1961. 'Ownership', in *Oxford Essays in Jurisprudence*, ed. Anthony G. Guest. Oxford: Oxford University Press, 107–47. Reprinted in the *Journal of Institutional Economics* 9 (2), June 2013, 227–55.

Hoppit, Julian. 1987. 'Financial Crises in Eighteenth-Century England', *Economic History Review*, New Series 39 (1), February, 39–58.

————. 2011. 'Compulsion, Compensation and Property Rights in Britain, 1688–1833', *Past and Present* 210 (1), February, 93–128.

Hoskins, W. G. 1968) 'Harvest Fluctuations and English Economic History, 1620–1759', *Agricultural History Review* 16 (10), 15–31.

Hoston, Germaine A. 1991. 'Conceptualizing Bourgeois Revolution: The Prewar Japanese Left and the Meiji Restoration', *Comparative Studies in Society and History* 33 (3), July, 539–81.

Houle, David. 1992. 'Comparing Evolvability and the Variability of Quantitative Traits', *Genetics* 130, January, 195–284.

Hudson, Pat. 1986. *The Genesis of Industrial Capital: A Study of the West Riding Wool Textile Industry c. 1750–1850*. Cambridge: Cambridge University Press.

Hull, David L. 1988. *Science as a Process: An Evolutionary Account of the Social and Conceptual Development of Science*. Chicago: University of Chicago Press.

Hume, David. 1983 [1778]. *The History of England from the Invasion of Julius Caesar to the Revolution in 1688*, ed. W. B. Todd, 6 vols. Indianapolis, IN: Liberty Fund.

Humphries, Jane, and Benjamin Schneider. 2019. 'Spinning the Industrial Revolution', *Economic History Review* 72 (1), February, 1–30.

Hutchins, Edwin. 1995. *Cognition in the Wild*. Cambridge, MA: MIT Press.

Hutchinson, Martin, and Kevin Dowd. 2018. 'The Apotheosis of the Rentier: How Napoleonic War Finance Kick-Started the Industrial Revolution', *Cato Journal* 38 (3), Fall, 655–78.

Ingham, Geoffrey. 1984. *Capitalism Divided? The City and Industry in British Social Development*. London: Macmillan.

————. 2004. *The Nature of Money*. Cambridge: Polity Press.

————. 2008. *Capitalism*. Cambridge: Polity Press.

Inikori, Joseph E. 1992. 'Slavery and Atlantic Commerce, 1650–1800', *American Economic Review* 82 (2), May, 151–57.

International Monetary Fund. 2022. *World Economic Outlook Database*. https://www.imf.org/en/Publications/WEO/weo-database/2022/April/weo-report?.

Israel, Jonathan I. 1989. *Dutch Primacy in World Trade 1585–1740*. Oxford: Oxford University Press.

————, ed. 1991. *The Anglo-Dutch Moment: Essays on the Glorious Revolution and Its World Impact*. Cambridge: Cambridge University Press.

Jakab, Zoltan, and Michael Kumhof. 2015. 'Banks Are Not Intermediaries of Loanable Funds— and Why This Matters', Bank of England Working Paper No. 529, London.

Jardine, Lisa. 2008. *Going Dutch: How England Plundered Holland's Glory*. London: Harper.

Jessop, Robert. 1990. *State Theory: Putting the Capitalist State in Its Place*. Oxford: Basil Blackwell.

Joas, Hans. 1996. *The Creativity of Action*, trans. from German edition of 1992. Chicago: University of Chicago Press.

John, A. H. 1953. 'Insurance Investment and the London Money Market of the Eighteenth Century', *Economica* 20 (78), May, 137–58.

Johnson, Chalmers. 1982. *MITI and the Japanese Miracle: The Growth of Industrial Policy, 1925–1975*. Stanford, CA: Stanford University Press.

———. 1995. *Japan, Who Governs? The Rise of the Developmental State*. New York: Norton.

Jones, Eric L. 2003. *European Miracle: Environments, Economies and Geopolitics in the History of Europe and Asia*, 3rd ed. Cambridge: Cambridge University Press.

Jones, J. R., ed. 1992. *Liberty Secured? Britain Before and After 1688*. Stanford, CA: Stanford University Press.

Jordan, William C. 1996. *The Great Famine: Northern Europe in the Early Fourteenth Century*. Princeton, NJ: Princeton University Press.

Joslin, D. M. 1954. 'The London Private Bankers, 1720–1785', *Economic History Review*, New Series, 7 (2), 167–86.

———. 1960. 'London Bankers in Wartime 1739–84', in *Studies in the Industrial Revolution*, ed. Leslie S. Pressnell. London: Athlone, 156–77.

Kahan, Arcadius. 1973. 'Notes on Serfdom in Western and Eastern Europe', *Journal of Economic History* 33 (1), March, 86–99.

Karaman, K. Kivanç, Sevket Pamuk and Seçil Yildirim-Karaman. 2020. 'Money and Monetary Stability in Europe, 1300–1914', *Journal of Monetary Economics* 115, November, 279–300.

Kelly, Patrick. 1985. 'Ireland and the Critique of Mercantilism in Berkeley's "Querist"', *Hermathena*, no. 139, Winter, 101–16.

Kendal, Jake. 2012. 'Local Financial Development and Growth', *Journal of Banking and Finance* 36 (5), May, 1548–62.

Kennedy, Paul. 1988. *The Rise and Fall of the Great Powers: Economic Change and Military Conflict from 1500 to 2000*. London: Unwin Hyman.

Kenworthy, Lane. 2019. *Social Democratic Capitalism*. Oxford: Oxford University Press.

Keynes, John Maynard. 1921. *A Treatise on Probability*. London: Macmillan.

———. 1930. *A Treatise on Money, Vol. 1: The Pure Theory of Money, Vol. 2: The Applied Theory of Money*. London: Macmillan.

———. 1936. *The General Theory of Employment, Interest and Money*. London: Macmillan.

———. 1937. 'The General Theory of Employment', *Quarterly Journal of Economics* 51 (1), February, 209–23.

Khanna, Sushil. 1978. 'Capital and Finance in the Industrial Revolution: Lessons for the Third World', *Economic and Political Weekly* 13 (46), 18 November, 1889–98.

Keen, Steve. 2022. *The New Economics: A Manifesto*. Cambridge: Polity.

Keijzer, Fred. 2001. *Representation and Behavior*. Cambridge, MA: MIT Press.

Kelton, Stephanie. 2020. *The Deficit Myth: Modern Monetary Theory and How to Build a Better Economy*. London: John Murray.

Kim, Jongchul. 2014. 'Identity and the Hybridity of Modern Finance: How a Specifically Modern Concept of the Self Underlies the Modern Ownership of Property, Trusts and Finance', *Cambridge Journal of Economics* 38 (2), 425–46.

Kindleberger, Charles P. 1984. *A Financial History of Western Europe*. London: George Allen and Unwin.

King, Robert G., and Ross Levine. 1993. 'Finance and Growth: Schumpeter Might Be Right', *Quarterly Journal of Economics* 108 (3), August, 717–37.

King, Steven, and Geoffrey Timmins. 2001. *Making Sense of the Industrial Revolution: English Economy and Society 1700–1850*. Manchester, UK: Manchester University Press.

Kingston, Chris, and Gonzalo Caballero. 2009. 'Comparing Theories of Institutional Change', *Journal of Institutional Economics* 5 (2), August, 161–80.

Kitcher, Philip. 1993. *The Advancement of Science: Science without Legend, Objectivity without Illusions*. Oxford: Oxford University Press.

Kitson, Peter M., L. Shaw-Taylor, E. A. Wrigley, R. S. Davies, G. Newton, and A. E. M. Satchell. 2012. 'The Creation of a "Census" of Adult Male Employment for England and Wales for 1817', Cambridge Group for the History of Population and Social Structure, Working Paper, University of Cambridge.

Knapp, Georg F. 1924. *The State Theory of Money*, trans. and abridged from fourth German edition of 1923. London: Macmillan.

Knight, Frank H. 1921. *Risk, Uncertainty and Profit*. New York: Houghton Mifflin.

Knight, Jack. 1992. *Institutions and Social Conflict*. Cambridge: Cambridge University Press.

Knudsen, Thorbjørn, Phanish Puranam and Marlo Raveendran. 2012. 'Organization Design: The Epistemic Interdependence Perspective', *Academy of Management Review* 37 (3), 419–40.

Knutsen, Carl Henrik. 2015. 'Why Democracies Outgrow Autocracies in the Long Run: Civil Liberties, Information Flows and Technological Change', *Kyklos* 68 (3), August, 357–84.

Kocher, Paul H. 1957. 'Francis Bacon and the Science of Jurisprudence', *Journal of the History of Ideas* 8 (1), January, 3–26.

Kornai, János. 1971. *Anti-Equilibrium: On Economic Systems Theory and the Tasks of Research*. Amsterdam: North-Holland.

Koyama, Mark, and Jared Rubin. 2022. *How the World Became Rich: The Historical Origins of Economic Growth*. Cambridge: Polity Press.

Kuhn, Thomas S. 1962. *The Structure of Scientific Revolutions*. Chicago: University of Chicago Press.

Laeven, Luc, Ross Levine and Stelios Michalopoulos. 2015. 'Financial Innovation and Endogenous Growth', *Journal of Financial Intermediation* 24 (1), January, 1–24.

Laibman, David. 2019. 'Forces of Production and Relations of Production', in *The Oxford Handbook of Karl Marx*, ed. Matt Vidal, Tony Smith, Tomás Rotta and Paul Prew. Oxford: Oxford University Press, 77–96.

Lane, David, Franco Malerba, Robert Maxfield and Luigi Orsenigo. 1996. 'Choice and Action', *Journal of Evolutionary Economics* 6 (1), 43–76.

Langbein, John H. 1976. *Torture and the Law of Proof*. Chicago: University of Chicago Press.

Latour, Bruno. 2005. *Reassembling the Social: An Introduction to Actor-Network-Theory*. Oxford: Oxford University Press.

Lave, Jean, and Etienne Wenger. 1991. *Situated Learning: Legitimate Peripheral Participation.* Cambridge: Cambridge University Press.

Lawrence, William H. 2002. *Understanding Negotiable Instruments and Payment Systems.* Newark, NJ: Matthew Bender.

Lay, Paul. 2020. *Providence Lost: The Rise and Fall of Cromwell's Protectorate.* London: Head of Zeus.

Lee, Keun. 2013. *Schumpeterian Analysis of Economic Catch-up: Knowledge, Path-Creation, and the Middle-Income Trap.* Cambridge: Cambridge University Press.

Leijonhufvud, Axel. 1986. 'Capitalism and the Factory System', in *Economic as a Process: Essays in the New Institutional Economics,* ed. Richard N. Langlois. Cambridge: Cambridge University Press, 203–23.

Leontief, Wassily W. 1966. *Input-Output Economics.* Oxford: Oxford University Press.

Lerner, Abba P. 1947. 'Money as a Creature of the State', *American Economic Review* 37 (2), June, 312–17.

Lessnoff, Michael H. 1994. *The Spirit of Capitalism and the Protestant Ethic: An Enquiry into the Weber Thesis.* Aldershot, UK: Edward Elgar.

Levine, Ross. 2005. 'Finance and Growth: Theory, Mechanisms and Evidence', in *Handbook of Economic Growth, Volume 1,* ed. Philippe Aghion and Steven N. Durlauf. Amsterdam: Elsevier, 865–934.

Libet, Benjamin. 1985. 'Unconscious Cerebral Initiative and the Role of Conscious Will in Voluntary Action', *Behavioral and Brain Sciences* 8, 529–66.

———. 2004. *Mind Time: The Temporal Factor in Consciousness.* Cambridge, MA: Harvard University Press.

Libet, Benjamin, Curtis A. Gleason, Elwood W. Wright and Dennis K. Pearl. 1983. 'Time of Conscious Intention to Act in Relation to Onset of Cerebral Activity (Readiness-Potential): The Unconscious Initiation of a Freely Voluntary Act', *Brain* 106 (3), 623–42.

Lin, Justin Yifu. 2012. *Demystifying the Chinese Economy.* Cambridge: Cambridge University Press.

Lindert, Peter H. 1986. 'Unequal English Wealth since 1670', *Journal of Political Economy* 94 (6), December, 1127–62.

Lindert, Peter H., and Jeffrey G. Williamson. 1982. 'Revising England's Social Tables, 1688–1812', *Explorations in Economic History* 19 (4), October, 385–408.

Lockwood, William W. 1954. *The Economic Development of Japan: Growth and Structural Change 1868–1938.* Princeton, NJ: Princeton University Press.

Lovell, Michael C. 1957. 'The Role of the Bank of England as Lender of Last Resort in the Crises of the Eighteenth Century', *Explorations in Entrepreneurial History* 10 (1), October, 8–21.

Luo, Jianxi, Carliss Y. Baldwin, Daniel E. Whitney and Christopher L. Magee. 2012. 'The Architecture of Transaction Networks: A Comparative Analysis of Hierarchy in Two Sectors', *Industrial and Corporate Change* 21 (6), 1307–35.

Mackie, John D. 1952. *The Early Tudors 1495–1558.* Oxford: Oxford University Press.

MacLeod, Christine. 2002. *Inventing the Industrial Revolution: The English Patent System, 1660–1800.* Cambridge: Cambridge University Press.

MacLeod, Henry Dunning. 1858. *Elements of Political Economy.* London: Longmans Green.

———. 1872. *The Principles of Economic Philosophy,* 2nd ed. London: Longmans Green.

Macpherson, Crawford B. 1962. *The Political Theory of Possessive Individualism: Hobbes to Locke.* Oxford: Oxford University Press.

Maddison, Angus. 2003. *The World Economy: Historical Statistics.* Paris: OECD.

———. 2007. *Contours of the World Economy, 1–2030 AD: Essays in Macro-Economic History.* Oxford: Oxford University Press.

Mann, Michael. 1986. *The Sources of Social Power, Volume 1: A History of Power from the Beginning to A.D. 1760.* Cambridge: Cambridge University Press.

Manning, Brian. 1976. *The English People and the English Revolution, 1640–1649.* London: Heinemann.

Mantzavinos, Chris. 2001. *Individuals, Institutions, and Markets.* Cambridge: Cambridge University Press.

Marshall, Alfred. 1920. *Principles of Economics: An Introductory Volume,* 8th ed. London: Macmillan.

Marx, Karl. 1971. *A Contribution to the Critique of Political Economy,* trans. from German edition of 1859. London: Lawrence and Wishart.

———. 1973a. *The Revolutions of 1848: Political Writings—Volume 1,* ed. and intro. David Fernbach. Harmondsworth, UK: Penguin.

———. 1973b. *Grundrisse: Foundations of the Critique of Political Economy,* trans. Martin Nicolaus. Harmondsworth, UK: Penguin.

———. 1976. *Capital,* vol. 1, trans. from fourth German edition of 1890. Harmondsworth, UK: Pelican.

———. 1981. *Capital,* vol. 3, trans. from German edition of 1894. Harmondsworth, UK: Pelican.

Marx, Karl, and Frederick Engels. 1962. *Selected Works in Two Volumes.* London: Lawrence and Wishart.

———. 1975. *Karl Marx and Frederick Engels, Collected Works, Vol. 3, Marx and Engels: 1843–1844.* London: Lawrence and Wishart.

———. 1976a. *Karl Marx and Frederick Engels, Collected Works, Vol. 5, Marx and Engels: 1845–1847.* London: Lawrence and Wishart.

———. 1976b. *Karl Marx and Frederick Engels, Collected Works, Vol. 6, Marx and Engels: 1845–1848.* London: Lawrence and Wishart.

———. 1978. *Karl Marx and Frederick Engels, Collected Works, Vol. 10, Marx and Engels: 1849–1851.* London: Lawrence and Wishart.

———. 1982. *Karl Marx and Frederick Engels, Collected Works, Vol. 38, Letters 1844–1851.* London: Lawrence and Wishart.

Mason, Shena. ed. 2009. *Matthew Boulton: Selling What All the World Desires.* (New Haven and London: Yale University Press).

Mathias, Peter. 1969. *The First Industrial Nation: An Economic History of Britain 1700–1914.* London: Methuen.

———. 1983. *The First Industrial Nation: An Economic History of Britain 1700–1914,* 2nd ed. London: Routledge.

Mayfield, John E. 2013. *The Engine of Complexity: Evolution as Computation.* New York: Columbia University Press.

Maynard Smith, John, and Eörs Szathmáry. 1995. *The Major Transitions in Evolution.* Oxford: Freeman.

Mayr, Ernst. 1960. 'The Emergence of Evolutionary Novelties', in *Evolution after Darwin (I): The Evolution of Life*, ed. Sol Tax. Chicago: University of Chicago Press, 349–80.

———. 1982. *The Growth of Biological Thought: Diversity, Evolution, and Inheritance*. Cambridge, MA: Harvard University Press.

———. 1988. *Toward a New Philosophy of Biology: Observations of an Evolutionist*. Cambridge, MA: Harvard University Press.

———. 1991. *One Long Argument: Charles Darwin and the Genesis of Modern Evolutionary Thought*. Cambridge, MA: Harvard University Press and London: Allen Lane.

McCloskey, Deirdre N. 2010. *Bourgeois Dignity: Why Economics Can't Explain the Modern World*. Chicago: University of Chicago Press.

———. 2016a. 'Max U vs. Humanomics: A Critique of Neo-Institutionalism', *Journal of Institutional Economics* 12 (1), March, 1–27.

———. 2016b. *Bourgeois Equality: How Ideas, Not Capital or Institutions, Enriched the World*. Chicago: University of Chicago Press.

———2019. *Why Liberalism Works: How True Liberal Values Produce a Freer, More Equal, Prosperous World for All*. New Haven, CT: Yale University Press.

McCloskey, Deirdre Nansen, and Paolo Silvestri. 2021. 'Beyond Behaviorism, Positivism, and Neo-institutionalism in Economics: A Conversation with Deirdre Nansen McCloskey', *Journal of Institutional Economics* 17 (5), October, 717–28.

McFarland, Floyd B. 1985. 'Thorstein Veblen versus the Institutionalists', *Review of Radical Political Economics* 17 (4), Winter, 95–105.

———. 1986. 'Clarence Ayres and His Gospel of Technology', *History of Political Economy* 18 (4), Winter, 593–613.

McLeay, Michael, Amar Radia and Ryland Thomas. 2014. 'Money Creation in the Modern Economy', *Bank of England Quarterly Bulletin* Q1, 14–27.

Mehrling, Perry G. 2000. "Modern Money: Fiat or Credit?" *Journal of Post Keynesian Economics* 22 (3), Spring, 397–406.

Meiksins Wood, Ellen. 2002. *The Origin of Capitalism: A Longer View*. London: Verso.

Menger, Carl. 1888. 'Zur Theorie des Kapitals', *Jahrbücher für Nationalökonomie und Statistik* 17, 1–49.

Merton, Robert K. 1996. *On Social Structure and Science*. Chicago: University of Chicago Press.

Miles, M. 1981. 'The Money Market in the Early Industrial Revolution: The Evidence from West Riding Attorneys c. 1750–1800', *Business History* 23 (2), 127–46.

Milgram, Stanley. 1974. *Obedience to Authority: An Experimental View*. New York: Harper and Row and London: Tavistock.

Mill, John Stuart. 1909. *Principles of Political Economy with Some of Their Applications to Social Philosophy*, 7th ed., ed. William Ashley. London: Longmans, Green.

Miller, Seumas. 2010. *The Moral Foundations of Social Institutions: A Philosophical Study*. Cambridge: Cambridge University Press.

Mingay, G. E. 1963. *English Landed Society in the Eighteenth Century*. London:Routledge and Kegan Paul and Toronto: University of Toronto Press.

Minsky, Hyman P. 1991. 'Endogeneity of Money', in *Nicholas Kaldor and Mainstream Economics: Confrontation or Convergence?*, ed. Edward J. Nell and Willi Semmler. London: Palgrave Macmillan, 207–20.

Mirowski, Philip. 1989. *More Heat than Light: Economics as Social Physics, Physics as Nature's Economics*. Cambridge: Cambridge University Press.

Mises, Ludwig von. 1949. *Human Action: A Treatise on Economics*. London: William Hodge and New Haven, CT: Yale University Press.

———. 1981. *Socialism: An Economic and Sociological Analysis*, trans. J. Kahane from second (1932) German edition of *Die Gemeinwirtschaft*. Indianapolis, IN: Liberty Classics.

Mitchell Innes, Alfred. 1914. 'The Credit Theory of Money', *Banking Law Journal* 31, December–January, 151–68.

Mokyr, Joel. 1990a. *The Lever of Riches: Technological Creativity and Economic Progress*. Oxford: Oxford University Press.

———1990b. 'Punctuated Equilibria and Technological Progress', *American Economic Review (Papers and Proceedings)* 80 (2), May, 350–54.

———. 1991. 'Evolutionary Biology, Technical Change and Economic History', *Bulletin of Economic Research* 43 (2), April, 127–49.

———, ed. 1993. *The British Industrial Revolution: An Economic Perspective*. Boulder, CO: Westview Press.

———. 1994a. 'Technological Change, 1700–1830', in *The Economic History of Britain since 1700: Volume 1: 1700–1860*, 2nd ed., ed. Roderick Floud and Deirdre McCloskey. Cambridge: Cambridge University Press, 12–43.

———. 1994b. 'Cardwell's Law and the Political Economy of Technological Progress', *Research Policy* 23 (5), 561–74.

———. 2002. *The Gifts of Athena: Historical Origins of the Knowledge Economy*. Princeton, NJ: Princeton University Press.

———. 2009. *The Enlightened Economy: An Economic History of Britain 1700–1850*. New Haven, CT: Yale University Press.

———. 2016. *A Culture of Growth: The Origins of the Modern Economy*. Princeton, NJ: Princeton University Press.

———. 2022. 'Institutions, Ideas and Economic Change: Some Reflections on Geoffrey Hodgson's "Culture and Institutions"', *Journal of Institutional Economics* 18 (1), February, 169–74.

Moore, Barrington, Jr. 1966. *Social Origins of Dictatorship and Democracy: Lord and Peasant in the Making of the Modern World*. London: Allen Lane.

Moore, Basil J. 1988. *Horizontalists and Verticalists: The Macroeconomics of Credit Money*. Cambridge: Cambridge University Press.

Morgan, E. Victor, and W. A. Thomas. 1962. *The Stock Exchange, Its History and Functions*. London: Elek Books.

Morley, John. 1920. *The Life of Richard Cobden*. London: Unwin.

Morrill, John. 1992. 'The Sensible Revolution', in *The Anglo-Dutch Moment: Essays on the Glorious Revolution and Its World Impact*, ed. Jonathan I. Israel. Cambridge: Cambridge University Press, 73–104.

Morris-Suzuki, Tessa. 1996. *The Technological Transformation of Japan: From the 17th to the 21st Century*. Cambridge: Cambridge University Press.

Muldrew, Craig. 1998. *The Economy of Obligation*. Basingstoke, UK: Palgrave.

Murphy, Anne L. 2009. *The Origins of English Financial Markets: Investment and Speculation before the South Sea Bubble*. Cambridge: Cambridge University Press.

————. 2013. 'Demanding "Credible Commitment": Public Reactions to the Failures of the Early Financial Revolution', *Economic History Review* 66 (1), February, 178–97.

Murray, Patrick. 1985. 'Money, Wealth, and Berkeley's Doctrine of Signs: A Reply to Patrick Kelly', *Hermathena*, no. 139, Winter, 152–56.

Murrell, Peter. 2017. 'Design and Evolution in Institutional Development: The Insignificance of the English Bill of Rights', *Journal of Comparative Economics* 45 (1), February, 36–55.

Nakamura, James I. 1966. 'Meiji Land Reform, Redistribution of Income, and Saving from Agriculture', *Economic Development and Cultural Change* 14 (4), July, 428–39.

Narsey, Wadan. 2016. *British Imperialism and the Making of Colonial Currency Systems*. London: Palgrave Macmillan.

Neal, Larry. 1990. *The Rise of Financial Capitalism: International Capital Markets in the Age of Reason*. Cambridge: Cambridge University Press.

————. 1994. 'The Finance of Business During the Industrial Revolution', in *The Economic History of Britain since 1700: Volume 1: 1700–1860*, 2nd ed., ed. Roderick Floud and Deirdre McCloskey. Cambridge: Cambridge University Press, 151–81.

————. 2015. *A Concise History of International Finance: From Babylon to Bernanke*. Cambridge: Cambridge University Press.

Neild, Robert R. 2002. *Public Corruption: The Dark Side of Social Evolution*. London: Anthem.

Nenner, Howard, ed. 1997. *Politics and Political Imagination in Later Stuart Britain*. Rochester, NY: University of Rochester Press.

Newman, Peter R. 1983. 'The Royalist Officer Corps 1642–1660: Army Command as a Reflexion of the Social Structure', *Historical Journal* 26 (4), December, 945–58.

Nonaka, Ikujiro, and Hirotaka Takeuchi. 1995. *The Knowledge-Creating Company: How Japanese Companies Create the Dynamics of Innovation*. Oxford: Oxford University Press.

Nonaka, Ikujiro, Groeg von Krogh and Sven Voelpel. 2006. 'Organizational Knowledge Creation Theory: Evolutionary Paths and Future Advances', *Organization Studies* 27 (8), 1179–1208.

North, Douglass C. 1971. 'Institutional Change and Economic Growth', *Journal of Economic History* 31 (1), March, 118–25.

————. 1981. *Structure and Change in Economic History*. New York: Norton.

————. 1990a. *Institutions, Institutional Change and Economic Performance*. Cambridge: Cambridge University Press.

————. 1990b. 'A Transactions Cost Theory of Politics', *Journal of Theoretical Politics* 2 (4), October, 355–67.

————. 1994. 'Economic Performance through Time', *American Economic Review* 84 (3), June, 359–67.

————. 2005. *Understanding the Process of Economic Change*. Princeton, NJ: Princeton University Press.

North, Douglass C., and Robert P. Thomas. 1971. 'The Rise and Fall of the Manorial System: A Theoretical Model', *Journal of Economic History* 31 (4), 777–803.

————. 1973. *The Rise of the Western World: A New Economic History*. Cambridge: Cambridge University Press.

North, Douglass C., John Joseph Wallis and Barry R. Weingast. 2009. *Violence and Social Orders: A Conceptual Framework for Interpreting Recorded Human History*. Cambridge: Cambridge University Press.

North, Douglass C., and Barry R. Weingast. 1989. 'Constitutions and Commitment: The Evolution of Institutions Governing Public Choice in Seventeenth-Century England', *Journal of Economic History* 49 (4), December, 803–32.

O'Brien, Patrick Karl. 1988. 'The Political Economy of British Taxation, 1660–1815', *Economic History Review*, New Series, 41 (1), February, 1–32.

———. 1996. 'Path Dependency, or Why Britain Became an Industrialized and Urbanized Economy Long before France', *Economic History Review*, New Series, 49 (2), May, 213–49.

———. 2006. 'Provincializing the First Industrial Revolution', Working Paper 17/06, Global Economic History Network (GEHN), London School of Economics, January 2006. http://eprints.lse.ac.uk/22474/1/wp17.pdf.

———. 2011. 'The Nature and Historical Evolution of an Exceptional Fiscal State and Its Possible Significance for the Precocious Commercialization and Industrialization of the British Economy from Cromwell to Nelson', *Economic History Review* 64 (2), May, 408–46.

Oda, Hiroshi. 1992. *Japanese Law*. London: Butterworths.

Ogburn, William F. 1922. *Social Change: With Respect to Culture and Original Nature*. New York: Huebsch.

Ogilvie, Sheilagh, and André W. Carus. 2014. 'Institutions and Economic Growth in Historical Perspective', in *Handbook of Economic Growth*, Vol. 2A, ed. Philippe Aghion and Steven Durlauf. Amsterdam: Elsevier, 403–513.

O'Gorman, Frank. 1997. *The Long Eighteenth Century: British Political and Social History 1688–1832*. New York: Arnold Press.

Okazaki, Tetsuji, and Masahiro Okuno-Fujiwara, eds. 1999. *The Japanese Economic System and Its Historical Origins*. Oxford: Oxford University Press.

Olson, Mancur, Jr. 1993. 'Dictatorship, Democracy, and Development', *American Political Science Review* 87 (3), September, 567–76.

———. 2000. *Power and Prosperity: Outgrowing Communist and Capitalist Dictatorships*. New York: Basic Books.

Organisation for Economic Cooperation and Development (OECD). 2021. 'OECD Income and Wealth Distribution Databases'. http://www.oecd.org/social/income-distribution-database.htm.

Orlikowski, Wanda J. 2010. 'The Sociomateriality of Organisational Life: Considering Technology in Management Research', *Cambridge Journal of Economics* 34 (1), January, 125–41.

Ostrom, Elinor 1990. *Governing the Commons: The Evolution of Institutions for Collective Action*. Cambridge: Cambridge University Press.

———. 2005. *Understanding Institutional Diversity*. Princeton, NJ: Princeton University Press.

Ostrom, Elinor, and Xavier Basurto. 2011. 'Crafting Analytical Tools to Study Institutional Change', *Journal of Institutional Economics* 7 (3), September, 317–43.

Ott, David J. 1961. 'The Financial Development of Japan, 1878–1958', *Journal of Political Economy* 69 (2), April, 122–41.

Overton, Mark. 1996. *Agricultural Revolution in England: The Transformation of the Agrarian Economy 1500–1850*. Cambridge: Cambridge University Press.

Parra, Carlos M. 2005. 'Rules and Knowledge', *Evolutionary and Institutional Economics Review* 2 (1), October, 81–111.

Parsons, Talcott. 1983. *On Institutions and Social Evolution: Selected Writings*, intro. Leon H. Mayhew. Chicago: University of Chicago Press.

Peirce, Charles Sanders. 1878. 'How to Make Our Ideas Clear', *Popular Science Monthly* 12, January, 286–302.

Pelteret, David A. E. 1995. *Slavery in Early Mediaeval England from the Reign of Alfred until the Twelfth Century*. Woodbridge, UK: Boydell Press.

Penner, James E. 1997. *The Idea of Property in Law*. Oxford: Oxford University Press.

Perez, Carlota. 2010. 'Technological Revolutions and Techno-economic Paradigms', *Cambridge Journal of Economics* 34 (1), January, 185–202.

Peters, Margaret. 2018. 'Government Finance and Imposition of Serfdom After the Black Death'. SSRN. http://dx.doi.org/10.2139/ssrn.3320807.

Petty, William. 1927. *The Petty Papers*, ed. Marquis of Landowne, 2 vols. London: Constable.

Phillips, John A., and Charles Wetherell. 1995. 'The Great Reform Act of 1832 and the Political Modernization of England', *American Historical Review* 100 (2), April, 411–36.

Piketty, Thomas. 2014. *Capital in the Twenty-First Century*. Cambridge, MA: Belknap Press.

Pincus, Steven C. A. 2009. *1688: The First Modern Revolution*. New Haven, CT: Yale University Press.

Pincus, Steven C. A., and James A. Robinson. 2014. 'What Really Happened During the Glorious Revolution?', in *Institutions, Property Rights, and Economic Growth: The Legacy of Douglass North*, ed. Sebastian Galiani and Itai Sened. Cambridge: Cambridge University Press, 192–222.

Pincus, Steven C. A., and Alice Wolfram. 2013. 'A Proactive State? The Land Bank, Investment and Party Politics in the 1690s', in *Regulating the British Economy, 1660–1850*, ed. Perry Gaucci. Aldershot, UK: Ashgate, 41–62.

Pipes, Richard. 1999. *Property and Freedom*. New York: Knopf.

Pistor, Katharina. 2019. *The Code of Capital: How the Law Creates Wealth and Inequality*. Princeton, NJ: Princeton University Press.

Planck, Max K. E. L. 1949. *Scientific Autobiography and Other Papers by Max Planck*, trans. from German by Frank Gaynor. New York: Philosophical Library.

Plotkin, Henry C. 1994. *Darwin Machines and the Nature of Knowledge: Concerning Adaptations, Instinct and the Evolution of Intelligence*. Harmondsworth, UK: Penguin.

Polanyi, Karl. 1944. *The Great Transformation: The Political and Economic Origins of Our Time*. New York: Rinehart.

Polanyi, Michael. 1958. *Personal Knowledge: Towards a Post-Critical Philosophy*. London: Routledge and Kegan Paul.

———. 1962. 'The Republic of Science: Its Political and Economic Theory', *Minerva* 1, 54–73.

———. 1966. *The Tacit Dimension*. New York: Doubleday.

Pollard, Sidney. 1958. 'Investment, Consumption and the Industrial Revolution', *Economic History Review*, New Series, 11 (2), 215–26.

———. 1964. 'Fixed Capital in the Industrial Revolution in Britain', *Journal of Economic History* 24 (3), September, 299–314.

Pollock, Frederick, and Frederic William Maitland. 1898) *The History of English Law Before the Time of Edward I*, 2nd ed., 2 vols. Cambridge: Cambridge University Press.

Popkin, Richard H. 1970. 'Hume and Isaac de Pinto', *Texas Studies in Literature and Language* 12 (3), Fall, 417–30.

Postan, Michael M. 1935. 'Recent Trends in the Accumulation of Capital', *Economic History Review* 6 (1), October, 1–12.

———. 1972. *The Medieval Economy and Society: Economic History of Britain, 1100–1500.* Harmondsworth, UK: Penguin.

Potts, Jason. 2000. *The New Evolutionary Microeconomics: Complexity, Competence and Adaptive Behaviour.* Cheltenham, UK: Edward Elgar.

Potts, Richard. 1996. *Humanity's Descent: The Consequences of Ecological Instability.* New York: Morrow.

Powell, Ellis T. 1915. *The Evolution of the Money Market (1385–1915): An Historical and Analytical Study of the Rise and Development of Finance as a Centralised, Co-ordinated Force.* London: Financial Press.

Pozuelo, Julia Ruiz, Amy Slipowitz and Guillermo Vuletin. 2016. 'Democracy Does Not Cause Growth: The Importance of Endogeneity Arguments', Inter-American Development Bank, IDB Working Paper Series No IDB-WP-694.

Pressnell, Leslie S. 1958. *Country Banking in the Industrial Revolution.* Oxford: Clarendon.

———. 1960. 'The Rate of Interest in the Eighteenth Century', in *Studies in the Industrial Revolution*, ed. Leslie S. Pressnell. London: Athlone, 178–214.

Price, George R. 1995. 'The Nature of Selection', *Journal of Theoretical Biology* 175, 389–96.

Quinn, Stephen. 2001. 'The Glorious Revolution's Effect on English Private Finance: A Microhistory 1680–1705', *Journal of Economic History* 61 (3), September, 593–615.

Raftis, J. Ambrose. 1964. *Tenure and Mobility: Studies in the Social History of the Mediaeval English Village.* Toronto: Pontifical Institute of Mediaeval Studies.

Raghutla, Chandrashekar, and Krishna Reddy Chittedi. 2021. 'Financial Development, Real Sector and Economic Growth: Evidence from Emerging Market Economies', *International Journal of Finance and Economics* 26 (4), October, 6156–67.

Rajan, Raghuram G., and Luigi Zingales. 1998. 'Financial Development and Growth', *American Economic Review* 88 (3), June, 559–86.

Reber, Arthur S. 1993. *Implicit Learning and Tacit Knowledge: An Essay on the Cognitive Unconscious.* Oxford: Oxford University Press.

Reid, Charles J., Jr. 1995. 'The Seventeenth-Century Revolution in the English Land Law', *Cleveland State Law Review* 43, 221–302.

Reinert, Erik S. 2007. *How Rich Countries Got Rich . . . and Why Poor Countries Stay Poor.* London: Constable.

Richards, Richard D. 1929. *The Early History of Banking in England.* London: P. S. King and Son.

Richards, Robert J. 1987. *Darwin and the Emergence of Evolutionary Theories of Mind and Behavior.* Chicago: University of Chicago Press.

Richerson, Peter J., and Robert Boyd. 2004. *Not by Genes Alone: How Culture Transformed Human Evolution.* Chicago: University of Chicago Press.

Richerson, Peter J., Robert Boyd and Robert L. Bettinger. 2001. 'Was Agriculture Impossible during the Pleistocene but Mandatory during the Holocene? A Climate Change Hypothesis', *American Antiquity* 66, 387–411.

Riley, James C. 2001. *Rising Life Expectancy: A Global History.* Cambridge: Cambridge University Press.

Roberts, Clayton. 1977. 'The Constitutional Significance of the Financial Settlement of 1690', *Historical Journal* 20 (1), March, 59–76.

Robertson, D. B. 1951. *The Religious Foundations of Leveller Democracy*. New York: Kings Crown Press, Columbia University.

Robertson, Dennis H. 1928. 'Theories of Banking Policy', *Economica*, no. 23, June, 131–46.

Robinson, Joan. 1952. *The Rate of Interest and Other Essays*. London: Macmillan.

———. 1953. 'The Production Function and the Theory of Capital', *Review of Economic Studies* 21 (1), 81–106.

———. 1979a. *Collected Economic Papers—Volume Five*. Oxford: Basil Blackwell.

———. 1979b. *The Generalization of the General Theory and Other Essays*. London: Macmillan.

Rodrik, Dani, ed. 2003. *In Search of Prosperity: Analytic Narratives on Economic Growth*. Princeton, NJ: Princeton University Press.

Rodrik, Dani, and Romain Wacziarg. 2005. 'Do Democratic Transitions Produce Bad Economic Outcomes?' *American Economic Review* 95 (2), 50–55.

Roland, Gérard. 2004. 'Understanding Institutional Change: Fast-Moving and Slow-Moving Institutions', *Studies in Comparative International Development* 38 (4), December, 109–31.

Roll, Eric. 1930. *An Early Experiment in Industrial Organisation: Being a History of the Firm of Boulton and Watt 1775–1805*. London: Longmans, Green.

Romer, Paul M. 1994. 'The Origins of Endogenous Growth', *Journal of Economic Perspectives* 8 (1), Winter, 3–22.

Rose, Mary B. 1977. 'The Role of the Family in Providing Capital and Managerial Talent in Samuel Greg and Company 1784–1840', *Business History* 19 (1), 37–54.

———. 1986. *The Greggs of Quarry Bank Mill: the Rise and Decline of a Family Firm, 1750–1914*. Cambridge: Cambridge University Press.

Rosenberg, Alexander. 1995. *The Philosophy of Social Science*, 2nd ed. Boulder, CO: Westview Press.

———. 1998. 'Folk Psychology', in *Handbook of Economic Methodology*, ed. John B. Davis, D. Wade Hands and Uskali Mäki. Cheltenham, UK: Edward Elgar, 195–97.

Rosenberg, Nathan. 1969. 'The Direction of Technological Change: Inducement Mechanisms and Focusing Devices', *Economic Development and Cultural Change* 18 (1), October, 1–24.

Rosenberg, Nathan, and Luther E. Birdzell, Jr. 1986. *How the West Grew Rich: The Economic Transformation of the Industrial World*. New York: Basic Books.

Rosenblatt, Helena. 2018. *The Lost History of Liberalism: From Ancient Rome to the Twenty-First Century*. Princeton, NJ: Princeton University Press.

Roseveare, Henry G. 1991. *The Financial Revolution, 1660–1760*. Harlow, UK: Longman.

Rousseau, Peter L. 2003. 'Historical Perspectives on Financial Development and Economic Growth', *Federal Research Bank of St. Louis*, July–August, 81–106.

Rowe, Nicholas. 1989. *Rules and Institutions*. London: Philip Allan.

Rubin, Jared. 2017. *Rulers, Religion, and Riches: Why the West Got Rich and the Middle East Did Not*. Cambridge: Cambridge University Press.

Rubini, Dennis. 1970. 'Politics and the Battle for the Banks, 1688–1697', *English Historical Review* 85 (337), October, 693–714.

Rudolph, Jenny W., J. Bradley Morrison and John S. Carroll. 2009. 'The Dynamics of Action-Oriented Problem Solving: Linking Interpretation and Choice', *Academy of Management Review* 34 (4), October, 733–56.

Ruffhead, Owen. 1763. *The Statutes at Large: Volume 3: From the First Year of King James the First to the Tenth Year of the Reign of King William the Third*. London: Mark Basket.

Ruttan, Vernon W. 1997. 'Induced Innovation, Evolutionary Theory and Path Dependence: Sources of Technical Change', *Economic Journal* 107 (5), September, 1520–29.

Ruttan, Vernon W. 2003. *Social Science Knowledge and Economic Development: An Institutional Design Approach*. Ann Arbor: University of Michigan Press.

———. 2006. 'Social Science Knowledge and Induced Institutional Innovation: An Institutional Design Perspective', *Journal of Institutional Economics* 2 (3), December, 249–72.

Samuels, Warren J. 1971. 'Interrelations Between Legal and Economic Processes', *Journal of Law and Economics* 5, 435–50.

———. 1973. 'The Economy as a System of Power and Its Legal Bases: The Legal Economics of Robert Lee Hale', *University of Miami Law Review* 27 (3–4), Spring–Summer, 261–371.

———. 1989. 'The Legal-Economic Nexus', *George Washington Law Review* 57 (6), August, 1556–78.

Sarma, Mandira, and Jesim Pais. 2011. 'Financial Inclusion and Development', *Journal of International Development* 23 (5), July, 613–28.

Scanlan, Padraic X. 2020. *Slave Empire: How Slavery Built Modern Britain*. London: Robinson.

Schäffle, Albert E. F. 1870. *Kapitalismus und Sozialismus: mit besonderer Rücksicht auf Geschäfts und Vermögensformen*. Tübingen, Ger.: Laupp.

Schumpeter, Joseph A. 1934. *The Theory of Economic Development: An Inquiry into Profits, Capital, Credit, Interest, and the Business Cycle*, trans. Redvers Opie from second German edition of 1926. Cambridge, MA: Harvard University Press.

———. 1939. *Business Cycles: A Theoretical Statistical and Historical Analysis of the Capitalist Process*, 2 vols. New York: McGraw-Hill.

———. 1954. *History of Economic Analysis*. Oxford: Oxford University Press).

Scott, Bruce R. 2011. *Capitalism: Its Origins and Evolution as a System of Governance*. Berlin: Springer.

Scott, Jonathan. 1991. *Algernon Sydney and the Restoration Crisis, 1677–1683*. Cambridge: Cambridge University Press.

Scott, W. Richard. 1995. *Institutions and Organizations*. Thousand Oaks, CA: Sage.

Seabury, Samuel. 1861. *American Slavery Justified by the Law of Nature*. New York: Mason.

Sen, Amartya K. 1999. *Development as Freedom*. New York: Knopf and Oxford: Oxford University Press.

Senn, Mark A. 2003. 'English Life and Law in the Time of the Black Death', *Real Property, Probate and Trust Journal* 38 (3), Fall, 507–88.

Shannon, Claude E., and Warren Weaver. 1949. *The Mathematical Theory of Communication*. Urbana: University of Illinois Press.

Sheppard, Francis, and Victor Belcher. 1980. 'The Deeds Registries of Yorkshire and Middlesex', *Journal of the Society of Archivists* 6, April, 274–86.

Sheppard, Francis, Victor Belcher and Philip Cottrell. 1979. 'The Middlesex and Yorkshire Deeds Registries and the Study of Building Fluctuations', *London Journal* 5, November, 176–217.

Shientag, Bernard L. 1941. 'Lord Mansfield Revisited—A Modern Assessment', *Fordham Law Review* 10 (3), November, 345–88.

Shrubsole, Guy. 2019. *Who Owns England? How We Lost Our Land and How to Take It Back.* London: William Collins.

Simpson, A. W. B. 1961. *An Introduction to the History of the Land Law.* Oxford: Clarendon Press.

Smith, Adam. 1976. *An Inquiry into the Nature and Causes of the Wealth of Nations,* 2 vols., originally published 1776, ed. Roy H. Campbell and Andrew S. Skinner. London: Methuen.

Smith, Merritt Roe, and Leo Marx, eds. 1994. *Does Technology Drive History? The Dilemma of Technological Determinism.* Cambridge, MA: MIT Press.

Smith, Thomas C. 1988. *Native Sources of Japanese Industrialization, 1750–1920.* Berkeley: University of California Press.

Smithin, John, ed. 2000. *What Is Money?* London: Routledge.

Smitka, Michael. 1998. *Japanese Prewar Growth: Lessons for Development Theory.* New York: Garland.

Sober, Elliott. 1980. 'Evolution, Population Thinking and Essentialism', *Philosophy of Science* 47, 350–83.

Solow, Barbara L. 1987. 'Capitalism and Slavery in the Exceedingly Long Run', *Journal of Interdisciplinary History* 17 (4), 711–37.

Solow, Robert M. 1956. 'A Contribution to the Theory of Economic Growth', *Quarterly Journal of Economics* 70 (1), February, 65–94.

———. 1957. 'Technical Change and the Aggregate Production Function', *Review of Economics and Statistics* 39, 312–20.

Sombart, Werner. 1913. *Krieg und Kapitalismus.* Munich: Duncker und Humblot.

———. 1919. *Der moderne Kapitalismus: Historisch-systematische Darstellung des gesamteuropäischen Wirtschaftslebens von seinen Anfängen bis zur Gegenwart,* 3rd ed., vol 1. Munich: Duncker und Humblot.

Sorenson, André. 2010. 'Land, Property Rights, and Planning in Japan: Institutional Design and Institutional Change in Land Management', *Planning Perspectives* 25 (3), July, 279–302.

Sousa, Wayne P. 1984. 'The Role of Disturbance in Natural Communities', *Annual Review of Ecology and Systematics* 15, 353–91.

Sowell, Thomas. 1985. *Marxism, Philosophy and Economics.* London: George Allen and Unwin.

Spring, Eileen. 1993. *Law, Land, and Family: Aristocratic Inheritance in England, 1300 to 1800.* Chapel Hill: University of North Carolina Press.

Sraffa, Piero. 1960. *Production of Commodities by Means of Commodities: Prelude to a Critique of Economic Theory.* Cambridge: Cambridge University Press.

Star, Susan Leigh, ed. 1995. *Ecologies of Knowledge: Work and Politics in Science and Technology.* Albany: State University of New York Press.

Staubwasser, Michael, and Harvey Weiss. 2006. 'Holocene Climate and Cultural Evolution in Late Prehistoric-Early Historic West Asia', *Quaternary Research* 66 (3), 372–87.

Steiger, Otto. 2006. 'Property Economics versus New Institutional Economics', *Journal of Economic Issues* 40 (1), March, 183–208.

———, ed. 2008. *Property Economics: Property Rights, Creditor's Money and the Foundations of the Economy.* Marburg, Ger.: Metropolis.

Steinmo, Sven. 2010. *The Evolution of Modern States: Sweden, Japan and the United States.* Cambridge: Cambridge University Press.

Stephens, W. B. 1990. 'Literacy in England, Scotland, and Wales, 1500–1900', *History of Education Quarterly* 30 (4), Winter, 545–71.

Stich, Stephen P. 1983. *From Folk Psychology to Cognitive Science*. Cambridge, MA: MIT Press.

———. 1996. *Deconstructing the Mind*. Oxford: Oxford University Press.

Stone, Lawrence. 1967. *The Crisis of the Aristocracy 1558–1641*. Oxford: Oxford University Press.

———. 1980. 'The Results of the English Revolutions of the Seventeenth Century', in *Three British Revolutions: 1641, 1688, 1776*, ed. J. G. A. Pocock. Princeton, NJ: Princeton University Press, 23–108.

———. 1985. 'The Bourgeois Revolution of Seventeenth-Century England Revisited', *Past and Present*, no. 109, November, 44–54.

Suchman, Lucy A. 1987. *Plans and Situated Actions: The Problem of Human-Machine Communication*. Cambridge: Cambridge University Press.

———. 2007. *Human-Machine Reconfigurations: Plans and Situated Actions*. Cambridge: Cambridge University Press.

Sugarman, David, and Ronnie Warrington. 1995. 'Land Law, Citizenship and the Invention of "Englishness": The Strange World of the Equity of Redemption', in *Early Modern Conceptions of Property*, ed. John Brewer and Susan Staves. London: Routledge, 111–44.

Sullivan, Richard J. 1989. 'England's "Age of Invention": The Acceleration of Patents and of Patentable Invention during the Industrial Revolution', *Explorations in Economic History* 26 (4), October, 424–52.

Sussman, Nathan, and Yishay Yafeh. 2006. 'Institutional Reforms, Financial Development and Sovereign Debt: Britain 1690–1790', *Journal of Economic History* 66 (4), December, 906–35.

Sylla, Richard. 1969. 'Federal Policy, Banking Market Structure, and Capital Mobilization in the United States, 1863–1913', *Journal of Economic History* 29 (4), December, 657–86.

Taira, Koji. 1971. 'Education and literacy in Meiji Japan: An Interpretation', *Explorations in Economic History* 8 (4), Summer, 371–94.

Tate, W. E. 1944. 'The Five English District Statutory Registries of Deeds', *Historical Research* 20 (60), 97–105.

Tawney, Richard H. 1912. *The Agrarian Problem in the Sixteenth Century*. London: Longmans Green.

———. 1936. *Religion and the Rise of Capitalism: An Historical Study*, 2nd ed. London: John Murray.

———. 1941. 'The Rise of the Gentry, 1558–1640', *Economic History Review* 11 (1), 1–38.

Taylor, Frederick Winslow. 1911. *The Principles of Scientific Management*. New York: Harper.

Taylor, George V. 1967. 'Noncapitalist Wealth and the Origins of the French Revolution', *American Historical Review* 72 (2), January, 469–96.

Temin, Peter, and Hans-Joachim Voth. 2005. 'Credit Rationing and Crowding Out during the Industrial Revolution: Evidence from Hoare's Bank, 1702–1862', *Explorations in Economic History* 42, 325–48.

———. 2013. *Prometheus Shackled: Goldsmith Banks and England's Financial Revolution after 1700*. London: Cambridge University Press.

Thirsk, Joan. 1952. 'The Sales of Royalist Land during the Interregnum', *Economic History Review* 5 (2), December, 188–207.

Thompson, Edward P. 1978. *The Poverty of Theory and Other Essays*. London: Merlin.

Thompson, F.M.L. 1966. 'The Social Distribution of Landed Property in England since the Sixteenth Century', *Economic History Review*, 2nd series, 19 (3), 505–17.

Thornton, Henry. 1802. *An Enquiry into the Nature and Effects of the Paper Credit of Great Britain*. London: Hatchard.

Tilly, Charles. 1992. *Coercion, Capital, and European States, AD 990–1992*. Oxford: Blackwell.

Trevelyan, George Macaulay. 1938. *The English Revolution: 1688–1689*. London: Thornton Butterworth.

Trevor-Roper, Hugh R. 1957. 'The Social Causes of the Great Rebellion', in *Historical Essays*, 195–205. London: Macmillan.

———. 1992. *Counter-Reformation to Glorious Revolution*. Chicago: University of Chicago Press.

Trew, Alex. 2010. 'Infrastructure Finance and Industrial Takeoff in England', *Journal of Money, Credit and Banking* 42 (6), September, 985–1010.

Turner, Michael. 1981. 'Cost, Finance, and Parliamentary Enclosure', *Economic History Review* 34 (2), May, 236–48.

———. 1986. 'English Open Fields and Enclosures: Retardation or Productivity Improvements', *Journal of Economic History* 46 (3), September, 669–92.

Turner, Michael, and D. Mills, eds. 1986. *The English Land Tax, 1692–1832*. New York: St Martin's.

Tylecote, Andrew. 2016. 'Institutions Matter: But Which Institutions? And How and Why Do They Change?' *Journal of Institutional Economics* 12 (3), September, 721–42.

Tyler, Tom R. 1990. *Why People Obey the Law*. New Haven, CT: Yale University Press.

Underhill, Arthur. 1901. *A Century of Law Reform: Twelve Lectures on the Changes in the Law of England during the Nineteenth Century*. London: Macmillan.

van Bavel, Bas. 2016. *The Invisible Hand? How Market Economies Have Emerged and Declined since AD 500*. Oxford: Oxford University Press.

van Bochove, Christiaan, Heidi Deneweth and Jaco Zuijderduijn. 2015. 'Real Estate and Mortgage Finance in England and the Low Countries, 1300–1800', *Continuity and Change* 30 (1), 9–38.

van der Ploeg, Frederick, and George S. Alogoskoufis. 1994. 'Money and Endogenous Growth', *Journal of Money Credit and Banking* 26 (4), February, 771–91.

van Zanden, Jan Luiten. 2009. *The Long Road to the Industrial Revolution. The European Economy in a Global Perspective, 1000–1800*. Leiden: Brill Academic Publishers.

Vanberg, Viktor J. 2002. 'Rational Choice versus Program-Based Behavior: Alternative Theoretical Approaches and Their Relevance for the Study of Institutions', *Rationality and Society* 14 (1), Summer, 7–53.

———. 2004. 'The Rationality Postulate in Economics: Its Ambiguity, Its Deficiency and Its Evolutionary Alternative', *Journal of Economic Methodology* 11 (1), March, 1–29.

Veblen, Thorstein B. 1898a. 'Why Is Economics Not an Evolutionary Science?' *Quarterly Journal of Economics* 12 (3), July, 373–97.

———. 1898b. 'The Instinct of Workmanship and the Irksomeness of Labor', *American Journal of Sociology* 4 (2), September, 187–201.

———. 1898c. 'The Beginnings of Ownership', *American Journal of Sociology* 4 (3), November, 352–65.

———. 1899. *The Theory of the Leisure Class: An Economic Study in the Evolution of Institutions.* New York: Macmillan.

———. 1904. *The Theory of Business Enterprise.* New York: Scribners.

———. 1906a. 'The Place of Science in Modern Civilization', *American Journal of Sociology* 11 (5), March, 585–609.

———. 1906b. 'The Socialist Economics of Karl Marx and His Followers I: The Theories of Karl Marx', *Quarterly Journal of Economics* 20 (3), August, 578–95.

———. 1907. 'The Socialist Economics of Karl Marx and His Followers II: The Later Marxism', *Quarterly Journal of Economics* 21 (1), February, 299–322.

———. 1908a. 'Professor Clark's Economics', *Quarterly Journal of Economics* 22 (2), February, 147–95.

———. 1908b. 'On the Nature of Capital II: Investment, Intangible Assets, and the Pecuniary Magnate', *Quarterly Journal of Economics* 23 (1), November, 104–36.

———. 1908c. 'The Evolution of the Scientific Point of View', *University of California Chronicle* 10 (4), October, 395–416.

———. 1913a. 'The Mutation Theory and the Blond Race', *Journal of Race Development* 3 (4), April, 491–507. Reprinted in Camic and Hodgson (2011).

———. 1915. *Imperial Germany and the Industrial Revolution.* New York: Macmillan.

Veitch, John M. 1986. 'Repudiations and Confiscations by the Medieval State', *Journal of Economic History* 46 (1), March, 31–36.

Ventura, Jaume, and Hans-Joachim Voth. 2015. 'Debt into Growth: How Sovereign Debt Accelerated the First Industrial Revolution', NBER Working Paper 21280, National Bureau for Economic Research, Cambridge, MA.

Vermeij, Geerat J. 1995. 'Economics, Volcanoes, and Phanerozoic Revolutions', *Paleobiology* 21 (2), 125–52.

Vestal, James E. 1993. *Planning for Change: Industrial Policy and Japanese Economic Development, 1945–1990.* Oxford: Oxford University Press.

Vries, Jan de, and Ad van der Woude. 1997. *The First Modern Economy. Success, Failure, and Perseverance of the Dutch Economy, 1500–1815.* Cambridge: Cambridge University Press.

Waddington, Conrad H. 1976. 'Evolution in the Sub-Human World', in *Evolution and Consciousness: Human Systems in Transition,* ed. Erich Jantsch and Conrad H. Waddington. Reading, MA: Addison-Wesley, 11–15.

Wagner, Gunter P., and Lee Altenberg. 1996. 'Perspective: Complex Adaptations and the Evolution of Evolvability', *Evolution* 50 (3), June, 967–76.

Wallast, Len H. 2013. *Evolvodynamics—The Mathematical Theory of Economic Evolution: A Coherent Way of Interpreting Time, Scarceness, Value and Economic Growth.* Berlin: Springer.

Walvin, James. 2011. *The Zong: A Massacre, the Law and the End of Slavery.* New Haven, CT: Yale University Press.

Ward, J. R. 1974. *The Finance of Canal Building in Eighteenth-Century England.* Oxford: Oxford University Press.

Ward, William R. 1953. *The English Land Tax in the Eighteenth Century.* Oxford: Oxford University Press.

Waswo, Ann. 1977. *Japanese Landlords: The Decline of a Rural Elite.* Berkeley: University of California Press.

Weber, Bruce H., and David J. Depew. 2003. *Evolution and Learning: The Baldwin Effect Reconsidered*. Cambridge, MA: MIT Press.

Weber, Max. 1930. *The Protestant Ethic and the Spirit of Capitalism*, trans. from German edition of 1905. London: Allen and Unwin.

———. 1968. *Economy and Society: An Outline of Interpretative Sociology*, 2 vols., trans. from German edition of 1921–22. New York: Bedminster Press.

Wedgwood, Cicely V. 1955. *The King's Peace 1637–1641*. London: Constable.

———. 1974. *The King's War 1641–1647*. London: Constable.

Wegner, Daniel M. 2002. *The Illusion of Conscious Will*. Cambridge, MA: MIT Press.

———. 2003. 'The Mind's Best Trick: How We Experience Conscious Will', *Trends in Cognitive Sciences* 7 (2), February, 65–69.

Wegner, Daniel M., and T. Wheatley. 1999. 'Apparent Mental Causation: Sources of the Experience of the Will', *American Psychologist* 54, 480–92.

Weiner, Martin J. 2004. *English Culture and the Decline of the Industrial Spirit, 1850–1980*, 2nd ed. Cambridge: Cambridge University Press.

Wenger, Etienne. 1998. *Communities of Practice: Learning, Memory and Identity*. Cambridge: Cambridge University Press.

Wennerlind, Carl. 2011. *Casualties of Credit: The English Financial Revolution 1620–1720*. Cambridge, MA: Harvard University Press.

Werner, Richard A. 2014. 'How Do Banks Create Money, and Why Can Other Firms Not Do the Same? An Explanation for the Coexistence of Lending and Deposit-Taking', *International Review of Financial Analysis* 36, December, 71–77.

Western, John R. 1972. *Monarchy and Revolution: The English State in the 1680s*. London: Blandford.

Whately, Warren C. 2018. 'The Gun-Slave Hypothesis and the 18th Century British Slave Trade', *Explorations in Economic History* 67, January, 80–104.

Wicken, Jeffrey S. 1987. *Evolution, Thermodynamics, and Information: Extending the Darwinian Paradigm*. Oxford: Oxford University Press.

Williams, Eric. 1944. *Capitalism and Slavery*. Chapel Hill: University of North Carolina Press.

Williamson, Jeffrey G. 1984. 'Why Was British Growth So Slow during the Industrial Revolution?' *Journal of Economic History* 44 (3), September, 687–712.

———. 1987. 'Did English Factor Markets Fail during the Industrial Revolution?' *Oxford Economic Papers*, New Series, 39 (4), December, 641–78.

Williamson, Oliver E. 2000. 'The New Institutional Economics: Taking Stock, Looking Ahead', *Journal of Economic Literature* 38 (3), September, 595–613.

Wills, Christopher. 1989. *The Wisdom of the Genes: New Pathways in Evolution*. New York: Basic Books.

Wimsatt, William C., and Jeffrey C. Schank. 1988. 'Two Constraints on the Evolution of Complex Adaptations and the Means of Their Avoidance', *Evolutionary Progress*, ed. Matthew H. Nitecki. Chicago: University of Chicago Press, 231–73.

Winthrop, William. 1920. *Military Law and Precedents*, 2nd ed. Washington, DC: Government Printing Office.

Wolfe, Don M. 1944. *Leveller Manifestoes of the Puritan Revolution*. New York: Nelson.

Wolferen, Karel van. 1993a. *The Enigma of Japanese Power*. Tokyo: Tuttle. First published 1989.

Woodhouse, A. S. P., ed. 1951. *Puritanism and Liberty: Being the Army Debates of 1647–9*. Chicago: University of Chicago Press.

Wordie, J. R. 1983. 'The Chronology of English Enclosure, 1500–1914', *Economic History Review* 36 (4), November, 483–505.

World Bank. 2021. 'GDP per Capita (PPP Current International $)', *World Bank Data*. https://data.worldbank.org/indicator/NY.GDP.PCAP.PP.CD?year_high_desc=true.

Wray, L. Randall. 1998. *Understanding Modern Money: The Key to Full Employment and Price Stability*. Cheltenham, UK: Edward Elgar.

———. ed. (2004. *Credit and State Theories of Money: The Contribution of A. Mitchell Innes*. Cheltenham, UK: Edward Elgar.

———. 2012. *Modern Money Theory: A Primer on Macroeconomics for Sovereign Monetary Systems*. London: Palgrave Macmillan.

Yamada, Makio. 2022. 'Making Reform and Stability Compatible with Each Other: Elite Redeployment in Meiji Japan', *Journal of Institutional Economics* 18 (5), October, 861–75.

Yoo, Dongwoo, and Richard Steckel. 2016. 'Property Rights and Economic Development: The Legacy of Japanese Colonial Institutions', *Journal of Institutional Economics* 13 (3), September, 623–50.

Zagorin, Perez. 1959. 'The Social Interpretation of the English Revolution', *Journal of Economic History* 19 (3), September, 376–401.

Ziegler, Philip. 1991. *The Black Death*. Stroud, UK: Sutton.

INDEX

Acemoglu, Daron, 22, 70, 79, 81, 109, 115, 226

Act of Revocation (1625), 91

Act of Settlement (1701), 118

Act of Supremacy (1534), 89

Act of Union (1707), 3, 124

adaptations, x, 17–18, 71, 73, 150, 190–201, 224–8

administrative revolution, 23, 124, 151

Africa, 109, 148

Aghion, Philippe, 10–11, 15, 20

agrarian law, 99

Agreement of the People, 98, 108

agricultural productivity, 2, 84, 88, 139, 142–3, 177, 217

agriculture, 2, 44, 72, 77, 84, 88, 99, 126, 139–43, 151, 175, 177, 181, 195, 201, 217–19, 222

Alchian, Armen A., 14

Aldrich, Howard E., 63

Alesina, Alberto, 202

Allen, Douglas W., 81, 101

Allen, Robert C., 42–5, 78–9, 83, 86–9, 99–101, 106–7, 111, 118, 125, 139–43, 146, 160, 170–1, 222

Alogoskoufis, George S., 11

Altenberg, Lee, 228

American War of Independence, *See* War of American Independence

Amsterdam, 121, 128, 169

Amsterdam stock exchange, 121

Anderson, B. L., 106, 160, 175–6

Anderson, Perry, 40–1, 111, 216, 221–2

Angeles, Luis, 80, 117

Anglo-Dutch Wars, 123

Anglo-Saxon period, 81, 202

Anglo-Spanish War, 122

Anne, Queen, 132, 163

Aoki, Masahiko, 27

Archimedes, 68

aristocracy, 27, 37, 39–42, 44, 77, 80, 94–5, 99–106, 110–11, 119, 122, 135, 145–6, 150, 174, 197, 218, 222

Aristotle, 43, 68

Arkwright, Richard, 146–7, 158, 175

Armada, 114

armies, 72, 88, 91–7, 100, 111–14, 123, 151, 196, 218

    standing, 87, 114–15

Arruñada, Benito, x, 14, 171, 174, 212, 223, 226–7

Arthur, W. Brian, 17, 27, 71

Ashley, Maurice, 113–14

Ashton, Thomas S., 4, 143, 146, 159, 163–4, 168–9, 175

Athens, 127

attorneys, 160, 175–6, 181

Aurelius, 68

Austen, Jane, 103–4, 142

authority, 25, 63, 67–8, 84, 100, 135, 155, 193, 208–9

    arbitrary, 94

    legal, 14, 25, 58, 201

    moral, 65

    parental, 85

    religious, 83, 89, 196

Ayres, Clarence E., 21, 52–3, 59, 71

Planck, Max, 19
Plato, 68
Plotkin, Henry C., 18–19, 188, 191
Plymouth, 83
Polanyi, Karl, 102
Polanyi, Michael, 19, 26, 34, 54, 67, 209
Pollard, Sidney, 8, 138, 166–8, 180–1
Pollock, Frederick, 78–9, 83
Popkin, Richard H., 138
Portugal, 86, 148, 213
possessive individualism, 92
postal network, 164
Postan, Michael M., 42, 158–9, 162, 168–81
Postan-Pollard story, the, 168, 180
Potts, Jason, 17
Potts, Richard, 73
Powell, Ellis T., 109, 121, 177
power, 14, 23–5, 34–48, 53, 57–60, 70, 73, 77,
    80–4, 88, 91–5, 98–103, 106–7, 110–16,
    119–25, 135, 139, 145–6, 150–5, 158, 160, 168,
    175, 177, 195–201, 205, 211, 214–22
        countervailing, 44, 57, 70, 216, 221
pragmatism, x, 188
preference functions, 190–1
Pressnell, Leslie S., 138, 141, 166, 172, 175
Pride and Prejudice, 103–4, 142
Pride's Purge, 100
Priestley, Joseph, 208
printing, 10, 55, 68, 209
private ownership, ix, 6, 12–13, 23, 37, 47,
    90–8, 115, 149, 177, 217, 225
problem solving, 18, 24, 40, 72–3, 103, 107,
    120, 130–2, 136, 150, 154, 170, 188–96,
    201–2, 210
production functions, 8, 14–16, 20, 182
production, nature of, 18
productive forces, 31–8, 47–8
productivity growth, 55, 90, 110–11, 118,
    142–3, 147, 152, 173, 217
proletariat, 37–9, 42, 45, 171
promissory notes, 131–2, 178, 199
property, ix, 5–6, 11–14, 19–26, 33, 39, 41,
    45–9, 52–4, 59, 68, 72, 77–81, 85, 92, 94–8,
    101–20, 133, 135, 139–45, 147, 151–7, 160,

163–4, 167–9, 171–5, 181, 198–200, 212,
    216–18, 221–6
    intellectual, 52–4, 147, 156, 163–4,
        168
    landed, 39, 41, 77–81, 85, 92, 97–8,
        104–10, 118–19, 139–141, 145, 151,
        154, 160, 174, 181, 198, 212, 217
    unequal distribution of, ix, 23, 101,
        139–45, 199, 218, 223
property rights, ix, 5–6, 11–14, 19–26, 33, 39,
    41, 45–9, 52–4, 59, 68, 72, 79–81, 92, 103,
    114–20, 133, 140, 151–7, 167, 171–2, 175, 181,
    200, 216–17, 221–6
Protectorate, 22, 99–100, 106, 108, 135, 153,
    198
Protestantism, 21, 50, 55–8, 71, 91, 111–14, 135,
    150, 197–8
Prussia, 26, 56, 60, 218
psychology, x, 24, 188–9
    folk, 24
public debt, See debt, public
punctuated equilibria, 70
Purcell, Henry, 66
Puritanism, 56, 94
purveyance, 91
Putney Debates, 97–9
Putterman, Louis, 193
Pym, John, 92

Quakers, 97, 146
Quarry Bank Mill, 160
Quinn, Stephen, 122, 138, 166

Raftis, J. Ambrose, 83
Raghutla, Chandrashekar, 9, 161, 212
Rajan, Raghuram G., 161, 165, 212
Raleigh, Walter, 92, 108, 110
rationality, 12, 15–16, 35, 57, 150, 191, 210
Reber, Arthur S., 18–19, 34
recognition, 24, 73, 154, 187
Rees, Geraint, 190
Reformation, 22, 56–7, 66, 81, 89, 195, 197
Reid, Charles J., 52, 81, 86–7, 90–3, 100–4,
    140

THE PRINCETON ECONOMIC HISTORY
OF THE WESTERN WORLD

Joel Mokyr, Series Editor

Recent titles

A NOTE ON THE TYPE

This book has been composed in Arno, an Old-style serif typeface in the classic Venetian tradition, designed by Robert Slimbach at Adobe.